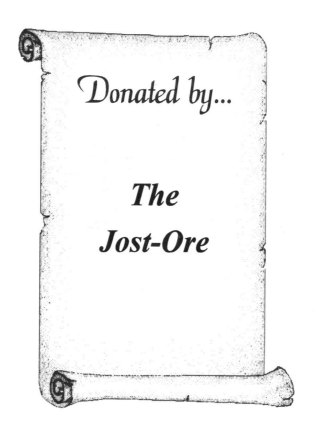

Donated by...

The

Jost-Ore

DAVID DAICHES is Professor of English and Dean of the School of English and American Studies at the University of Sussex. Educated at Edinburgh University, and with a D. Phil. from Oxford, he has taught English at Edinburgh, Oxford, Chicago, Cornell, Indiana, Cambridge, and the Sorbonne. He is the author of some twenty books, including *The Novel and the Modern World; Robert Burns; A Critical History of English Literature,* and works on Virginia Woolf, Robert Louis Stevenson, and George Eliot. He is also one of the editors of *The Norton Anthology of English Literature.*

David Daiches is one of the editors of
The Norton Anthology of English Literature

Norton paperbacks by David Daiches are
A Study of Literature for Readers and Critics
Critical Approaches to Literature

MILTON

DAVID DAICHES

The Norton Library
W · W · NORTON & COMPANY · INC ·
NEW YORK

W. W. Norton & Company, Inc. is also the publisher of *The Norton Anthology of English Literature,* edited by M. H. Abrams, Robert M. Adams, David Daiches, E. Talbot Donaldson, George H. Ford, Samuel Holt Monk, and Hallett Smith; *The American Tradition in Literature,* edited by Sculley Bradley, Richmond Croom Beatty, and E. Hudson Long; *World Masterpieces,* edited by Maynard Mack, Kenneth Douglas, Howard E. Hugo, Bernard M. W. Knox, John C. McGalliard, P. M. Pasinetti, and René Wellek; and the paperbound Norton Critical Editions—authoritative texts, together with the leading critical interpretations, of *Adventures of Huckleberry Finn, The Ambassadors, Crime and Punishment, Gulliver's Travels, Hamlet, Heart of Darkness, Henry IV, Part 1, Madame Bovary, The Red Badge of Courage, The Scarlet Letter,* and *Wuthering Heights.*

PRINTED IN THE UNITED STATES OF AMERICA

1 2 3 4 5 6 7 8 9 0

CONTENTS

I

EARLY POEMS

'ANNO DOMINI 1619, he was ten years old; and was then a Poet.' So wrote John Aubrey in his 'brief life' of Milton, and though he may have exaggerated somewhat the information is essentially true, for Milton was dedicated to literature from early childhood more consciously and more deliberately than any other English poet. 'My father destined me from a child to the pursuits of literature,' he confided to his readers in his *Defensio Secunda pro Populo Anglicano*. Again and again in those autobiographical asides which stud his political pamphlets Milton stressed both his early and continuous poetical ambition and his careful and thorough literary training. 'After I had from my first yeeres . . . bin exercis'd to the tongues, and some sciences, as my age would suffer, . . . it was found that whether aught was impos'd me by them that had the overlooking, or betak'n to of mine own choise in English, or other tongue, prosing or versing, but chiefly by this latter, the style, by certain vital signes it had, was likely to live.' This passage, from *The Reason of Church-Government*, can be paralleled by many others. Milton recalls no moment of revelation and dedication such as Wordsworth describes in Book IV of *The Prelude* :

> I made no vows, but vows
> Were then made for me; bond unknown to me
> Was given, that I should be, else sinning greatly,
> A dedicated Spirit.

For Milton the process seems to have been continuous and his early years a period of steady preparation to be a great English poet. He shared with Wordsworth, however, his high view of the poet's mission, though the source of Wordsworth's ethical idealism was very different from the Protestant Christian Humanism which led Milton to declare that the poet's abilities 'are of power beside the office of a pulpit, to inbreed and cherish in a great

people the seeds of vertu, and publick civility, to allay the
perturbations of the mind, and set the affections in right tune'.
Yet Wordsworth's half-mystic pantheism and Milton's Puritan
assimilation of the functions of poetry and of preaching produced
very similar views of the ultimate purpose of poetry.

From the beginning Milton's sense of literature was both
passionately humanist and passionately Christian. He was born
in London on 9 December, 1608, and attended St. Paul's School,
whose Christian humanist curriculum had been devised by Colet
and Erasmus. 'I wolde they were taught all way in good littera-
ture both laten and greke, and good auctors suych as have the
veray Romayne eliquence joyned with wisdome, specially Cristen
auctors that wrote theyre wysdome with clene and chast laten,'
wrote Colet. The mediaeval *trivium* of grammar, logic and
rhetoric became at St. Paul's both a critical training in the gram-
matical, logical and rhetorical analysis of Latin and Greek texts
and a training in the art of writing and discoursing in those
languages. Dr. Alexander Gill, headmaster of the school in
Milton's time, was the author of an English grammar entitled
Logonomia Anglica, in which the structure and qualities of the
English language were explained in Latin and by analogy with
Latin but which illustrated the potentialities of English expression
by quotations from English poets—Spenser, Sidney and George
Wither. We may assume, therefore, that the formal training in
grammar and rhetoric which Milton received was not confined
entirely to work with Latin and Greek texts and that his attention
was directed to the way in which English poets had handled their
native language.

The primary object of the movement known as Humanism
was the recovery of all that was best in the thought and expression
of the Greek and Latin classics. The worship and almost exclusive
imitation of Ciceronian Latin prose (and the concomitant rejection, as models of style, of all Latin prose that did not belong to
the 'golden' Ciceronian age) has been condemned as narrow and
arbitrary; but it should be remembered that Cicero was more
than a stylistic hero—he was also an exponent of natural law and
an orator who showed how to persuade in the cause of virtue. To
the Renaissance humanist, rhetoric was an important and practical study of the 'complete' man, whose knowledge and virtue

might be useless if he could not communicate it persuasively to others. Rhetoric to Plato was suspect as dealing with opinion rather than with truth; it was the art of the opportunist, who knew how to make the worse appear the better reason. To Aristotle rhetoric meant the laws of persuasion based on the nature of language and the facts of human psychology; it was an art neutral in itself, and he was interested in it as a scientist. But to the later Greek rhetoricians, and to Cicero and Quintilian in Rome, rhetoric was a necessary art for a citizen, for it enabled him to maintain his point of view effectively in public assembly. The complete Renaissance man had to be trained in public affairs among other things, and this meant trained in rhetoric. The view that rhetoric was a necessary skill for a citizen of a free state was thus an essential part of the Renaissance humanist attitude, and the study of Cicero as an orator and of Quintilian as a literary critic both flowed from this view and further encouraged it.

It is worth pausing at this question of rhetoric in considering the young Milton, for his view of rhetoric was to shift significantly under the pressure of events, with important results on his poetry. The great debate in Hell, in *Paradise Lost*, shows Milton illustrating the perversion of public debate by a skilful but un- scrupulous use of all the tricks of the orator's trade. He had done the same thing, in a different way and on a different scale, in *Comus*, where the conflict between Comus and the Lady is shown as in some degree a conflict between rhetoric and logic. That is why Comus, like Satan, has all the most obviously persuasive speeches. Indeed, the style often known as 'Miltonic' is, it is hardly an exaggeration to say, the high Satanic style of perverted rhetoric which led so many romantic critics to acclaim Satan as a hero. In his early and middle life Milton, though acutely aware of the dangers of a perverted rhetoric, nevertheless saw it also in the humanist light of an essential weapon for democratic man, and there is 'good' rhetoric as well as 'bad' rhetoric in *Paradise Lost*. But it seems that disillusion with the Long Parliament and with the course of public affairs in England eventually led Milton from the Ciceronian and humanist view of rhetoric back to the neutral Aristotelian view and finally to the Platonic view of rhetoric as misleading and corrupting. In *Paradise Regained* all the rhetoric is on Satan's side; Christ repudiates both public

ambition and public speech and His quiet and simple utterances
are in marked contrast to the artfully seductive tones of Satan.
Thus Milton began by accepting rhetoric as an essential tool for
a free citizen and employed it himself as such, but his own implication in the political scene of his day progressively disillusioned
him with its possibilities and in the end he repudiated it and
denied the possibility in contemporary political terms of the
brave new world it was to help to bring to birth. To put the
matter in another way: Milton was educated as a Christian
humanist and in early life found no difficulty in accepting with
equal enthusiasm both parts of this term, but in the light of his
experience he felt called upon to modify the humanist element
until in the end, the problem of reconciling a full-blooded classical humanism with Protestant Christianity having now become
well-nigh insoluble, it emerges as something very different from
what he began with.

No study of Milton can avoid discussing the relation between
his Christianity and his humanism and the effect of his Christian
humanist idealism on his poetic ideals and his poetic practice.
For Milton, poet and prophet were combined in a very special
way. In *The Reason of Church-Government* he urged the magistrates to consider organizing public festivals that 'may civilize,
adorn and make discreet our minds by the learned and affable
meeting of frequent Academies, and the procurement of wise and
artfull recitations, sweetned with eloquent and gracefull inticements to the love and practice of justice, temperance and fortitude, instructing and bettering the Nation at all opportunities,
that the call of wisdom and vertu may be heard everywhere'.
Such couplings of words as 'learned and affable', 'wise and
artfull', 'wisdom and vertu' provide an important clue to the way
in which Milton associated the aesthetic and the ethical and saw
an art based on classical models as a means of encouraging a life
of Christian virtue. In 'Lycidas' the poet and the priest are both
assimilated to the image of the shepherd, the pastor who tends
his flock. And in the *Apology for Smectymnuus* Milton told how
in his youth he 'was confirm'd in this opinion, that he who would
not be frustrate of his hope to write well hereafter in laudable
things, ought him selfe to be a true Poem, that is, a composition
and patterne of the best and honorablest things; not presuming

to sing praises of heroick men, or famous Cities, unlesse he have
in himselfe the experience and practice of all that which is praise-
worthy'.

All this argues a high idealistic cast of mind and an interesting
coming together of the Greek notion of epic poetry as *paideia*
(education) and its Latin and Renaissance modifications, the
Renaissance ideal of combining the life of action and the life of
contemplation, and the Puritan view of the nature and function
of preaching. Milton's own temperament was in large measure
responsible for this, but of course his education and the times he
lived in were also important factors. He was lucky, too, in his
father, a man of unusual culture though his occupation of
scrivener (which involved miscellaneous legal activities as well,
sometimes, as collecting and money-lending, and was more a
business than a profession) would not normally suggest an
interest in the arts. The elder Milton was an accomplished
musician—'an ingeniose man; delighted in musique; composed
many Songs now in print', noted Aubrey—and apparently an
occasional writer of verse as well. He prospered in his occupation,
making enough money to allow his son to live a life of leisured
self-preparation for poetry for some years after completing his
formal education. It was during this period of self-preparation
that Milton addressed to his father a charming Latin poem which
is an important confirmation of the view that his father encouraged his poetic ambitions from the beginning and shows an
attractive relationship between father and son:

> Tu tamen ut simules teneras odisse camoenas,
> Non odisse reor, neque enim, pater, ire iubebas
> Quà via lata patet, quà pronior area lucri,
> Certaque condendi fulget spes aurea nummi;
> Nec rapis ad leges, malè custoditaque gentis
> Iura, nec insulsis damnas clamoribus aures.
> Sed magis excultam cupiens ditescere mentem,
> Me procul urbano strepitu, secessibus altis
> Abductum Aoniae iucunda per otia ripae,
> Phoebaeo lateri comitem sinis ire beatum.
> Officium chari taceo commune parentis,
> Me poscunt maiora, tuo, pater optime, sumptu
> Cum mihi Romuleae patuit facundia linguae,

Et Latii veneres, et quae Iovis ora decebant
Grandia magniloquis elata vocabula Graiis,
Addere suasisti quos iactat Gallia flores,
Et quam degeneri novus Italus ore loquelam
Fundit, Barbaricos testatus voce tumultus
Quaeque Palaestinus loquitur mysteria vates.

Though you pretend to dislike the delicate Muses, I do not think you really do so. For you did not, father, order me to go where the broad way lies open, where opportunities for gain are easier and the golden hope of accumulating money shines steadily. Nor did you force me to study law and the ill-guarded legal principles of the nation; and you do not condemn my ears to meaningless clamour. But you are eager to enrich still further my cultivated mind, and so you have taken me far away from the noise of the city into these high retreats of delightful leisure by the banks of the Aonian stream and you let me walk there by Phoebus' side, his happy comrade.

I do not mention the usual favours of a dear father; greater things make their demands on me. After the eloquence of the language of Romulus and the graces of Latin had been revealed to me—at your expense, best of fathers—and I had learned also the lofty speech of the magniloquent Greeks, befitting the mouth of Jove himself, you persuaded me to add the flowers which France boasts and the speech which the modern Italian utters with degenerate mouth (testifying by his speech to the barbarian invasions) as well as the mysteries uttered by the prophets of Palestine.

This was written in the 1630's when Milton's father was apparently becoming just a trifle impatient with his son's slow programme of reading and meditating, but its tone reveals clearly a warmly affectionate relationship and also Milton's confidence that his father, who had encouraged his literary interests from the beginning, would understand his present attitude. It also shows that Milton learned as a child Greek, Latin, French, Italian and Hebrew. Latin and Greek were taught thoroughly at St. Paul's. Hebrew was taught in the last year, but from 1618 until 1620 Milton also had private tuition in that language from Thomas Young, a Puritan divine from Scotland. It may be that Milton did not enter Paul's until 1620, or perhaps Young's tutoring went on side by side with his school work; perhaps again there were other tutors before Young. (In his *Defensio Secunda* Milton summed up this phase of his career thus : 'My father had me instructed daily in the grammar school, and by other masters at home.') Later, Milton was to claim that from the age of twelve he pursued his literary studies voraciously, hardly ever going to bed before midnight, and this, he argued in the *Defensio Secunda*, was the primary cause of his ultimate blindness. In spite of or perhaps because of his hard private studying, Milton was behind his age at school. Perhaps illness or eye trouble made him start late, or he may have begun early and been taken out of school for a year or two because of illness ; but the fact remains that, in the words of Milton's modern biographer, James Holly Hanford, 'Milton, though brilliant, was retarded.' He came up to Cambridge at a later age than was usual at that time. His close friend at St. Paul's, Charles Diodati—a member of a distinguished Italian Protestant family—was his own age but two years ahead of him at school. It is interesting that the other friend Milton made at St. Paul's, Alexander Gill, son of the headmaster and assistant master at the school, was nine years Milton's senior.

There can be no doubt that Milton acquired a mastery of the classical and other languages far greater in depth and scope than was usual among educated persons in his day, and that his facility in writing Latin verse was quite remarkable. But he was not a prodigy of learning, though he may seem so to modern eyes, and it is salutary to remember that he was two years behind his age at school. The curriculum at St. Paul's was severe, and in any case educated people learned languages in sixteenth- and seventeenth-century England to a degree they do not do today. England was a small country and English a relatively unimportant tongue in Europe. French, Italian and Dutch were demanded of anybody who wanted to get about freely in Europe in the seventeenth century (Shakespeare scatters puns and allusions in these three languages throughout his plays). Hebrew had been developed by the so-called 'trilingual' movement of the sixteenth century as an important humanistic study beside Latin and Greek and its study had also been encouraged by that strain in Protestantism (and it was a very lively strain in England) which emphasized the importance of the original text of the Bible as the only true repository of God's word. Hebrew scholarship among Puritan divines was formidable in Milton's youth, and there were equally learned Anglican Hebraists, as the Authorized Version of the Bible testifies. So while it is true that Milton is the most learned of our English poets, it is less the quantity than the quality of his learning that is impressive. Also, his learning often enters into the fabric of his poetry in a way that poses some unusual critical questions.

Milton went up to Cambridge in 1625, already a dedicated spirit. The extant poems that he had written by this time show, however, no special precocity, though they sometimes exhibit an impressive technical assurance. Inevitably, in an early seventeenth-century English Protestant household, he had been introduced at a tender age to Joshua Sylvester's *Divine Weeks and Works*, a version of the French Protestant epic on the Creation by Guillaume de Salluste du Bartas. Sylvester's free poetic rendering appeared in 1605, and immediately began to exercise enormous influence. Milton succumbed as others did, and traces of du Bartas can be seen throughout much of his work. The young Dryden also read Sylvester with enthusiastic admiration, but repudiated him later; his style of deliberate 'quaintness', his daring and sometimes incongruous imagery, his mixture of stylized Latinisms with plain English words, his ingenious ornamentation, seemed 'abominable fustian' to the mature Dryden and the style was never revived afterwards, yet much of eighteenth-century poetic diction really stems from Sylvester. His influence on English poetic style lasted longer than his reputation, but the direct and conscious influence continued only for some fifty years after publication of the *Divine Weeks*.

We can see Sylvester in Milton's early paraphrases of Psalms. In his rendering of Psalm 114, for example, done, he tells us, when he was fifteen years old, Milton expands his original with Sylvester-like epithets. 'The sea saw it, and fled' becomes 'That saw the *troubl'd* Sea, and *shivering* fled', and 'fled' is expanded quite gratuitously into 'And sought to hide his froth-becurled head', which is almost reminiscent of Sylvester's notorious line 'And periwig with Snow the bald-pate Woods'. But Milton's version of Psalm 136 is quite different. It is not great poetry, but it has assurance, cogency, and technical control :

Let us with a gladsom mind
Praise the Lord, for he is kind,
  For his mercies ay endure,
  Ever faithfull, ever sure. . . .

That by his all-commanding might,
Did fill the new-made world with light. . . .

He with his thunder-clasping hand,
Smote the first-born of *Egypt* land. . . .

The floods stood still like Walls of Glass,
While the Hebrew Bands did pass. . . .

'The floods stood still like Walls of Glass' is an effective poeticizing of the simple original : 'To him which divided the Red
Sea into parts . . . and made Israel to pass through the midst of
it.' But one can pay too much attention to this childish versifying
of Milton's : if he had not developed into a great poet nobody
would have thought it worth serious critical consideration.

With Milton at Christ's College, Cambridge, we get a clearer
picture of him both as man and as 'prentice poet. There can be
no doubt that his fastidious and idealistic temperament resented
the behaviour of the majority of his fellow-students, while his
early training in the Christian humanism of St. Paul's led him
to consider the curriculum at Cambridge as scholastic and re-
actionary. Instead of reading classical works with a view to
examining their rhetorical or poetic structure and learning the
nature of literary style, which is what he had done under Dr. Gill
at St. Paul's, he found himself expected to engage in scholastic
debates on purely formal subjects with a view, presumably, to
acquiring a training in logic. From the beginning Milton found
himself in opposition. 'His first Tutor there,' wrote Aubrey, 'was
Mr. Chapell ; from whom receiving some unkindnesse (whipt
him) he was afterwards (though it seemed contrary to the Rules
of the College) transferred to the Tuition of one Mr. Tovell, who
dyed Parson of Lutterworth.' Whether Milton was actually
whipped by William Chappell, his tutor, is doubtful : the phrase
'whipt him' was added by Aubrey later, between the lines of the
manuscript. But he certainly had a set-to with his tutor, with the

result that he was sent down for a short time, probably early in
1626, and was back again under a new tutor for the Lent Term
of that year.

Milton preserved a group of Latin 'prolusions' or oratorical
exercises which he delivered before his fellow-students in college,
and the first of these shows him conscious of the hostility of his
audience :

> ... What a plight I am in today! In the very first words of my
> speech I am afraid that I am going to say something improper in
> a speaker, and that I shall have to neglect an orator's first and
> most important duty. Indeed, what good will can I expect from
> you when in as great an assembly as this I recognize almost every
> face that I can see as unfriendly to me?

Milton goes on to refer to the rivalries and dissensions between
those who study different subjects or who study the same subjects
in different ways, and then adds significantly, 'But I do not wholly
despair, for, unless I am mistaken, I see here and there some
whose expressions show silently but definitely that they wish me
well.' There were both religious and political factions in Cambridge in Milton's time, Royalist high Anglicans, strict Puritans
and middle-of-the-road Christian humanists. It was to this last
party that Milton would naturally have gravitated, for his idealistic Puritanism was in the tradition of the Platonic Protestantism
of Spenser and Sidney, a tradition that was still maintained at
Cambridge, though the university was no longer the centre of
dissenting Protestantism that it had been under Elizabeth. But
Milton must have found few fellow-students really congenial and
the 'fit audience though few' which he noted among those who
listened to his first prolusion were almost certainly not intimate
friends.

Political and religious differences among members of the
university were probably at this time less interesting to Milton
than different views of the nature and function of knowledge.
Bacon's *Advancement of Learning* had appeared three years before
Milton's birth : it laid down a programme of intellectual advancement in all areas and bitterly attacked the kind of learning which
consisted of mere verbal ingenuity. 'This kind of degenerate
learning did chiefly reign amongst the schoolmen : who having

sharp and strong wits, and abundance of leisure, and small variety of reading, but their wits being shut up in the cells of a few authors (chiefly Aristotle their dictator) as their persons were shut up in the cells of monasteries and colleges, and knowing little history, either of nature or time, did out of no great quantity of matter and infinite agitation of wit spin out unto us those laborious webs of learning which are extant in their books.' The empirical scientist's attack on the scholastic philosophy was often echoed by humanists, who, though not necessarily sharing Bacon's view of the function of knowledge as 'the relief of man's estate', did tend to agree with him about the uselessness of mediaeval disputation. Milton's third prolusion, delivered 'in the public schools' at Cambridge, attacks the scholastic philosophy in terms very reminiscent of Bacon:

> Many times, gentlemen, when I have been forced to investigate these quibbles for a while, my eyes and my mind would be dulled by long reading and I would pause to take breath and try to alleviate my miserable boredom by looking to see how much of my task still remained. And when I saw that there was always more left than I had already got through I often wished that instead of having to stuff myself with this nonsense I had the task of cleaning out the Augean stables again; I considered Hercules a happy man, for good-natured Juno had never set him this sort of labour.

'Divine poetry,' Milton goes on, rouses the mind to high flight, rhetoric stirs the emotions, history, properly written, moves and pleases, 'but these useless and utterly dry controversies and verbal bickerings have no power at all to stir the soul'. They are utterly profitless, 'adding absolutely nothing to knowledge; they are both fruitless and unpleasant'. One is again reminded of Bacon, 'For the wit and mind of man, if it work upon matter, which is the contemplation of the creatures of God, worketh according to the stuff and is limited thereby; but if it work upon itself, as the spider worketh his web, then it is endless, and brings forth indeed cobwebs of learning, admirable for the fineness of thread and work, but of no substance or profit.' Milton's solution is not, however, the Baconian collection of data, but a study of history, geography and the manners of men as well as physics and astronomy:

How much better it would be and how much more worthy of
your academic status to take a view of the whole world set out
on a map, visit in your imagination the places trodden by ancient
heroes, travel through the regions made famous by renowned
poets' tales of wars and triumphs, now crossing the raging
Adriatic, now approaching flame-capped Etna unhurt; and then
observe the manners of men and the well ordering of national
governments, investigate the nature of all living creatures and
thence descending to study the secret properties of stones and
plants. And do not hesitate to rise up to the heavens and behold
there the varied shapes of the clouds, the massive piles of snow
stored up there and the source of early morning dew; then examine
the coffers where hail is kept and survey the arsenals of the thunder-
bolts. And do not let the secrets of Jupiter or Nature escape you
when a large and dreadful comet keeps threatening a conflagration
from heaven, nor let even the smallest stars be hidden from you
in spite of the enormous number of them scattered between the
two poles. . . .

It is interesting that geography should come first in this list.
Milton always had a fondness for maps, and his imagination was
easily kindled by thoughts of different countries spread over the
globe, each with its own geographical features and social customs.
He was to use geographical imagery in *Paradise Lost* as a means
of universalizing the human implications of a story set in Eden
and in ancient Palestine. Geography for him was always a human
rather than a physical study.

There was of course a long Christian tradition of attacks on
vain learning going back to Bernard of Clairvaux's twelfth-
century attack on 'curiositas' and beyond. Curiosity about the
hidden mysteries of the universe was contrasted with the proper
moral knowledge of oneself. The humanists, however, attacked
scholasticism not because it strove after forbidden knowledge
but because it was mere verbalizing or at most 'vain' or useless
knowledge, and in doing so they were joined by the Baconians.
It was Bacon's spirited defence of learning and its high destiny
that captured Milton's imagination. 'Let us conclude with the
dignity and excellence of knowledge and learning in that where-
unto man's nature doth most aspire, which is immortality or con-
tinuance,' wrote Bacon at the end of Book I of the *Advancement*,
and Milton echoed him in his seventh prolusion, arguing that

'knowledge renders man happier than ignorance'. It is true that these prolusions were exercises on set subjects, but Milton was certainly not asked to attack the Cambridge system of education and in any case there is no mistaking the note of personal excitement when he talks of these subjects.

Bacon had looked forward to a steady progress of the arts and sciences in the interests of human happiness and man's control over his environment. Milton, too, was on the side of progress in the great seventeenth-century debate on whether the world was getting better or worse. Political disillusionment was to force a sharp modification of his view later in life, but at this stage he was certainly on the side of the optimists and was to continue there for some time. The argument for the decay of nature had been put in its most elaborate form by Godfrey Goodman in his work *The Fall of Man, or the Corruption of Nature*, published in 1616, and the most comprehensive statement of the case against this (argued from the religious rather than the Baconian point of view), George Hakewill's *An Apologie of the Power and Providence of God*, appeared in 1627, early in Milton's Cambridge career. Milton was with Hakewill, although much later, in the opening of Book IX of *Paradise Lost*, he was to voice one of the arguments of those who believed in the progressive decay of the world :

> . . . unless an age too late, or cold
> Climate, or Years damp my intended wing
> Deprest, . . .

But his view of this question during his Cambridge days was well summed up in a poem in Latin hexameters he wrote for a Fellow of Christ's in 1628 : the set subject was 'Naturam not pati senium', 'that Nature is not subject to old age', and it concludes :

> Sic denique in aevum
> Ibit cunctarum series iustissima rerum,
> Donec flamma orbem populabitur ultima, . . .

Thus, in brief, the perfect sequence of all things shall go on for ever, until the final conflagration shall destroy the world.

Milton also wrote Latin poems for his own amusement, and
some of these give us more intimate glimpses of him than anything he wrote in English. He wrote a series of Ovidian elegiacs,
of which the first, addressed to his friend Charles Diodati, shows
him keeping up his spirits in London during his brief period of
rustication from Cambridge. He professes to be perfectly happy
in his dear native city and not to be interested in the least in returning to the sedgy Cam and the charmless bare fields so un-
congenial to worshippers of Apollo. 'Nor am I disposed to endure
the constant threats of a harsh master and other things not to be
borne by a man of my spirit.' He goes on to paint a picture of
himself leading a life of cultivated leisure, reading, and when he
is tired of that visiting the theatre to see comedies or tragedies.
Or he goes for walks in the spring sunshine and admires the
beauty of the girls he sees:

> Ah quoties dignae stupui miracula formae
>   Quae possit senium vel reparare Iovis;
> Ah quoties vidi superantia lumina gemmas,
>   Atque faces quotquot volvit uterque polus;
> Collaque bis vivi Pelopis quae brachia vincant,
>   Quaeque fluit puro nectare tincta via,
> Et decus eximium frontis, tremulosque capillos,
>   Aurea quae fallax retia tendit Amor; . . .

> Ah, how often have I been struck by the miracle of a beautiful
> form which might even make old Jove young again! Ah, how
> often have I seen eyes brighter than gems and all the stars that
> either pole moves round, necks which excel the arms of the twice-
> living Pelops and the Way which flows coloured with pure nectar,
> a brow of superb beauty, waving tresses thàt are golden nets flung
> by deceiving Love . . .

This section of the poem concludes with an eloquent picture of
'Alma Venus', Venus the giver of life, deserting her traditional
haunts to come to London. This was a side of his nature which
he never revealed in his English poetry. And it is not to be thought
that it is merely an Ovidian exercise; other Latin poems of
Milton's youth show the same excited interest in female beauty
and in sex. Paradoxical though it may seem to the modern reader,

Milton used Latin to express intimate feelings that he could never bring himself to reveal in English. His skill in writing Ovidian elegiacs was remarkable, though it is perhaps surprising that he should have chosen as a model a Latin poet so different from himself in temperament and one whose style, for all its artfulness, was so limited in range. Milton, who in many respects was more of an Elizabethan than a man of the seventeenth century, shared the Elizabethan feeling for Ovid as the great narrator of classical myth, the poet who transmitted in lively and picturesque form the whole achievement of the classical imagination.

Meanwhile, he was trying his hand at English poetry. About the same time as his first Latin Elegy he produced a poem on the death of his niece, 'On the Death of a Fair Infant Dying of a Cough'. This, probably Milton's earliest English poem except for the two Psalm paraphrases already discussed, is an ambitious work in an Elizabethan rhetorical style; there are echoes of Ovid as well as of Phineas Fletcher (from whom he probably derived the stanza-form he uses), and there is a liberal sprinkling of conceits that are not really functional in the poem. The poem is indeed a mass of separate conceits, obviously the work of a young poet indulging in an exhibitionist use of language. It opens with a not ineffective rhetorical formality:

> O fairest flower no sooner blown but blasted,
> Soft silken Primrose fading timelesslie,
> Summers chief honour if thou hadst out-lasted
> Bleak winters force that made thy blossome drie;
> For he being amorous on that lovely die
>   That did thy cheek envermeil, thought to kiss
> But kill'd alas, and then bewayl'd his fatal bliss.

The force of the opening line is diminished somewhat by the alternative descriptions that follow: the consecutive descriptions do not rise to a climax but simply play variations on the initial statement. Nevertheless, the first four lines do achieve a certain cogency: it is only when a new kind of thought, with its deliberate ingenuity, is introduced in the fifth line that we begin to wonder whether this is not an exercise rather than a true poem. It is, in its way, artful enough, with the paradoxical sequence—thought to *kiss*, but *kill'd*, then *bewayl'd*, *fatal bliss*, with the final word

coming round again to an association with the word it rhymes
with (bliss, kiss) after the open, plangent vowels in between
(bewayl'd, fatal). But the whole notion of winter being in love
with the dye on the infant's cheek and so kissing and involun-
tarily killing her is strained and even absurd. It needs a certain
kind of Elizabethan *bravura* or else genuine metaphysical wit to
bring off such a conceit, and Milton as yet had neither.

It is interesting that Milton's impulse is to make a classical
myth out of the whole situation. Winter, he explains in the second
stanza, wanted 'some fair one' to marry, 'to wipe away th'in-
famous blot, / Of long-uncoupled bed, and childless eld'. It was
not simply a sudden passion for the red dye on the infant's cheek,
but a well-thought-out policy that led him to kiss and kill the
infant. The third stanza continues:

> So mounting up in ycie-pearled carr,
> Through middle empire of the freezing aire
> He wandered long, till thee he spy'd from farr,
> There ended was his quest, there ceast his care.
> Down he descended from his Snow-soft chaire,
>   But all unwares with his cold-kind embrace
> Unhous'd thy Virgin Soul from her fair biding place.

This is skilfully done. There is a rhythmic ease in Milton's handling of the actual words and lines that is impressive. 'Down he
descended from his Snow-soft chaire' is very well contrived. But
the 'cold-kind embrace' is a tedious echo of the end of the first
stanza, and 'her fair biding place' lacks conviction; it sounds
padded out for the sake of the rhythm and rhyme.

The rest of the poem is largely taken up with ingenious
mythological speculations intended to provide comfort. 'Yet art
thou not inglorious in thy fate'—because Apollo slew Hyacinth
accidentally injust the same way, and 'transform'd him to a
purple flower'. The next stanza repeats the 'Yet' in a different
context:

> Yet can I not perswade me thou art dead
> Or that thy coarse corrupts in earths dark wombe,
> Or that thy beauties lie in wormie bed,

Hid from the world in a low delved tombe:
Could Heav'n for pity thee so strictly doom?
Oh no! for something in thy face did shine
Above mortalitie that shew'd thou wast divine

The question and answer here (especially the reply, 'Oh no!')
hover on the brink of the ridiculous. But it is interesting that only
in this, the fifth stanza of the poem, does the imagery begin, in
however slight a degree, to be Christian rather than classical. The
sixth stanza develops the Christian implications:

Resolve me then oh Soul most surely blest
(If so it be that thou these plaints dost hear)
Tell me bright Spirit where e're thou hoverest
Whether above that high first-moving Spheare
Or in the Elisian fields (if such there were.)
Oh say me true if thou wert mortal wight
And why from us so quickly thou didst take thy flight.

Having accepted Apollo, Hyacinth and other mythological
figures, Milton suddenly feels a Christian compunction about the
Elysian fields and adds the significant qualification 'if such there
were', reminding us of what he was to do in *Paradise Lost* in
comparing Eden to the Garden of the Hesperides:

Hesperian Fables true,
If true, here only, . . .

The concluding lines of this stanza are very Spenserian in tone,
but there is a Miltonic ring in

Whether above that high first-moving Spheare

that reminds us of lines in *Comus* and 'Lycidas'.

The speculative questions which follow are purely pagan
again:

Wert thou some Starr which from the ruin'd roofe
Of shak't Olympus by mischance didst fall;
Which carefull *Jove* in natures true behoofe
Took up, and in fit place did reinstall?

Or perhaps the infant was the 'just Maid', Astraea, returning to
earth again for a visit, or Mercy (though this is an editorial
conjecture to complete a defective line) or Truth,

> Or any other of that heav'nly brood
> Let down in clowdie throne to do the world some good.

Or was she a Christian angel visiting from Heaven? We could do
with angels on earth to intercede against the plague:

> But oh why didst thou not stay here below
> To bless us with thy heav'n-lov'd innocence,
> To slake his wrath whom sin hath made our foe,
> To turn Swift-rushing black perdition hence,
> Or drive away the slaughtering pestilence,
>   To stand 'twixt us and our deserved smart?
> But thou canst best perform that office where thou art.

Although this stanza has a certain eloquence and assurance, there
is nothing at all Miltonic about it. It might have been written by
any one of half a dozen late Elizabethan or early Jacobean minor
poets. The same can be said of the concluding stanza, where
Milton addresses the mother of the child (his own elder sister)
with grave sententiousness:

> Then thou the mother of so sweet a child
> Her false imagin'd loss cease to lament,
> And wisely learn to curb thy sorrows wild;
> Think what a present thou to God hast sent,
> And render him with patience what he lent;
>   This if thou do he will an off-spring give,
> That till the worlds last-end shall make thy name to live.

This first full-dress English poem of Milton's is not, taken as
a whole, successful, but it has many features of interest. It shows
him as yet unable to integrate pagan classical imagery into a
Christian theme; each element exists in the poem separately. It
shows Spenserian and post-Spenserian influences, together with
an occasional line which rings out with a new kind of gravity and
eloquence. It has echoes of Ovid and of Ovid's way of handling

mythological stories. It reveals an experimental ear for rhetorical and decorative devices and at the same time a 'sage and serious' temperament.

But Milton was writing many more Latin than English poems at this time. The second and third of his Latin elegies are dated by him, as was the 'Ode on the Death of a Fair Infant', *Anno Aetatis 17*, by which he probably meant 'at the age of 17'. The 'Elegia Secunda' is a poem in Ovidian elegiacs on the death of the Cambridge University Beadle : it is an ingenious piece of mythologizing, where the beadle is likened to a whole series of classical mythological figures. It was presumably intended to be mock-heroic, though the elaborate comparisons of a university official to figures in Greek and Roman legend may well have been meant more seriously by the young Milton than it is taken by us today. There can be no doubt, however, that the 'Elegia Tertia' is wholly serious. It is on the death of the Bishop of Winchester, Lancelot Andrewes, for whom Milton shared the almost universal respect and affection. Here there is a deliberate difference in tone and depth of meaning between the classical and the Christian elements. The former are used in similes for purely decorative purposes, but the latter, which emerge towards the end of the poem when the poet describes his dream of the bishop entering Heaven amid the applause of the angels, carry much greater weight. He ends by exclaiming 'Talia contingant somnia saepe mihi'—'May such dreams come to me often', which seems a remarkably egotistical ending to a poem of this sort until one realizes that (as Professor Rand has suggested) Milton is probably adapting, with an almost impudent audacity, Ovid's line praying for the return of another happy day with Corinna, 'Proveniant medii sic mihi saepe dies.'

Milton also wrote poems in Horatian metres during his eighteenth year. The poem on the death of the Bishop of Ely, 'In Obitum Praesulis Eliensis', is (except for one allusion to Elijah's ascent to Heaven) entirely classical in its imagery as the poet tells how he heard 'in the gently moving air' the voice of the bishop describing how he was borne aloft through the skies until he reached the shining portals of Olympus. The rhetorical elaboration in the poem is somewhat excessive, though there are some fine imaginative touches. The Alcaics he wrote on the death of the Vice-Chancellor are again full of classical imagery—the goddess of Fate, Tartarus, Styx, Nessus, Hercules, Troy, Hector, Athene, are all mentioned in the first fifteen lines—but a more personal note emerges in the conclusion, which has a fine benedictory eloquence:

> Colende praeses, membra precor tua
> Molli quiescant cespite, et ex tuo
>   Crescant rosae, calthaeque busto,
>   Purpureoque hyacinthus ore.
>
> Sit mite de te judicium Aeaci,
> Subrideatque Ennaea Proserpina,
>   Interque felices perennis
>   Elysio spatiere campo.

Revered President, I pray that your limbs may rest in soft turf and that from your grave may grow roses and marigolds and the purple-mouthed hyacinth. May the judgment of Aeacus on you be gentle, and may Sicilian Proserpine smile on you. And may you walk forever among the blessed in the Elysian Fields.

One of the most interesting of the Latin poems Milton wrote at this time is his mock-epic poem on the gunpowder plot, 'In Quintum Novembris', which shows the influence of Phineas Fletcher's *Locustae* (a Latin poem on the same theme) and, in parts, of Giles Fletcher's elaborate allegorical poem, *The Purple Island*. Milton's poem, in hexameters, opens with an account of Satan's determination to stir up hatred and disturbance in the peaceful realm of King James. Satan journeys to England, to find there a pious, God-fearing people; he grinds his teeth in rage and goes off to Rome to rouse the Pope in a dream against the English so that a Catholic monarch may be restored to the English throne. The following morning the 'Babylonish priest' (i.e. the Pope) gives orders for the English King and nobles alike to be blown into thin air. But God looks down and smiles; he orders Rumour to spread reports of the treachery that is afoot; and so (in a most perfunctory ending) the plot is discovered and the culprits arrested and punished. There is a naïve violence about the poem which has its own appeal, though not at a very serious level. Satan observing in rage the prosperous and pious

English people who alone continue to rebel against him is the
faintest of sketches for the self-torturing Satan of *Paradise Lost*
peering jealously at Adam and Eve in Eden. But there is a wonderful relish in the descriptions of darkness and evil. A papal procession in Rome is described in terms of black orgies—'Cimmeriis
nati in tenebris, vitamque trahentes'—'they are born and pass their
lives in Cimmerian darkness'—and Satan's speech at the ear of
the sleeping Pope has the true note of whispered conspiracy. The
description of Satan's journey from England to Rome has some
vivid touches, but the core of the poem is the lurid scenes in Rome.
There is a kind of poetic high spirits in the poem which Milton
preferred to exhibit in Latin rather than in English. Milton also
wrote a number of Latin epigrams on the gunpowder plot.

Milton's fourth Latin elegy was written when he was eighteen
to his former tutor Thomas Young. Young was in Hamburg, and
Milton employs elaborate Ovidian machinery in speeding his
letter across the sea:

> Curre per immensum subitò, mea littera, pontum,
>   I, pete Teutonicos laeve per aequor agros, . . .

> Speed quickly over the vast sea, oh my letter;
> Go, and over the smooth sea seek German fields, . . .

This goes on for some fifteen lines crowded with imagery from
classical story, and then the poem turns into an account of the
poet's friendship for Young and of all that Young had done for
him:

> Primus ego Aonios illo praeeunte recessus
>   Lustrabam, et bifidi sacra vireta jugi,
> Pieriosque hausi latices, Clioque favente,
>   Castalio sparsi laeta ter ora mero.

> Under his guidance I first visited the Aonian vales and the
> sacred sward of the twin-peaked mountains, drank of the Pierian
> spring and by Clio's grace thrice wet my joyful lips with Castalian
> wine.

This, it must be remembered, was a letter to a Presbyterian divine
who was later to join in the pamphlet war against episcopacy,

thus encouraging Milton to join the battle in his defence. That Milton, passionately idealist Christian and dedicated poet-priest that he was, should have written in this strain to his old teacher is a reminder that Puritanism was not the simple phenomenon it is sometimes taken to have been and that there were classical humanists among the Puritan camp as well as on the other side. The poem, which is one hundred and twenty-six lines long, is written throughout in a vein of exhibitionist classicism. Milton was showing off to a Scottish Presbyterian divine by demonstrating how well he could write like a pagan author.

Of course Milton himself had not yet clearly defined his religious position *vis-à-vis* the conflicting sects of his time, and there is no evidence that at this stage he had any thought of repudiating the Anglican mode of worship—indeed, such evidence as exists is entirely the other way. In *The Reason of Church Government*, published in 1641, Milton explained that he had been originally destined to the Church 'by the intentions of my parents and friends . . . and in mine own resolutions, till comming to some maturity of yeers and perceaving what tyranny had invaded the Church, that he who would take Orders must subscribe slave, and take an oath withall, which unlesse he took with a conscience that would retch, I thought it better to preferre a blamelesse silence before the sacred office of speaking bought, and begun with servitude and forswearing'. Nevertheless, his high Protestant idealism manifested itself in many ways during his years at Cambridge, and if he was not yet in the strict sense a Puritan (i.e. one who desired a simpler and 'purer' form of church worship than the Church of England allowed), his dedicated way of life, his mystical view of chastity, his withdrawal from every kind of undergraduate horseplay and the delicacy of bearing and behaviour which earned him the name of 'the Lady of Christ's', bore ample witness to the central part that Christianity played in his attitude and conduct. If in spite of this he could write pagan poems, both Latin and English, with such relish, and if heightened emotion of loss or friendship again and again sought expression in terms of classical mythology, this only shows the central part which a classical humanism could, in the seventeenth century or in the sixteenth, play in the mind of a strict Protestant Christian.

Milton began his poetic career by completely separating the Christian and the classical elements in his education: he wrote English verse paraphrases of Psalms and Latin imitations of Ovid. But it was not long before he began to make a variety of attempts to accommodate the two within the same context. One of the most interesting of his early combinations of classical and Christian elements is his view of the music of the spheres and its relation to virtue and chastity. In the second of his Latin prolusions Milton discussed the music of the spheres. The idea is Pythagorean and Platonic in origin, but Milton developed it in his own way. 'What though no one on earth has ever heard this symphony of the stars,' asked Milton, 'does that mean that everything beyond the moon's sphere is absolutely silent in benumbing sleep? No, let us rather blame our own feeble ears, which cannot catch the songs or are not worthy to overhear such sweet strains. . . . If our hearts were as pure, spotless and snowy white as that of Pythagoras was, then indeed our ears would resound and be filled with that most delightful music of the circling stars. Then indeed all things would seem to return to the age of gold.' Milton developed the theory that each of the planetary spheres sounded a note so that a perfect harmony resulted, symbolizing the divine order of things, by associating with it the vision in the fourteenth chapter of Revelation describing the 'new song before the throne' which could be heard only by the hundred and forty and four thousand which were not defiled with women. Music, divine order and chastity became associated in his mind, and we shall find evidence of this association in the 'Nativity Ode', in *Arcades* and in *Comus*. In 1642, in the *Apology for Smectymnuus*, Milton recalled the development of his own views on this subject. He is defending himself against a charge of loose living:

This that I have hitherto related, hath bin to shew, that though Christianity had bin but slightly taught me, yet a certain reserv'd-nesse of naturall disposition, and morall discipline learnt out of the noblest Philosophy was anough to keep me in disdain of farre lesse incontinences then this of the Burdello. But having had the doctrine of holy Scripture unfolding those chaste and high mysteries with timeliest care infus'd, that *the body is for the Lord and the Lord for the body*, thus also I argu'd to my selfe; that if unchastity

in a woman whom Saint *Paul* termes the glory of man, be such a
scandall and dishonour, then certainly in a man who is both the
image and glory of God, it must, though commonly not so thought,
be much more deflouring and dishonourable. . . . Nor did I slumber
over that place expressing such high rewards of ever accompanying
the Lambe, with those celestiall songs to others inapprehensible,
but not to those who were not defil'd with women, which doubtless
meanes fornication: For mariage must not be call'd a defilement.

Milton may well not have subscribed to this last clause in his
student days at Cambridge. At any rate, it is clear that as a young
man he worked out a doctrine of chastity based on a combination
of classical and Christian sources and he seems to have really
believed that if he kept himself chaste the divine music of the
spheres might become audible to him. The Pythagorean harmonies
eventually became for him

> That undisturbed Song of pure concent,
> Ay sung before the saphire-colour'd throne
> To him that sits theron
> With Saintly shout, and solemn Jubily,
> Where the bright Seraphim in burning row
> Their loud up-lifted Angel trumpets blow,
> And the Cherubick host in thousand quires
> Touch their immortal Harps of golden wires,
> With those just Spirits that wear victorious Palms,
> Hymns devout and holy Psalms
> Singing everlastingly; . . .

In the second prolusion he explained that it was the robber
Prometheus, by his theft of fire from Heaven, who was responsible for man's being deprived of the privilege of hearing the
divine harmony, but a few years later it was the Fall of Man that
was to blame. The passage from 'At a Solemn Musick' quoted
above continues:

> That we on Earth with undiscording voice
> May rightly answer that melodious noise;
> As once we did, till disproportion'd sin
> Jarr'd against natures chime, and with harsh din

Broke the fair musick that all creatures made
To their great Lord, whose love their motion sway'd
In perfet Diapason, whilst they stood
In first obedience, and their state of good.

It took no great effort of the Christian humanist mind to associate the Prometheus myth with the Christian story of the Fall—
indeed, such associations had long been a commonplace of
Christian thought. Similarly, the association of Christ with Pan
in the Nativity Ode implies a Christian symbolism in a pagan
story. But the music-chastity doctrine that Milton forged for himself had a quality all its own, and was deeply rooted in the sources
of Milton's moral imagination. It is significant that in 'At a
Solemn Musick' he describes the divine harmony as having been
audible to men 'whilst they stood in first obedience', and *Paradise
Lost* begins, 'Of Mans First Disobedience, . . .'

Milton's sixth prolusion is in some ways the most interesting
of all, for at the end he breaks off the Latin and moves into
English verse, to express his intention of writing poetry in his
native language. The subject set was 'that sometimes sportive
exercises are not prejudicial to philosophic studies' and he delivered the oration in 1627 (if his own dating is correct) in the
summer holidays, but, according to custom, with almost all of
the young men of the college assembled. It was a 'vacation
exercise', and Milton was expected to amuse his audience. He
begins his Latin oration by complaining that he has been torn
away from his literary and philosophical studies in order to take
part in this annual foolery, but he goes on to say that members
of his College had been very courteous to him recently, so he is
ready to play the part assigned to him. Evidently his relations
with his fellow-students had improved since the time of his first
prolusion. He develops his theme at considerable length, with a
rather ponderous humour, and then proceeds with an 'exercise'
in which he amuses himself by playing with personifications of
Aristotelian and scholastic notions; it is in the course of this
'exercise' that he refers to the nickname of 'the Lady' given him
by his fellow-students and remarks that this must be because he
cannot quaff huge bumpers or because his hand has not become
calloused by holding the plough, or because he never lay on his

back under the sun at noon like an ox-driver or 'never proved myself a man in the same way as those brothellers'. Then suddenly, 'leaping over academic laws as though they are the walls of Romulus' and asking for his listeners' careful attention, he breaks into English verse:

> Hail native Language, that by sinews weak
> Didst move my first endeavouring tongue to speak,
> And mad'st imperfect words with childish tripps,
> Half unpronounc't, slide through my infant-lipps, . . .
> Here I salute thee and thy pardon ask,
> That now I use thee in my latter task: . . .
> I pray thee then deny me not thy aide
> For this same small neglect that I have made:
> But haste thee strait to do me once a Pleasure,
> And from thy wardrope bring thy chiefest treasure;
> Not those new fangled toys, and trimming slight
> Which take our late fantasticks with delight,
> But cull those richest Robes, and gay'st attire
> Which deepest Spirits, and choicest Wits desire:
> I have some naked thoughts that rove about
> And loudly knock to have their passage out; . . .

It is typical of Milton that he should proclaim his resolution to devote himself to English rather than Latin poetry in a public oration to his fellow-students. The resolution itself was not so obvious as it may seem to us. Milton had proved his ability at Latin verse, for which there was still a European audience, while English was the comparatively little-known language of a small island. One must not think of Latin as an important international medium in Europe only in the Middle Ages. Renaissance humanism revived Latin as a medium for imaginative literature, and Milton would not have despised the reputation of a Mantuan (Baptista Spanuoli, the fifteenth-century Vicar-General of the Carmelites in Mantua) whose Latin eclogues had long been a standard book for schoolboys, or a George Buchanan, the sixteenth-century Scotsman, whose Latin poems and dramas were known throughout Europe.

The terms in which Milton hails the English language are most interesting. The emphasis on the fact that it is his own native tongue, on which he was brought up, suggests that he felt that he could express his 'naked thoughts' more fully and immediately in a language that had been his from infancy and that a foreign tongue, however well mastered, could never mean the same to him. There is clearly more here than a careerist resolve to be an English rather than a Latin poet : deep emotional factors are involved. Those who accuse Milton of forcing English into a Latin mould should at least realize that he expressed the sense of the *nativeness* of his native English more forcefully than any English poet has ever done.

In dismissing 'those new fangled toys, and trimming slight/ Which takes our late fantasticks with delight', Milton may have been thinking of the Metaphysical style or perhaps he was repudiating a fashion of over-fancy word play among some of the Cambridge young men (he had attacked such a 'ridiculous foam of words' in his first prolusion). He seeks a richer and deeper utterance : the terms 'richest Robes', 'deepest Spirits' and 'choicest Wits' are significant. He goes on to discuss the kind of subject that interests him :

> Yet I had rather if I were to chuse,
> Thy service in some graver subject use,
> Such as may make thee search thy coffers round,
> Before thou cloath my fancy in fit sound :
> Such where the deep transported mind may soare
> Above the wheeling poles, and at Heav'ns dore
> Look in, and see each blissful Deitie
> How he before the thunderous throne doth lie,
> Listening to what unshorn *Apollo* sings
> To th'touch of golden wires, . . .
> Then sing of secret things that came to pass
> When Beldam Nature in her cradle was ;
> And last of Kings and Queens and *Hero's* old,
> Such as the wise *Demodocus* once told
> In solemn Songs at King *Alcinous* feast,
> While sad *Ulisses* soul and all the rest
> Are held with his melodious harmonie
> In willing chains and sweet captivitie.

The verse sings out in quiet eloquence at the close of this passage ; Milton's imagination is now really involved. He is thinking in

terms of cosmic imagery involving the whole created universe, and
the origin of things ; but he wants not only to impress but also to
move to tears, as Demodocus, the bard of King Alcinoüs, moved
Ulysses to tears : 'but the heart of Ulysses was melted, and tears
wet his cheeks beneath his eyelids' (*Odyssey*, VIII, 522). It seems
that he wants to be Homer and Lucretius and Ovid all in one.
So far, it is worth noting, he is content to express his poetic
ambitions in images that are at least outwardly wholly classical
and pagan.

Milton did not, in spite of his public profession of allegiance
to his native language, give up Latin poetry. Perhaps the finest
of his Latin poems was written in 1628 or 1629 when he was
nineteen or twenty years of age. This is his fifth elegy, the 'In
Adventum Veris', a poem on the coming of spring which pulses
with a kind of sensual excitement in the renewal of life and growth
that we never find to the same degree in the English poems. The
idiom is again Ovidian, as the opening lines at once establish :

> In se perpetuo Tempus revolubile gyro
> Iam revocat Zephyros, vere tepente novos.
> Induiturque brevem Tellus reparata juventam,
> Iamque soluta gelu dulce virescit humus.

> Time, turning in its eternal circle, now as the spring grows
> warmer brings back the zephyrs anew. Earth, with her strength
> renewed, puts on her brief youth, and the ground, now freed
> from frost, grows sweetly green.

Spring, poetry and love are all associated in the excited poet's
mind :

> Fallor ? an et nobis redeunt in carmina vires,
> Ingeniumque mihi munere veris adest ?

> Am I deceived ? Or are my powers of song also returning, and
> is my inspiration here by the grace of spring ?

It is true that Milton's nephew, Edward Philips, who had lived
with his uncle and been educated by him, wrote in his *Life of
Milton* that 'his vein never happily flowed but from the autumnal

equinoctial to the vernal', which suggests that he wrote poetry
most easily in the winter, but we must not take this as evidence
that the statement in this poem is a piece of imitative poeticizing.
Tillyard is surely right in repudiating Masson's view that the
poem is laborious and the mood simulated, and in maintaining
that 'it is curiously turgid and swift, and pulsates like not a single
other in the elegiac metre'. The crowded and ecstatic imagery
carries its own conviction :

> Quid tam grande sonat distento spiritus ore ?
> Quid parit haec rabies, quid sacer iste furor ?

> What lofty strain does my spirit utter with full throat ?
> What will this madness, this divine frenzy, bring forth ?

He can modulate the tone, too, as in the liquid lines about the
nightingale :

> Iam, Philemela, tuos foliis adoperta novellis
> Instituis modulos, dum silet omne nemus,

which can be roughly translated by the opening lines of the sonnet
to the nightingale which he wrote about the same time :

> O Nightingale, that on yon bloomy Spray
> Warbl'st at eve, when all the Woods are still, . . .

The picture of the passionate earth craving for the embraces of
Phoebus is heavily sensuous in movement and imagery, and the
account of Cupid going forth to stir up love throughout the world
has a kind of gaiety we do not normally associate with Milton.
There is a pastoral scene, with the shepherd piping to Phyllis who
adds her songs to his, and a carefully wrought picture of the
satyrs dancing through the flowery fields as the evening shadows
lengthen :

> Nunc etiam Satyri cum sera crepuscula surgunt,
> Pervolitant celeri florea rura choro, . . .

The poem ends with a characteristic plea (we are to find it often

in the early Milton) for a return of the Golden Age—or at least
for the spring to pass slowly and the long nights of winter to come
later than usual.

A similar mood, though lighter and fresher, is to be found in
a charming English fragment, 'On May Morning', which he wrote
about this time or a little later:

> Now the bright morning Star, Dayes harbinger,
> Comes dancing from the East, and leads with her
> The Flowry *May*, who from her green lap throws
> The yellow Cowslip, and the pale Primrose. . . .

This is in the best tradition of Elizabethan song. The nightingale
sonnet is another of the group of poems written probably in
1628, many of them in Italian, which show a special feeling for
Nature and for love.

It was probably in 1628 also that Milton wrote a group of
sonnets in Italian celebrating his love for a lady apparently called
Emilia who, we gather, was a singer and was perhaps foreign (he
talks of her 'pellegrina bellezza', which may mean 'foreign beauty'
or, less literally, 'rare beauty'). The love affair may not have been
any more serious than the attack by Cupid which he celebrated
in Ovidian elegiacs in his 'Elegia Septima'—perhaps both the Latin
and the Italian poems celebrate the same event. The sonnets are
a weaving together of Petrarchan fancies with an occasional flash
of original phrasing and perception. They have a calm and gentle
gravity which the Latin poem lacks. The finest is the charming
sonnet 'Qual in colle aspro', which is both more original and more
gracefully phrased than the others:

> Qual in colle aspro, a l'imbrunir di sera,
>   L'avezza giovinetta pastorella
>   Va bagnando l'herbetta strana e bella,
>   Che mal si spande a disusata spera,
> Fuor di sua natia alma primavera,
>   Così Amor meco insù la lingua snella
>   Desta il fior novo di strania favella,
>   Mentre io di te, vezzosamente altera,
> Canto, . . .

As on a rugged hill when the evening darkens
The young shepherdess, brought up there,
Is wont to water the strange and beautiful little plant
Which feebly spreads its leaves in the unfamiliar clime
Far from its native fostering springtime,
So Love on my prompt tongue
Calls forth the novel flower of a strange speech
When of you, gracious and noble lady,
I sing, . . .

Another of these sonnets, 'Giovane piano, e semplicetto amante',
is an interesting mixture of conventional Petrarchan imagery and
an original self-portrait of the poet as constant in mood and
gracious, courteous and virtuous in thought, confident and stead-
fast amid worldly changes and keenly ambitious for intellectual
and poetic distinction. Among these Italian sonnets Milton included a charming canzone on the same theme : he tells how young
men and women ask him why he writes in a strange tongue when
another kind of immortal guerdon is awaiting him (i.e. as a poet
in English), and he replies :

> Dice mia Donna, e'l suo dir e il mio cuore,
> Questa è lingua di cui si vanta Amore.

> My Lady says, and her speech is my heart,
> 'This is the language of which Love boasts.'

Milton's interest in Italian poetry extended far beyond
Petrarchan love sonnets. Italian literature played an important
part in his poetic development, and the influence of Della Casa
on his English sonnets and of Bembo, Della Casa and Tasso on
the development of his epic style will be discussed later. Meanwhile, it is worth noting that the young Milton, while still a
student at Cambridge, wrote a series of Italian love poems inspired if not by a passionate love affair at least by admiration
for an attractive dark-eyed singer who knew Italian among other
languages.

Milton took his B.A. degree at Cambridge in March 1629,
but he remained at the university until the summer of 1632, when

he took his M.A. In December, 1629, he wrote a set of Latin elegiacs—the 'Elegia Sexta'—to his friend Diodati. It is a genial and fluent poem, full of the usual mythologizing, but the conclusion strikes a different note. If you want to know what I am doing, he tells Diodati,

> Paciferum canimus caelesti semine regem,
> Faustaque sacratis saecula pacta libris.

I am singing the heaven-born King, the peace-bearer, and the blessed times promised in Holy Scripture.

These lines, he goes on, are to be his birthday gift to Christ. He also has ready to recite to Diodati a simpler poem played on his native pipes. The latter is probably the lines 'On May Morning', and the Christmas poem is the ode 'On the Morning of Christ's Nativity', generally known as the Nativity Ode.

The Nativity Ode shows Milton working within the Spenserian tradition: there are clear echoes of Spenser himself, of Phineas Fletcher, and others. The ode is in two parts, a more heavily orchestrated introduction, in the same stanza that he had used in 'On the Death of a Fair Infant', and the hymn, in a lighter eight-lined stanza. Both stanzas conclude with a Spenserian alexandrine. The poem opens in solemn, declaratory tones:

> This is the Month, and this the happy morn
> Wherin the Son of Heav'ns eternal King,
> Of wedded Maid, and Virgin Mother born,
> Our great redemption from above did bring;
> For so the holy sages once did sing,
>   That he our deadly forfeit should release,
>   And with his Father work us a perpetual peace.

The emphatic opening *This*, repeated twice in the first line, has the effect of an arresting gesture. The stanza has a solidity throughout; phrases like 'great redemption from above' and 'work us a perpetual peace' give a sense of largeness and assurance. The tone is sustained in the second stanza, which ends with a characteristic reference to Christ as hero:

>   ... and here with us to be,
> Forsook the Courts of everlasting Day,
> And chose with us a darksom House of mortal Clay.

The fourth and last stanza of the introduction brings in a sense
of movement which provides the external framework of the poem.
The Wise Men from the East are bringing their gifts to the child;
Milton will anticipate ('prevent', in its Latin sense of 'come
before') them, bringing his ode as a gift. At the end of the poem
the Wise Men have arrived and the guiding star now stands still
over the stable. The change of rhythm and of stanza-form which
comes with the opening of the hymn sets off the 'gift' from the
introductory explanation almost in the same way that Shakespeare sets off the play within the play from the main action in
Hamlet. The hymn is the set-piece which the introduction talks
about; it is therefore more stylized, more deliberately artful, than
the introduction. The suggestion of baroque about the imagery,
the use of elaborate pathetic fallacies and similar conceits, mark
at once the difference between the tone of the hymn and that of
the preceding introduction:

>   It was the Winter wilde,
>   While the Heav'n-born-childe,
>   All meanly wrapt in the rude manger lies;
>   Nature in aw to him
>   Had doff't her gawdy trim,
>   With her great Master so to sympathize:
>   It was no season then for her
>   To wanton with the Sun her lusty Paramour.

We are reminded of the *Elegia Quinta*:

>   Exuit invisam Tellus rediviva senectam,
>   Et cupit amplexus, Phoebe, subire tuos.

>   The reviving earth casts off hateful old age and eagerly seeks
> thy embraces, O Phoebus.

For Milton at this stage, the more classical the more artful. The
imagery of the introduction is purely Christian, but that of the
hymn, being a more consciously artful set-piece, has more

elaborate artifice, which means among other things more classical references. The picture of the earth hiding her guilty front
with innocent snow, in the second stanza of the hymn, is again
artificial in the sense appropriate to a poem-within-a-poem.
Similarly, the imagery in the third stanza is consciously ornate:

> But he her fears to cease,
> Sent down the meek-eyd Peace,
>   She crown'd with Olive green, came softly sliding
> Down through the turning sphear
> His ready Harbinger,
>   With Turtle wing the amorous clouds dividing,
> And waving wide her mirtle wand,
> She strikes a universall Peace through Sea and Land.

Peace sliding down through the turning sphere on wings of love,
meek-eyed, crowned with olive green, and waving a myrtle wand,
is a deliberately baroque image; but it is not only the image that
arrests—the distribution of the description between the lines of
varying lengths is most cunningly done, and the whole stanza
coaxes the idea as well as the image into the reader's imagination, to prepare him for the hushing of the poem into silence in
the next two stanzas. First the images of war—

> No War, or Battels sound
> Was heard the World around:
>   The idle spear and shield were high up hung;
> The hooked Chariot stood
> Unstain'd with hostile blood,
>   The trumpet spake not to the armed throng,—

and then the whole poem is arrested into stillness:

> But peacefull was the night
> Wherein the Prince of light
>   His raign of peace upon the earth began:
> The Windes with wonder whist,
> Smoothly the waters kist,
>   Whispering new joyes to the milde Ocean,
> Who now hath quite forgot to rave,
> While Birds of Calm sit brooding on the charmed wave.

The manipulation of words here—peaceful, peace, smoothly, mild, calm, brooding, and the more onomatopoeic whist, kist, whispering—hardly needs pointing out. There are subtler and more complex ways of handling poetic language, but none more effective for its purpose. The sense of arrested motion is emphasized in the following stanza, describing how even the influence of the stars (in the astrological sense) is frozen in one direction; the sun, too, is arrested in the heavens and hides his head before the greater Son. The stage of the heavens is set for some tremendous revelation. But before the revelation, we are shown the audience, with the deliberate paradox that this great scene in the history of man is first shown to a few humble shepherds:

> The Shepherds on the Lawn,
> Or e're the point of dawn,
>   Sate simply chatting in a rustick row;
> Full little thought they than,
> That the mighty *Pan*
>   Was kindly com to live with them below;
> Perhaps their loves, or els their sheep,
> Was all that did their silly thoughts so busie keep.

Milton momentarily lures us away from the celestial vision to look at the simple shepherds unaware of what is about to happen. (Christ is, significantly, the mighty Pan, an early classical-Christian synthesis.) And then—all the more effective because our attention has been turned away from it to the shepherds—the revelation comes. It is not, however, at first, a visual appearance, but something which strikes the ear; the music of the spheres is now heard:

> When such musick sweet
> Their hearts and ears did greet,
>   As never was by mortall finger strook,
> Divinely-warbl'd voice
> Answering the stringed noise,
>   As all their souls in blissfull rapture took:
> The Air such pleasure loth to lose,
> With thousand echo's still prolongs each heav'nly close.

Nature that heard such sound
Beneath the hollow round
  Of *Cynthia's* seat, the Airy region thrilling,
Now was almost won
To think her part was don,
  And that her raign had here its last fulfilling;
She knew such harmony alone
Could hold all Heav'n and Earth in happier union.

Milton allows his imagination to dwell on the congenial idea of
a restored Golden Age, when the divine harmony would be
heard by men as it was before the Fall and Heaven and Earth
be joined together again.

The whole effect is, one might say, theatrical. First, the
hushing into silence. Then a brief look at the audience. Then,
suddenly, the ravishing music. Finally, after the music has been
playing for some time, the curtain slowly rises and we actually
see the angelic choir singing:

At last surrounds their sight
A Globe of circular light,
  That with long beams the shame-fac't night array'd,
The helmed Cherubim
And sworded Seraphim,
  Are seen in glittering ranks with wings displaid,
Harping in loud and solemn quire,
With unexpressive notes to Heavens new-born Heir.

As we watch the angelic choir performing on their lighted stage
the music swells out louder and louder to the central climax of
the poem:

Ring out ye Crystall sphears,
Once bless our human ears,
  (If ye have power to touch our senses so)
And let your silver chime
Move in melodious time;
  And let the Base of Heav'ns deep Organ blow,
And with your ninefold harmony
Make up full consort to th'Angelike symphony.

Music symbolizes the divine order; when we hear the 'unexpressive' (i.e. inexpressible) notes we also see the cherubim and seraphim 'in glittering ranks', each in his proper place. Each of the nine spheres has its angelic note (the tenth sphere, the earth, is apparently being serenaded by the other nine) and Heaven's organ supplies the bass. Milton finds it hard to tear himself away from the contemplation of this divine concert; his imagination, haunted as it was in youth and young manhood by thoughts of prelapsarian bliss in Paradise, and its return in a new Golden Age, dwells on it:

> For if such holy Song
> Enwrap our fancy long,
>   Time will run back, and fetch the age of gold,
> And speckl'd vanity
> Will sicken soon and die,
>   And leprous sin will melt from earthly mould,
> And Hell it self will pass away,
> And leave her dolorous mansions to the peering day.

The last line of this stanza gives an extraordinarily vivid sense of an aerial view of a ruined city—anyone who has flown over a bombed city cannot help being struck by the accuracy of the image. Milton had a curiously aerial imagination; he liked to picture things as seen from a height, and he could describe flying with uncanny precision, as in the account in *Paradise Lost* of Satan's falling into an air pocket as he beat his way upwards through chaos.

He goes on for one further stanza describing the Golden Age which seems on the point of returning to men, then reluctantly pulls himself up:

> But wisest Fate says no,
> This must not yet be so.

The babe must grow up and be crucified in order to 'redeem our loss', and ultimate regeneration will not be possible before the Second Coming. Milton hurries over the reference to the Crucifixion, a theme on which he never preferred to dwell. It was not the suffering Christ but the heroic Christ which aroused his

imagination, and Christ emerges in the Nativity Ode as a character more like a classical hero than a divine sufferer. Milton had
never much use for martyrdom, certainly not in his younger days.

The poem then moves into a description of the banishment
of the classical gods by the arrival of the new-born babe. It is
remarkable how effectively Milton manages to suggest the
different evils of different kinds of pagan religion. A combination
of fraud and hysteria is suggested by his account of the cessation
of the Delphic oracle:

> The Oracles are dumm
> No voice or hideous humm
>   Runs through the arched roof in words deceiving.
> *Apollo* from his shrine
> Can no more divine,
>   With hollow shreik the steep of *Delphos* leaving.
> No nightly trance, or breathed spell,
> Inspire's the pale-ey'd Priest from the prophetic cell.

Milton's view of the classical pagan gods was that they were real,
but false; as *Paradise Lost* makes clear, they were really the fallen
angels who adopted these forms in order to deceive and betray
man. Yet he cannot restrain an occasional elegiac note in
describing their downfall:

> The lonely mountains o're,
> And the resounding shore,
>   A voice of weeping heard, and loud lament;
> From haunted spring, and dale
> Edg'd with poplar pale,
>   The parting Genius is with sighing sent,
> With flowre-inwov'n tresses torn
> The Nimphs in twilight shade of tangled thickets mourn.

The first three lines of this stanza are surely an echo (conscious
or unconscious) of Jeremiah's account of Rachel weeping for her
children, 'A voice was heard in Ramah, lamentation, and bitter
weeping; Rachel weeping for her children . . .' The nymphs and
the local deities, the *genii loci*, had a special place in Milton's
affections and he could not speak of their dismissal in the same

tone of voice as that which he used in talking of the senior pagan gods. After all, the English countryside was peopled with local pagan spirits whom Spenser and his followers had pressed into the service of a national poetry; and it was a water nymph who was to save the Lady in *Comus*. In any case, Milton had not and could not have the animosity against the Greek and Latin gods that he had against the gods of ancient Palestine against whom the Chosen People had fought and whom no literature that he knew of treated as anything but false and cruel misleaders of men or at best as empty names. There is almost a note of grim satisfaction in

> *Peor*, and *Baalim*,
> Forsake their Temples dim,
>   With that twise batter'd god of *Palestine*, . . .

and in the last two lines of this stanza—

> The Libyc *Hammon* shrinks his horn,
> In vain the *Tyrian* Maids their wounded *Thamuz* mourn—

we have that fascination with pre-Christian dying god myths and what might be called the 'Golden Bough' aspect of ancient mythology which Milton reveals so often in his poetry: he shows it, for example, in Book I of *Paradise Lost*:

> *Thammuz* came next behind,
> Whose annual wound in *Lebanon* allur'd
> The *Syrian* Damsels to lament his fate
> In amorous dittyes al a Summers day,
> While smooth *Adonis* from his native Rock
> Ran purple to the Sea, suppos'd with blood
> Of *Thammuz* yearly wounded; . . .

The picture of Moloch which follows reflects Milton's particular abomination of the god who demanded the sacrifice by fire of children (*see* 2 Kings xxiii, 10); he is thinking, too, of the description in George Sandys's *Relation of a Journey*, an account of travels in the East published in 1615, of the worship of an 'Idoll of brasse, having the head of a Calfe, the rest of a kingly

figure, with armes, extended to receive the miserable sacrifice',
while trumpets and timbrels are sounded to drown the 'lamentable
shrieks' of the children who are being sacrificed:

> And sullen *Moloch* fled,
> Hath left in shadows dred,
>   His burning Idol all of blackest hue;
> In vain with Cymbals ring,
> They call the grisly king,
>   In dismal dance about the furnace blue; ...

We meet him too again in *Paradise Lost*:

> First *Moloch*, horrid King besmear'd with blood
> Of human sacrifice, and parents tears,
> Though for the noyse of Drums and Timbrels loud
> Thir childrens cries unheard, that past through fire
> To his grim Idol.

A different kind of horror is reflected in the two lines with which
the stanza about Moloch in the Nativity Ode concludes:

> The brutish gods of *Nile* as fast,
> *Isis* and *Orus* and the Dog *Anubis* hast.

The long vowels in 'Isis', 'Orus' and 'Anubis' sing out in a
strangely seductive way, yet the feeling is clearly one of fascinated
repulsion. The animal gods of Egypt aroused Milton's peculiar
revulsion, but he also had a special antipathy to Egypt as the
land which had persecuted the Chosen People and a horror of
the elaborate rituals, monuments and death-customs of the
ancient Egyptians, the 'monstrous shapes and sorceries'.

The last god to depart is Osiris and then, the catalogue of
vanquished pagan deities being complete, Milton turns his and
our eyes to the source of all this:

> He feels from *Judahs* Land
> The dredded Infants hand,
>   The rayes of *Bethlehem* blind his dusky eyn;
> Nor all the gods beside,
> Longer dare abide,

> Not *Typhon* huge ending in snaky twine:
> Our Babe to shew his Godhead true,
> Can in his swadling bands controul the damned crew.

This is Christ the Hero routing his pagan opponents: the image
in the last two lines suggests Hercules strangling snakes in his
cradle.

Two more stanzes bring the ode to a conclusion, the first with
images of nature (but still highly 'conceited') suggesting the dawn
of Christianity banishing the pagan darkness:

> So when the Sun in bed,
> Curtain'd with cloudy red,
>   Pillows his chin upon an Orient wave,
> The flocking shadows pale,
> Troop to th'infernall jail,
>   Each fetter'd Ghost slips to his severall grave,
> And the yellow-skirted *Fayes*
> Fly after the Night-steeds, leaving their Moon-lov'd maze.

The image of the sun pillowing his chin upon an orient wave is
curiously precise and domestic for its cosmic context; yet it is
effective in its odd way, and helps to modulate the poem into a
new key. As the light of Christianity rises the pagan gods, who
had seemed so threatening and monstrous in the darkness, are
seen as pale shadows. In the morning, the nightmare fades. And
in the last two lines of the stanza Milton with quite remarkable
skill gently moves the whole situation into romantic English
folklore half-believed in the morning after a night of moonlit
fantasies.

The final stanza of the ode brings us into the stable in a neatly
contrived sudden movement:

> But see the Virgin blest,
> Hath laid her Babe to rest.
>   Time is our tedious Song should here have ending:
> Heav'ns youngest teemed Star,
> Hath fixt her polisht Car,
>   Her sleeping Lord with Handmaid Lamp attending;
> And all about the Courtly Stable,
> Bright-harnest Angels sit in order serviceable.

Everything is completed. In the stable, the babe is laid to rest. Above, the guiding star, having fulfilled its function, stops moving; and all around the angelic orders stand guard. Images of order, degree, stability conclude the poem. (One almost suspects a pun in 'Courtly Stable', for the idea of courtliness and stability is clearly present.) This is the divine harmony, guaranteeing that 'God's in his Heaven, all's right with the world'. The difference between Browning's way of putting it and Milton's 'Bright-harnest Angels sit in order serviceable' represents a radical difference between Milton's Christian humanism, with its mediaeval as well as classical roots, and Browning's romantic optimism, with its casual deistic use of a Christian terminology.

Milton wrote the Nativity Ode to celebrate Christmas of 1629. He was twenty-one on 9 December of that year, and the poem marks in many respects his literary as well as his legal coming of age. As a piece of deliberate craftsmanship it is a most remarkable achievement. It is, of course, limited in range and complexity, but it achieves its effects with admirable success, showing a precision in the handling of imagery and a virtuosity in the manipulation of rhythms that mark the self-conscious artist. Nevertheless, the ode is not a fair indication of the road Milton was to travel as a poet. He never wrote anything quite like this again. He was to develop a poetic style less Spenserian, less coyly artful in its manipulation of conceits, less exhibitionist, one might almost say, though this is perhaps unfair to the ode, which remains an impressive but isolated example of Milton's virtuosity.

Milton did not, however, intend it to be an isolated example. He evidently projected a series of poems to mark the different occasions in the Christian year, but the project was never carried through. He began a poem on 'The Passion', presumably for the Easter after the Christmas for which he wrote the Nativity Ode (i.e. Easter 1630), but left it uncompleted with the note, 'This Subject the Author finding to be above the yeers he had, when he wrote it, and nothing satisfi'd with what was begun, left it unfinisht.' Nevertheless, he thought well enough of the incomplete poem to include it in the volume of his poems which he published in 1645. He uses the same seven-line stanza that he had employed in the introduction to the Nativity Ode and the poem 'On the

Death of a Fair Infant'; the style suggests Spenser and Fletcher, not happily :

> Most perfet *Heroe*, try'd in heaviest plight
> Of labours huge and hard, too hard for human wight.

The Passion was not a congenial subject for Milton. He beats about the bush in a most infuriating way, announcing his grief in a variety of conventional hyperboles :

> The leaves should all be black wheron I write,
> And letters where my tears have washt a wannish white.

He simply cannot get down to his subject. He tries to get help from an image taken from Ezekiel :

> See see the Chariot, and those rushing wheels,
> That whirl'd the Prophet up at *Chebar* flood,
> My spirit som transporting *Cherub* feels,
> To bear me where the Towers of *Salem* stood, . . .

Anything to postpone coming to grips with his theme. He goes on to tell us that

> Mine eye hath found that sad Sepulchral rock
> That was the Casket of Heav'ns richest store,

and suggests that he might mourn there,

> For sure so well instructed are my tears,
> That they would fitly fall in order'd Characters.

There is no progression in the poem at all. The eighth and last stanza begins :

> Or should I thence hurried on viewles wing,
> Take up a weeping on the Mountains wilde, . . .

The poem ends abruptly in the midst of these alternative suggestions. The whole production is quite surprisingly bad for a poet who had already produced the Nativity Ode. The final alexandrines are mechanically constructed and often loaded with an exaggerated rhetoric; the conceits are conventional and generally functionless; and the poem does not move at all.

What appears to be the third poem in the projected religious group is 'Upon the Circumcision', written towards the end of Milton's Cambridge career or early in his stay at Horton. The theme was hardly more congenial to Milton than the Passion, but he was sensible enough not to attempt a long poem but to handle the theme in two fourteen-line stanzas which, as Mr. F. T. Prince has shown, follow closely the stanza used by Petrarch in his *canzone* to the Blessed Virgin. The poem is more interesting as a technical experiment than in its own right. It opens with an effective flourish, but as it proceeds we seem to be aware of a lack of centre to the poem, as though Milton had really nothing to say on the subject and was trying desperately to give it content.

A more interesting product of Milton's last years at Cambridge is the epitaph on Shakespeare prefixed to the Second Folio of 1632. Tillyard has called this 'the one poem of Milton than can be called metaphysical', and there is indeed an elaborate ingenuity in working out the conceit that Shakespeare's best monument is the wonder and astonishment of his readers in whose hearts 'those Delphick lines' are deeply engraved, not to be effaced because the imagination has been paralysed by the excessive demands on it made by the plays. The first half of the poem, however, has a Jonsonian combination of formality with a note of deep personal affection, and the metaphysical element is only developed in the second half:

> What needs my *Shakespear* for his honour'd Bones,
> The labour of an age in piled Stones,
> Or that his hallow'd reliques should be hid
> Under a Star-ypointing *Pyramid*?
> Dear son of memory, great heir of Fame,
> What need'st thou such weak witnes of thy name?
> Thou in our wonder and astonishment
> Hast built thyself a live-long Monument.
> For whilst to th' shame of slow-endeavouring art,
> Thy easie numbers flow, and that each heart

Hath from the leaves of thy unvalu'd Book,
Those Delphick lines with deep impression took,
Then thou our fancy of it self bereaving,
Dost make us marble with too much conceaving;
And so Sepulcher'd in such pomp dost lie,
That Kings for such a Tomb would wish to die.[1]

The tone of personal affection sounds strongly in the poem, and the formality (appropriate to an epitaph) only disciplines and strengthens it. 'My' Shakespeare establishes a special relationship at once, but the most impressive thing about the poem—more impressive than the working out of the ingenious conceit—is the way in which it rises to the highly formal 'Under a Star-ypointing Pyramid' and then, after a pause, turns suddenly with a clearly audible shift in tone of voice and an almost visible gesture of affection and admiration to the strong line

Dear son of memory, great heir of fame.

The accent falls strongly on the first syllable (which is also the first and most important word) of the line, reversing the normal iambic rhythm and at once arresting our attention; while the balance of 'dear son . . . great heir' helps to emphasize the grave emotion of the line.

The shift in tone is dramatic and Shakespearean, reminding us of those passages in Shakespeare where the speaker suddenly drops an argument and falls back on an appeal to love or friendship :

. . . And could it work so much upon your shape
As it hath much prevail'd on your condition,
I should not know you, Brutus. Dear my lord,
Make me acquainted with your cause of grief.

But the poem returns almost immediately to an even more elaborate style of formal compliment than that in which it began, rising to a conventional complimentary climax.

[1] This is the text as it appeared in the 1645 volume of Milton's poems; it differs in some respects from the text in the Second Folio.

Milton's two poems on the death of Hobson, the university carrier, who died in January 1631, show a mild metaphysical wit. but the punning epigram was a seventeenth-century poetic mode rather apart from the metaphysical tradition and there is no suggestion of any influence of Donne. Milton playfully uses images drawn from Hobson's occupation as carrier:

> And surely, Death could never have prevail'd,
> Had not his weekly cours of carriage fail'd;
> But lately finding him so long at home,
> And thinking now his journeys end was come,
> And that he had tane up his latest Inne,
> In the kind office of a Chamberlin
> Shew'd him his room where he must lodge the night,
> Pull'd off his Boots, and took away the light:
> If any ask for him, it shall be sed:
> Hobson has supt, and 's newly gon to bed.

The second poem on Hobson is in a similar vein.

More interesting, as well as more accomplished, is the epitaph Milton wrote on the Marchioness of Winchester, who died in April 1631. This has the quiet control and the firm lapidary quality of Ben Jonson's poetry in this vein. The chiselled words are perfectly suited for a formal epitaph:

> This rich Marble doth enterr
> The honour'd Wife of *Winchester*,
> A Vicounts daughter, an Earls heir,
> Besides what her vertues fair
> Added to her noble birth,
> More than she could own from Earth. . . .
> Gentle Lady may thy grave
> Peace and quiet ever have;
> After this thy travail sore,
> Sweet rest sease thee evermore, . . .

If this is not as polished and poised as the finest seventeenth-century poems in this *genre*—such as William Browne's poem on the Countess of Pembroke, whose opening lines Milton's opening seems to echo—it shows an assured handling of the octosyllabic couplet with interesting variations of the basic metrical pattern.

Among the poems written at Cambridge we must probably include the twin lyrics 'L'Allegro' and 'Il Penseroso', which were once thought to have been written during Milton's retirement at Horton but which seem rather to have been the product of a vacation during his last years at Cambridge. These poems are in a sense exercises, a poetic development of the formal debate on the relative claims of night and day which was the subject of his first prolusion, but they have a grace and freshness and a happy stylization which have helped to make them the most popular of Milton's poems. Each poem creates its own mood by appropriate imagery and tone. 'L'Allegro' ('the cheerful man') opens with a mock-violent dismissal of 'loathed Melancholy' in a crashing of chords, after which the smoothly tripping solo instrument takes up the main theme. The happily modulated lines in which Milton describes a day in the life of the cheerful man show appropriate mythological pastoral imagery developed in order to build up a mood of contented living. It is a carefully stylized picture, with the description of Euphrosyne, mirthful daughter of the west wind and the dawn, of a vine-covered rustic cottage, of milkmaids singing, mowers whetting their scythes, and shepherds making love under the hawthorn. The poem is full of light and movement. Its structure is chronological, beginning with 'the dappled dawn' rising to the accompaniment of the lark's song and going through a day of cheerful pastoral activities until sunset turns l'Allegro's thoughts to tournaments, pageants, poetry and music. Milton exploits classical mythology, English folklore and mediaeval romance in the course of this variegated poem. A sense of the dignity and orderliness of rustic labour, which was to emerge again and again in Milton's poetry, gives a certain weight of significance to the pastoral imagery, which remains nevertheless lighthearted in tone:

> While the Plowman neer at hand,
> Whistles ore the Furrow'd Land,
> And the Milkmaid singeth blithe,
> And the Mower whets his sithe,
> And every Shepherd tells his tale
> Under the Hawthorn in the dale.

The stylization here is deft and felicitous; it is even more deliberately cultivated in such an image as

> Hard by, a Cottage chimney smokes,
> From betwixt two aged Okes,

with its careful symmetry. This is a very formal art; every activity has its proper symbols, which link the poem up at all points with a complex tradition in both art and life. In 'Il Penseroso' ('the meditative man'), the images are organized to present a mood of contemplation and grave intellectual activity. The colouring of this poem is darker than that of 'L'Allegro': moonlight, dark woods, the song of the nightingale, are appropriate symbols here. The sound of the far-off curfew, the glowing embers of a dying fire half-lighting a gloomy room, the midnight lamp of the lonely student in the tower—these images are as stylized as their counterparts in 'L'Allegro', and distil a mood in the same way. Though the verse forms of the two poems are the same, the pace of 'Il Penseroso' is slower. Music is a pleasure to both l'Allegro and il Penseroso, but to the latter it is associated with religion and study:

> But let my due feet never fail,
> To walk the studious Cloysters pale,
> And love the high embowed Roof,
> With antick Pillars massy proof,
> And storied Windows richly dight,
> Casting a dimm religious light.
> There let the pealing Organ blow,
> To the full voic'd Quire below,
> In Service high, and Anthems clear,
> As may with sweetnes, through mine ear,
> Dissolve me into extasies,
> And bring all Heav'n before mine eyes.

There is an Anglican (if not a Catholic) feeling here: Milton had not yet become suspicious of cloisters and stained glass windows and the Anglican service.

Milton's Cambridge output is small for a dedicated poet. He was in no hurry to produce before he was ready, and more than once he found himself defending his policy of slow and deliberate self-preparation. There exist two drafts of a letter to a friend, written probably in December 1631 (but perhaps in December 1632[1]), in which he justifies himself against an admonishment that 'the howres of the night passe on . . . and the day with me is at hand wherin Christ commands all to labour while there is light'. He is not dreaming his time away, he protests. It is not mere love of learning and 'a poore regardlesse and unprofitable sin of curiosity' that is withholding him from a course which vanity, pride and ambition call him to. Further, 'a desire of honour and repute and immortall fame, seated in the breast of every true scholar' would also call him to action. It is not, therefore, 'the endlesse delight of speculation' that holds him back, 'but this very consideration of that great commandement' which 'does not presse forward, as soone as may be, to undergo, but keeps off, with a sacred reverence and religious avisement how best to under-goe—not taking thought of being late, so it give advantage to be more fit'. In the first of the two drafts he included the following sonnet:

> How soon hath Time the suttle theef of youth,
>> Stoln on his wing my three and twentith year!
>> My hasting dayes flie on with full career,
>> But my late spring no bud or blossom shew'th.
> Perhaps my semblance might deceive the truth,
>> That I to manhood am arriv'd so near,
>> And inward ripeness doth much less appear
>> That som more timely-happy spirits indu'th.
> Yet be it less or more, or soon or slow,
>> It shall be still in strictest measure eev'n,
>> To that same lot, however mean, or high,
> Toward which Time leads me, and the will of Heav'n;
>> All is, if I have grace to use it so,
>> As ever in my great task-Masters eye.

'The sonnet is perfect Puritanism,' Hanford has remarked, 'in its

---

[1] Milton was twenty-three on 9 December, 1631, but if the phrase 'three and twentith year' in the sonnet quoted here is used in the same way in which Milton habitually used equivalent Latin phrases in dating his Latin elegies, the sonnet was referring to his twenty-fourth, not his twenty-third, birthday. His three-and-twentieth year would be the year in which he was twenty-three.

soul-searching and its resignation, equally so in its assumption that God demands of His servants strenuousness as well as worship.' It is also characteristically Miltonic in its confidence that Milton himself was being led by God towards some significant destiny. And it is technically interesting in showing a new ease and confidence in the sonnet form, a careful poising and counterpointing of words and phrases, deriving from Milton's study of the Italian sonnets of Giovanni della Casa.

On taking his M.A. degree in July 1632, Milton retired to his father's estate at Horton, Buckinghamshire, to continue his self-preparation as a poet. He may indeed have gone to Horton soon after taking his B.A. and gone up to Cambridge only occasionally between 1629 and 1632. In any case, the dating of most of the poems at the end of his years at Cambridge and the early years at Horton is not certain. There seems to have been no emotional gap between Milton's later Cambridge and his Horton period. Gravely, deliberately, at his own pace, Milton was proceeding along the lines he laid down for himself. To anyone, friend or father, who remonstrated with him, he replied gently but firmly that he knew what he was doing. Perhaps, however, his grave deliberation covered a certain doubt, or a worry about the 'belatednesse' he confessed to the friend to whom he sent the sonnet, 'I . . . doe take notice of a certaine belatednesse in me.' Even in November 1637, when he was almost thirty, the opening lines of 'Lycidas' show that he did not yet consider himself ready, but was forced to produce the unripe berries of his art by the 'bitter constraint, and sad occasion dear' of Edward King's death.

II

COMUS, 'LYCIDAS' AND THE
ITALIAN JOURNEY

MILTON'S nearly six years at Horton were years of quiet preparation and maturing. 'On my father's estate,' he wrote in
Defensio Secunda, 'where he had determined to pass the remainder
of his days, I enjoyed an interval of uninterrupted leisure, which
I entirely devoted to the perusal of the Greek and Latin classics;
though I occasionally visited the metropolis, either for the sake
of purchasing books, or of learning something new in mathe-
matics or in music, in which I, at that time, found a source of
pleasure and amusement.' The rustic environment, with its
routine of seasonal agricultural activity, left a permanent mark
on his poetic imagery and on his view of productive labour. The
programme of reading he set himself during these years was to
be reflected in different ways in his poetry throughout his career.
He seems to have done a great deal of reading in history, both
ecclesiastical and political. Entries in a Commonplace Book which
he kept at this time and later reveal not only some of the books he
read at Horton but also his growing interest in civil and religious
freedom. He made no overt comment, however, on the growing
tension between King and Parliament or the conflict between the
Anglican bishops and their Puritan critics; but the attack on the
Anglican clergy which flashes out so fiercely in 'Lycidas' (1637)
shows in what direction his thoughts must have been moving for
some time.

Exactly why and under what conditions Milton gave up his
own ambitions to enter the Church is not clear. In the retrospective sketch of his early life which he gives in his *Reason of Church-
Government* he refers to himself as having been 'Church-outed by
the Prelats'; this may mean that he failed to get a fellowship at
Christ's because of his religious or political views, or he may even
have been offered a fellowship and declined it because of the professions its acceptance would have demanded of him. It is more
likely, however, that his general dissatisfaction with the state of

the Anglican clergy together with his own developing poetic ambitions led him to turn to that other method of edifying his generation which he was to describe also in *The Reason of Church-Government* : 'These [poetic] abilities, wheresoever they be found, are the inspired guift of God rarely bestow'd, but yet to some (though most abuse) in every Nation : and are of power beside the office of a pulpit, to inbreed and cherish in a great people the seeds of vertu, and publick civility, to allay the perturbations of the mind, and set the affections in right tune, to celebrate in glorious and lofty Hymns the throne and equipage of Gods Almightinesse, and what he works, and what he suffers to be wrought with high providence in his Church, to sing the victorious agonies of Martyrs and Saints, the deeds and triumphs of just and pious Nations doing valiantly through faith against the enemies of Christ, to deplore the general relapses of Kingdoms and States from justice and Gods true worship.'

Two short poems written either at the end of his Cambridge period or early in his stay at Horton show interestingly both the trend of his thought and the influence on his verse technique of his Italian studies. These are 'On Time' and 'At a Solemn Musick'. The former, originally intended, as the heading in the Trinity Manuscript shows, to be 'set on a clock case', is in one carefully modulated stanza or verse-paragraph of twenty-two lines. Its form derives, as Mr. Prince has pointed out, from the Italian madrigal as practised by Tasso and others. The madrigal, originally employed to reproduce Greek epigram and retaining even in its more developed form something of the wit and polish of the epigram, was in Italian a carefully shaped stanza of varying line-lengths. Milton did not follow the Italian form exactly, but attempted to achieve similar effects by handling his varying line-lengths in his own way. The result is a remarkably accomplished poem, in which variations of *tempo* and line-length are used most skilfully to carry the intellectual and emotional pattern to the reader. It begins slowly, with deliberate heaviness :

> Fly envious *Time*, till thou run out thy race,
> Call on the lazy leaden-stepping hours,
> Whose speed is but the heavy Plummets pace ;
> And glut thyself with what thy womb devours,

> Which is no more than what is false and vain,
> And meerly mortal dross;
> So little is our loss,
> So little is thy gain.

The rhythm, in Tillyard's phrase, 'dwindles grudgingly till the short last lines'. The change of thought, however, comes in the fifth line, with 'Which is no more . . .' What Time's womb devours is nothing after all, 'meerly mortal dross', and devouring Time is slowed almost to a standstill while the illusory nature of its triumphs is noted. Then the verse swells out again, looking to eternity and the reason for the emptiness of Time's triumph:

> For when as each thing bad thou hast entomb'd,
> And last of all, thy greedy self consum'd,
> Then long Eternity shall greet our bliss
> With an individual kiss;
> And Joy shall overtake us as a flood,
> When every thing that is sincerely good
> And perfetly divine,
> With Truth, and Peace, and Love shall ever shine
> About the supreme Throne
> Of him, t'whose happy-making sight alone,
> When once our heav'nly-guided soul shall clime,
> Then all this Earthy grosnes quit,
> Attir'd with Stars, we shall for ever sit,
>   Triumphing over Death, and Chance, and thee O Time.

The placing of the short lines, 'With an individual kiss', 'And perfetly divine', and the way in which the first of them ends in a second rhyming word while the second of them ends in a word which is itself echoed by the rhyming word in the following longer line, show real craftsmanship. The soaring conclusion reveals the poet's genuine excitement at the thought of the soul's final triumph over earthly change. It is interesting that Milton does not hesitate to use abstract nouns conveying a large, elemental meaning. A phrase like 'When every thing that is sincerely good / And perfetly divine' is deliberately both abstract and simple, as though the ultimate in virtue and divinity cannot be expressed in any other way. Attack on such abstractions on doctrinaire grounds is surely misguided. They are absolutely right for this kind of statement in this kind of verse. It is essentially the same kind of use of abstractions which Milton was to use so brilliantly in *Paradise Lost* in order to convey a sense of unearthly beauty or splendour :

> And all amid them stood the Tree of Life,
> High eminent, blooming Ambrosial Fruit
> Of vegetable Gold.

'At a Solemn Musick' is similarly constructed, with similarly cunning variations of line-length and an even more impressive modulation of tone until the final climax. Song and organ music together bring to our imagination the divine Music of the Spheres :

> Blest pair of *Sirens*, pledges of Heav'ns joy,
> Sphear-born harmonious Sisters, Voice, and Vers,
> Wed your divine sounds, and mixt power employ
> Dead things with inbreath'd sense able to pierce,
> And to our high-rais'd phantasie present,
> That undisturbed Song of pure concent,
> Ay sung before the saphire-colour'd throne
> To him that sits theron . . .

The gravity and stateliness of the verse yield gradually to a lighter and more ethereal tone. The account of the divine music then moves through the splendid to the haunting :

> . . . Where the bright Seraphim in burning row
> Their loud up-lifted Angel trumpets blow,
> And the Cherubick host in thousand quires
> Touch their immortal Harps of golden wires,
> With those just Spirits that wear victorious Palms,
> Hymns devout and holy Psalms
> Singing everlastingly ; . . .

The short, melodious line 'Singing everlastingly' ends the first part of the single complex stanza which forms the poem. The second part begins with a return to earth—

> That we on Earth with undiscording voice
> May rightly answer that melodious noise;
> As once we did, . . .

—and rises again to give an account of how man once, before the Fall, used to join in that great cosmic chorus, concluding with a prayer, uttered in ecstasy by the rapt poet as he listens to the real and the imaginary music, that we may soon again renew that song:

> O may we soon again renew that Song,
> And keep in tune with Heav'n, till God ere long
> To his celestial consort us unite,
> To live with him, and sing in endles morn of light.

These two poems are more than exercises: they are small works of art, perfectly controlled and cunningly modulated. They have not the complexity of much of Milton's later poetry, where he exhibits greater range and variety in his syntactical and metrical devices. But they do show that control over verse movement and some aspects at least of that 'architectonic' power which are such conspicuous qualities of Milton's greatest work.

Milton's musical interests, expressed with high religious passion in 'At a Solemn Musick', were responsible for a development in his poetic career that could not have been anticipated by anyone who had followed his career and his professions up to this point. Henry Lawes the musician had both an appointment at court and a position with the family of Sir John Egerton, first Earl of Bridgewater. Common musical interests apparently led to his acquaintance with Milton and this acquaintance led Lawes to ask Milton to provide the words for a dramatic entertainment to be presented at Harefield (not very far from Horton) before the Dowager Countess of Derby, step-mother of the Earl of Bridgewater. Milton's contribution was first published in the 1645 volume of his poems under the title *Arcades*, with the sub-title: 'Part of an entertainment presented to the Countess Dowager of *Darby* at *Harefield*, by som Noble persons of her Family, who appear on the Scene in pastoral habit, moving toward the seat of State, with this song'. The first song follows, a song of compliment to the Countess. Then 'As they com forward, the Genius of the

Wood appears, and turning toward them, speaks'. Two more songs follow this speech, which is some eighty lines long. Milton's model for this slight affair, for which Lawes wrote the music, was the Jonsonian masque, but there is an Elizabethan freshness about the songs, and a controlled grace about the aristocratic compliment which is the purpose of the whole entertainment, that are not quite Jonsonian. The whole thing is simple enough. The 'Noble persons of her Family' sing the first song of compliment:

> Look Nymphs, and Shepherds look,
> What sudden blaze of Majesty
> Is that which we from hence descry
> Too divine to be mistook:
>   This this is she
> To whom our vows and wishes bend,
> Heer our solemn search hath end. . . .

Three more stanzas follow, and then the Genius of the Wood (a part probably played by Lawes) approaches to speak his piece:

> Stay gentle Swains, for though in this disguise,
> I see bright honour sparkle through your eyes,
> Of famous *Arcady* ye are, and sprung
> Of that renowned flood, so often sung,
> Divine Alpheus, . . .
> I know this quest of yours, and free intent
> Was all in honour and devotion ment
> To the great Mistres of yon princely shrine, . . .

The blank verse is light yet formal, more like the blank verse of, say, *A Midsummer Night's Dream* than anything in later Shakespeare or in Jonson. The Genius goes on to describe how he is the protector of 'this fair Wood', where at night, when mortals are asleep, he listens

> To the celestial *Sirens* harmony,
> That sit upon the nine enfolded Sphears,
> And sing to those that hold the vital shears,
> And turn the Adamantine spindle round,
> On which the fate of gods and men is wound.

> Such sweet compulsion doth in musick ly,
> To lull the daughters of *Necessity*,
> And keep unsteddy Nature to her law,
> And the low world in measur'd motion draw
> After the heavenly tune, which none can hear
> Of human mould with grosse unpurged ear; . . .

It is the familiar theme, Platonic and Christian, and as the tone of courtly compliment modulates into these deeper strains the verse rises to a musical gravity before returning to a conventional compliment at the end.

Then comes the second song, the delicate, lightly dancing

> O're the smooth enameld green
> Where no print of step hath been.
>   Follow me as I sing,
>   And touch the warbled string. . . .

This has overtones of both Puck and Ariel. The final song, with its strangely moving opening

> Nymphs and Shepherds dance no more,

brings the entertainment to a close, concluding with a final compliment to the Countess:

> Such a rural Queen
> All *Arcadia* hath not seen.

This is an aristocratic art, Elizabethan in feeling, courtly in tone (except when it rises momentarily to mystical contemplation), yet essentially simple in manner. These songs give us some basis for speculating about what Milton might have developed into had he been a contemporary of Sidney and Spenser in fact as he was in many ways in spirit. One does not readily think of Milton as a courtly poet, or as writing from half-way up Fortune's Hill with an eye on the summit; but *Arcades* does show him for once in this role.

Milton's next aristocratic entertainment was a full-length

masque 'presented at Ludlow Castle, 1634: On Michaelmasse night, before the Right Honorable, John Earle of Bridgewater, Vicount Brackly, Lord Praesident of Wales, And one of His Majesties most honorable Privie Counsell'. (This is from the title page of the anonymous first edition of 1637, published by Lawes because, as he said in his dedication to the Earl of Bridgewater's son and heir, it was 'so much desired, that the often Copying of it hath tir'd my Pen'.) The occasion was the inauguration of the Earl as Lord President of Wales. Milton seems by this time to have been firm friends with Lawes and, presumably because of the success of *Arcades*, to have been favourably regarded by the Egerton family. This commission was a more serious one than that which he had executed for the Dowager Countess of Derby. Milton was expected to employ the masque form, which involved an allegorical theme treated through the presentation of mythological characters. The masque had developed from a visit by masked dancers (as Romeo and his friends visit the Capulets' party masked in *Romeo and Juliet*) to an elaborate private entertainment with music and often ambitious painted scenery as well as spoken dialogue ; masques were performed at court and at great houses as part of the celebration of a variety of occasions from weddings to the arrival of distinguished visitors. Spectacle, music and dancing were often more important than the dialogue, and different masques used these elements in different proportions. The Ludlow Castle masque (its popular title, *Comus*, is not Milton's, but first appears in an eighteenth-century acting edition) was directed by Lawes, whose producing hand can be seen in the extant stage version. Two manuscript copies of the masque survive, one in the Trinity Manuscript (a folio manuscript in which Milton kept drafts of English poems), which shows revisions in various stages (the 1637 edition was printed from the fully revised Trinity text) ; the other, not in Milton's hand, is the stage version just mentioned ; it was copied from the original acting version for the Earl of Bridgewater.

In his dedication of the 1637 edition, Lawes wrote of *Comus*: 'Although not openly acknowledg'd by the Author, yet it is a legitimate off-spring, so lovely, and so much desired, . . .' It was clearly popular, as Lawes' remarks about frequent copying show, yet to entertain an aristocratic audience with a masque which

preached passionately the sage and serious doctrine of virginity
was an enterprise that few but Milton would have thought of in
1634 (it was different when the Virgin Queen was alive). The
reason why Milton did not openly acknowledge the work is suggested by the quotation from Virgil's Eclogues which appears on
the title page of the 1637 edition and which Milton clearly chose
himself:

> Eheu quid volui misero mihi! floribus austrum——

> Alas, what wretchedness have I brought upon myself! I have
> let loose the south wind upon my flowers . . .

He had written the masque because he had been requested to do
so, but he did not feel really ready, any more than he was to feel
ready when the death of King wrung 'Lycidas' from him three
years later. In September 1637—two months before completing
'Lycidas' and a month and a half after King's death—he wrote in
a Latin letter to Charles Diodati: 'Do you ask me what I am
thinking of? With God's help, of immortal fame! And what
am I doing? Growing my wings and preparing for flight; but
as yet my Pegasus rises on very tender pinions.' It is the
familiar combination of intense ambition and deliberate holding
back.

Comus is in the Elizabethan masque tradition, one of the last
English works of its kind. Book X of the *Odyssey*, Platonic and
neo-Platonic philosophy, Spenser's description of the Bower of
Bliss in Book II of *The Faerie Queene*, William Browne's *Inner
Temple Masque* (treating of Circe and Ulysses), Jonson's *Pleasure
Reconciled to Virtue* (a masque where Comus figures as a glutton),
Peele's *Old Wives Tale*, Fletcher's *The Faithful Shepherdess*, each
appear to have suggested something to Milton, and Hanford has
suggested that the defence of chastity in *Comus* may have been a
deliberate reply on Milton's part to the libertine philosophy
expounded by his fellow-student Thomas Randolph in *The Muse's
Looking Glass*.

Comus opens with the attendant spirit (played by Lawes)
speaking, in the calm recitative of formal blank verse, the introductory expository speech:

Before the starry threshold of *Joves* Court
My mansion is, where those immortal shapes
Of bright aëreal Spirits live insphear'd
In Regions milde of calm and serene Ayr,
Above the smoak and stirr of this dim spot,
Which men call Earth, and with low-thoughted care
Confin'd, and pester'd in this pin-fold here,
Strive to keep up a frail, and Feaverish being
Unmindfull of the crown that Vertue gives
After this mortal change, to her true Servants
Amongst the enthron'd gods on Sainted seats.

He speaks of the tutelary deities of the region (managing to pay
a compliment to the Earl of Bridgewater while doing so), tells of
the peer's daughter and two sons coming 'through the perplex't
paths of this drear Wood' to greet their father, and warns of
Comus the enchanter, son of Bacchus and Circe (and thus, incidentally, a half-brother of Euphrosyne, daughter of Bacchus and
Venus, who is invoked in 'L'Allegro'). Comus lies in wait in 'this
ominous Wood' to trap the unwary into his 'sensual sty'. Comus
and his rout of monsters are heard approaching, and the attendant
spirit departs.

The entry of Comus 'with a Charming Rod in one hand, his
Glass in the other, with him a rout of Monsters headed like
sundry sorts of wilde Beasts, but otherwise like Men and
Women' must have been elaborately devised as an antic dance
in the tradition of the 'anti-masque'. 'They com in making a
riotous and unruly noise, with Torches in their hands' concludes
the stage direction. Then Comus speaks, in accents that are
sharply distinguished from the earlier formal blank verse; his
words go trippingly, almost tipsily, in their tones of revelry:

The Star that bids the Shepherd fold,
Now the top of Heav'n doth hold,
And the gilded Car of Day,
His glowing Axle doth allay
In the steep *Atlantick* stream,
And the slope Sun his upward beam
Shoots against the dusky Pole,
Pacing toward the other gole

> Of his Chamber in the East.
> Mean while welcom Joy, and Feast,
> Midnight shout, and revelry,
> Tipsie dance, and Jollity. . . .
> The Sounds, and Seas with all their finny drove
> Now to the Moon in wavering Morrice move,
> And on the Tawny Sands and Shelves,
> Trip the pert Fairies and the dapper Elves;
> By dimpled Brook, and Fountain brim,
> The Wood-Nymphs deckt with Daisies trim,
> Their merry wakes and pastimes keep:
> What hath night to do with sleep?

The lilt to this sounds innocent enough (though the ear accustomed to Milton's cadences will note the occasional drunken lurch); but one of the themes of the masque is the distinction between guilty and innocent mirth, and after some thirty-five lines the tone changes, to make clear that we are here dealing with the former variety:

> Com let us our rights begin,
> 'Tis onely day-light that makes Sin
> Which these dun shades will ne're report.
> Hail Goddesse of Nocturnal sport
> Dark vaild *Cotytto*, t'whom the secret flame
> Of mid-night Torches burns; mysterious Dame
> That ne're art call'd, but when the Dragon woom
> Of Stygian darknes spets her thickest gloom, . . .

The movement from revelry to witchcraft and the shift in tone from the gay to the sinister comes to a climax with the reference to Cotytto, whose obscene midnight orgies were attacked by Juvenal and burlesqued by Horace.

A dance by Comus and his company follows, broken off by the entry of the Lady, who has become separated from her brothers and is lost in the wood. (The Lady and her brothers were played by the Earl of Bridgewater's daughter and sons.) Comus falls into a more formal speech—

> Break off, break off, I feel the different pace
> Of som chast footing neer about this ground . . .

—and lays his plans. The Lady enters, and in flexible verse with
conversational overtones explains her plight:

> ... I should be loath
> To meet the rudenesse, and swill'd insolence
> Of such late Wassailers; yet O where els
> Shall I inform my unacquainted feet
> In the blind mazes of this tangl'd Wood?

As she dwells on her situation, the verse becomes more plangent
and stately:

> They left me then, when the gray-hooded Eev'n
> Like a sad Votarist in Palmers weed
> Rose from the hindmost wheels of *Phoebus* wain.

But she senses the presence of Comus, and the movement of the
verse changes again:

> What might this be? A thousand fantasies
> Begin to throng into my memory
> Of calling shapes, and beckning shadows dire,
> And airy tongues, that syllable mens names
> On Sands, and Shoars, and desert Wildernesses.

She recalls her virtue and her chastity, and announces in somewhat stilted verse her confidence in them, then sings a song, in
the hope of attracting her brothers' attention. The song is about
Echo and Narcissus, a perfect piece of mythological delicacy, with
the final two lines swelling out to a profounder meaning:

> Sweet Echo, sweetest Nymph that liv'st unseen
> Within thy airy shell
> By slow *Meander's* margent green,
> And in the violet-imbroider'd vale
> Where the love-lorn Nightingale
> Nightly to thee her sad Song mourneth well.
>
> Canst thou not tell me of a gentle Pair
> That likest thy *Narcissus* are?
> O if thou have
> Hid them in som flowry Cave,

> Tell me but where
> Sweet Queen of Parly, Daughter of the Sphear,
> So maist thou be translated to the skies,
> And give resounding grace to all Heav'ns Harmonies.

Comus is ravished by the song, which moves him to an eloquent expression of admiration:

> . . . But such a sacred, and home-felt delight,
> Such sober certainty of waking bliss
> I never heard till now.

He hails the Lady in tones reminiscent of Caliban's attitude to Miranda, and the ensuing dialogue shows him playing skilfully the role of guide and comforter to the Lady. He knows the wood, and will help her find her brothers, whom he saw recently:

> Two such I saw, what time the labour'd Oxe
> In his loose traces from the furrow came,
> And the swink't hedger at his Supper sate; . . .

If he is adroit enough to convince the Lady, it is no wonder that he also convinces the reader, who finds in this part of the masque some of the most charming verse, expressing the quiet joy in the English countryside and satisfaction in agricultural labour well done (which we know to have been Milton's own attitude), put into Comus' mouth. We have echoes of Puck:

> I know each lane, and every alley green
> Dingle, or bushy dell of this wilde Wood,

and of the Spenserian pastoralists. The Lady, not surprisingly, agrees to follow Comus, and as they depart the two brothers enter, searching for their sister. 'Unmuffle ye faint Stars,' cried the elder brother, in tones that might have been used by Romeo or some other of Shakespeare's early heroes, but as the dialogue between the brothers develops, and the elder preaches to the younger Milton's grand doctrine of the mystical virtues of chastity that always preserves from harm, something of the dramatic life goes out of the verse. The statement of the doctrine is eloquent enough, but didactically rather than dramatically.

The attendant spirit, disguised as the shepherd Thyrsis, then enters and tells of Comus, his nature and his threat, in a fine set-piece of descriptive verse. The younger brother is appalled at the danger to his sister, but the elder reaffirms the young Milton's view that virtue always guarantees the safety of its possessor:

> Vertue may be assail'd, but never hurt,
> Surpriz'd by unjust force, but not enthrall'd,

a view which his later contemplation of the nature of temptation led him to modify. Thyrsis explains about the magic herb which will undo Comus' enchantments, and they depart, the scene changing to Comus' palace, where the Lady is now confronted with Comus in his true colours. This is the most dramatic scene in the masque, and the give and take between Comus and the Lady is done with great spirit. The claims of sensual pleasure are pressed by Comus with a persuasive charm—this is the misuse of rhetoric which Milton was to show more profoundly in the speeches of Satan and his followers in *Paradise Lost*. Again we have the slightly tipsy lilt to the speech (faintly reminiscent of Eve's 'distempered' speech on returning to Adam after eating the fatal apple):

> Why are you vext Lady? why do you frown?
> Here dwel no frowns, nor anger, from these gates
> Sorrow flies farr: . . .

To the Lady's lively reply Comus returns an even more skilful speech, denouncing 'lean and sallow Abstinence' and painting a persuasive picture of Nature's bounty, meant to be used. He goes on:

>   if all the world
> Should in a pet of temperance feed on Pulse,
> Drink the clear stream, and nothing wear but Freize,
> Th'all-giver would be unthank't, would be unprais'd,
> Not half his riches known, and yet despis'd,
> And we should serve him as a grudging master,
> As a penurious niggard of his wealth,

> And live like Nature's bastards, not her sons,
> Who would be quite surcharg'd with her own weight,
> And strangl'd with her waste fertility ; . . .

and he proceeds to give a brilliant picture of Nature choked by her own unused abundance. This is effective dramatic verse. For a man of Milton's temperament, and his strongly held personal views, it is remarkable how he is able to get inside Comus' character (as later he was to get inside Satan's) and put some of his most persuasive verse into Comus' mouth. This is—perhaps it need hardly be said—a deliberate dramatic device, with Comus as with Satan, and to argue that because it is successful Satan is the 'real' hero of *Paradise Lost* is as absurd as to argue that Comus is the real hero of Milton's masque : both views show a basic misunderstanding of the nature of Milton's art.

The dramatic element in Milton is of a rather special kind. It was Milton's study of rhetoric that enabled him to voice persuasively views that he detested. With Comus as with Satan he builds up character not by innumerable little touches which cumulatively reveal the true quality of a personality, nor yet by means of deep inward soliloquies (though in *Paradise Lost* Satan occasionally soliloquizes), but by devising occasions which call from his characters their most persuasive statements of their position. Comus mingles brilliant generalization with urgent personal appeal. Here is the latter :

> List Lady be not coy, and be not cosen'd
> With that same vaunted name Virginity, . . .

But it moves immediately into generalization :

> Beauty is natures coyn, must not be hoorded,
> But must be currant, and the good thereof
> Consists in mutual and partak'n bliss,
> Unsavoury in th'injoyment of it self ;
> If you let slip time, like a neglected rose
> It withers on the stalk with languish't head.
> Beauty is natures brag, and must be shown
> In courts, at feasts, and high solemnities
> Where most may wonder at the workmanship ; . . .

And the speech concludes with the urgent personal appeal again, the movement of the verse rapid and colloquial:

> Think what, and be adviz'd, you are but young yet.

The Lady's reply is a lofty rhetorical statement of her position, beginning with a fine contemptuous reference to the tempter:

> I had not thought to have unlockt my lips
> In this unhallow'd air, but that this Jugler
> Would think to charm my judgment, as mine eyes,
> Obtruding false rules pranckt in reasons garb.

We need not follow the plot through. The Lady is rescued, Sabrina, the river nymph, is hailed, in another charming song, to come and release her from the chair to which she is magically bound, and *Comus* ends with a cluster of songs and dances, in true masque style. It is characteristic of Milton that after the dance—*innocent* mirth this time, but perhaps the distinction is not as clear as Milton intended—the attendant spirit, in his song, proclaims that 'enough is as good as a feast':

> Back Shepherds, back, anough your play,
> Till next Sun-shine holiday, . . .

Holidays are all very well if they are properly spaced and do not last too long. So *Arcades* had ended with

> Nymphs and Shepherds dance no more,

and so more than twenty years later, writing a sonnet to a young friend inviting him to dine with wine and music, he concluded:

> He who of those delights can judge, and spare [i.e. forbear]
> To interpose them oft, is not unwise.

The epilogue, spoken by the attendant spirit, suggests Ariel again:

To the Ocean now I fly,
And those happy climes that ly
Where day never shuts his eye,

but it ends with a Miltonic moral:

Mortals, that would follow me,
Love vertue, she alone is free,
She can teach you how to clime
Higher than the Spheary chime;
Or if Vertue feeble were,
Heav'n itself would stoop to her.

Comus is a remarkable performance. Its freshness, variety, sureness of touch, mastery of different tones, show how far Milton had gone in developing high technical skill. Its variety is perhaps excessive; the different styles—including a not very successful imitation of the Greek *stichomythia* in some of the dialogue—are not always adequately subdued to the total design. But we must remember that this is a masque, meant to be sung and acted, and without the music and the somewhat stylized dramatic action it loses a great deal.

It was not until his former fellow-student at Christ's was drowned in the Irish Sea in August 1637 that Milton was moved to write another English poem. This, too, was wrung from him before he felt himself ready, not this time by the request of an aristocratic family but by 'bitter constraint, and sad occasion deare'. Edward King does not appear to have been a very intimate friend of Milton's, but he had been a learned and virtuous young man dedicated to a career in the Church, and there must have been some sympathy and fellow feeling between them even though King, unlike Milton, was appointed to a college fellowship by royal mandate and was not 'Church-outed by the Prelats'. The shock to Milton of seeing a promising and dedicated contemporary cut off in his youth must have been great. Here he was, taking his time in preparing himself to become a poet who would 'leave something so written to after-times, as they should not willingly let die', and suddenly the prospect of sudden and premature death was violently brought before him. If he were to die as King had died, what would have been the use, then, of all

his laborious self-preparation? The very slowness and deliberation of Milton's progress towards his goal must have increased
the shock enormously. He might well have said, as Marvell was
to say in another context,

> Had we but World enough, and Time,
> This coyness Lady were no crime.

He had been acting on the assumption that he had world enough
and time; and perhaps, after all, he had not. This is not to say
that the elegy which Milton wrote for King was not about King
but about himself, but it does indicate one of the major streams
of feeling that flowed into the poem.

'Lycidas', Milton's elegy on King, appeared in a memorial
volume which came out in two parts in 1638, the first and larger
part containing Latin and Greek poems and the second containing poems in English. 'Lycidas' concludes the second part; it is
signed 'J. M.'. All but two of the other eleven English elegies are
signed with the author's name. It is strange to look at 'Lycidas'
as it first appeared, tucked away at the end of a collection of
poems most of which are uninspired and conventional laments.
Henry King's poem begins:

> No Death! I'le not examine Gods decree,
> Nor question providence, in chiding thee:
> Discreet Religion binds us to admire
> The wayes of providence, and not enquire.

Joseph Beaumont's piece began:

> When first this news, rough as the sea
> From whence it came, began to be
> Sigh'd out by fame, and generall tears
> Drown'd him again, my stupid fears
> Would not awake; . . .

Cleveland's opens:

> I like not tears in tune; nor will I prise
> His artificiall grief, that scannes his eyes:
> Mine weep down pious beads: but why should I
> Confine them to the Muses Rosarie?

> I am not Poet here; my pen's the spout
> Where the rain-water of my eyes run out
> In pitie of that name, whose fate we see
> Thus copied out in griefs Hydrographie.

Among this company, Milton's poem stands out at once for its gravity of utterance, its artfully modulated verse, and its formal use of the conventions of the pastoral elegy, as developed in Greek, Latin and Italian poetry.

The verse of 'Lycidas' owes much to Milton's study of Italian poetry. While Milton does not employ the *canzone* (which consists of a complex rhymed verse-paragraph repeated in the same form several times before the concluding *commiato*, which is a shorter stanza), nevertheless his handling of the verse-paragraphs and of varying line-lengths clearly derives from the *canzone*, and the concluding passage of eight lines is his own adaptation of the *commiato*. Mr. F. T. Prince has traced in detail the influence on 'Lycidas' of sixteenth-century Italian pastoral poetry, and he has shown how the structure of the *canzone*, as originally explained by Dante in the *De Vulgari Eloquentia*, with its stanza divided into two sections linked by a *chiave*, illuminates the sustained technical discipline shown by Milton in his handling of rhyme-pattern, pauses and transitions in their relation to the movement of thought and emotion.

'Lycidas' begins with a statement of the occasion which prompted it:

> Yet once more, O ye laurels, and once more,
> Ye myrtles brown, with ivy never-sere,
> I come to pluck your berries harsh and crude,
> And with forc'd fingers rude
> Shatter your leaves before the mellowing yeare.
> Bitter constraint, and sad occasion deare
> Compells me to disturb your season due:
> For Lycidas is dead, dead ere his prime,
> (Young Lycidas!) and hath not left his peere.
> Who would not sing for Lycidas? he knew
> Himself to sing, and build the lofty rhyme.
> He must not flote upon his watery biere
> Unwept, and welter to the parching wind
> Without the meed of some melodious tear.

The very first line introduces Milton in his capacity of young and ambitious poet: he is young because he has to pluck the berries of his art before they are ripe; he has already begun his career as a poet because this is not the first time he has plucked the unripe berries; and he thinks of himself (potentially at least) as a poet in the great classical tradition, as is made clear by his use of such images as laurel, myrtle and ivy with their traditional associations with triumphant art. The berries may be unripe, but they are the true berries of art. He has to interrupt his period of apprenticeship to attempt a mature poem, because the fate of a fellow-poet compels him.

The note of compulsion is urgent. 'Yet once more'—in these three opening words, three equally stressed monosyllables which take the reader into the poem suddenly and passionately yet which in themselves are very 'ordinary' words with no obvious poetic qualities, we have the first hint of that strongly felt personal concern with himself and his own fate which is to be fully developed later in the poem. Yet that concern is not with his fate simply as man: it is with that aspect of himself which links him with the dead Lycidas and in the light of which Lycidas is himself an impressive subject—they are both poets (or poet-priests: we have seen how the two concepts were linked for Milton).

> Who would not sing for Lycidas? he knew
> Himself to sing, and build the lofty rhyme.

If the subject of the poem is not simply Edward King as man, neither is it (as Tillyard would have it) simply Milton himself. It is man in his creative capacity, as Christian humanist poet-priest. Lycidas has been drowned before he could fulfil his potentialities as poet-priest: man is always liable to be cut off before making his contribution; hence the lament, hence the problem, hence the poem. In 'Lycidas' Milton circles round the problem, and with each circling he moves nearer the centre (he is spiralling rather than circling), and he reaches the centre only when he has found a solution, or at least an attitude in terms of which the problem can be faced with equanimity.

Of the many points worthy of detailed attention in these opening lines, only a few can be selected for brief comment. The image of the unripe berries and such phrases as 'season due' and 'mellowing yeare' introduce thus early in the poem the richly suggestive notion of the changing seasons with all the emotional implications of seedtime and harvest, of the death of the year being inevitably followed by its re-birth in the spring. These implications (which, it might almost be said, convey a suggestion of comfort even while introducing the cause for lament) are not over-stressed, but delicately handled by the rhymes and the rhythms. The first sentence of the poem moves up to a climactic autumn image :

> Shatter your leaves before the mellowing yeare.

'Yeare' rhymes with 'sere' (dry) at the end of the second line, and the two rhyme words echoing together form a contrast between the withered and the ripe, between death and hope. Thus not only is the theme fully presented in these opening lines ; there is also an anticipation of the way in which it is going to be worked out. In the very run of this fifth and just-quoted line there is an implication both of action and of hope, the sharp gesture of 'shatter' giving way to the image of 'mellowing yeare' as the line slows down, so that the 'forced' and 'rude' fingers plucking the unripe berries almost become, for a brief moment, harvesting images of active labourers gathering ripe fruit.

The young poet faces the premature death of the unfulfilled fellow-poet. His first reaction is to sing a lament for him :

> He must not flote upon his watery biere
> Unwept, and welter to the parching wind
> Without the meed of some melodious tear.

These three lines bring the first verse-paragraph to an end, on a note which combines resignation with resolve. This quiet close of the introduction not only provides a perfect balance for this opening paragraph, which rests, as it were, on these three lines ; it also holds a note of anticipation, and so draws the reader further into the poem.

It is with deliberate awareness of the classical pastoral

tradition that Milton begins the actual elegy in the second
verse-paragraph:

> Begin then, Sisters of the sacred well . . .

He is invoking the muses with an almost ironic deliberation, the
second word of the line, 'then', almost suggesting that this is the
thing to do, the proper routine. There is an echo of Theocritus'
first Idyll in the line, and this adds to the suggestion of routine,
of Milton doing his duty. But this is more than a conventional
elegy, and its subject is more than Lycidas—or rather, its subject
is Lycidas rather than Edward King, for when he has given his
dead friend a classical name, he has elevated him to the status of
fellow-poet and from there the expansion to creative man can
proceed. He does not stay long with these traditional sentiments,
but, with a significantly short line, turns the subject to himself as
poet:

> So may some gentle Muse
> With lucky words favour my destin'd urn,
> And as he passes, turn
> And bid fair peace be to my sable shroud.

He will do this for Lycidas so that it will be done in turn for him;
it is what is due to a poet. The death of Lycidas is now linked to
the inevitable death of all men, however talented, however great
their promise or achievements; even the present celebrator will in
his turn become the celebrated. There is a restrained note of self-
pity here, conveyed not so much by the actual words used as by
the suggestion given to the words by rhyme and metre. The short
lines in which he breaks off to draw the parallel with himself are
echoed by a later short line which is pure action or gesture—a
striking image of Milton's elegist turning to invoke peace on *his*
remains:

> And as he passes, turn
> And bid fair peace be to my sable shroud.

Nothing could better illustrate the importance of metrical and semantic context in poetic expression than the first of these two lines. In itself, it is a wholly 'neutral' line, containing no arresting word or phrase, no striking image. But in its context the very simplicity of the expression, the shortness of the line (echoing.in length the other short line two lines before, but rhyming with the immediately preceding long line), and its effect purely as sound (three light monosyllables followed by a leaning on the first syllable of 'passes' and then on 'turn') combine with the purely intellectual meaning to flash forth a significant and moving gesture. Milton has now substituted himself for Lycidas in the poem, but not before both men have been identified with a larger and more general conception of man. Having made the substitution, he again points out why he has done it:

> For we were nurst upon the self-same hill,
> Fed the same flock, by fountain, shade, and rill; ...

This is a re-statement of the earlier

> Who would not sing for Lycidas? He knew
> Himself to sing, and build the lofty rhyme.

But whereas the first time it was an explanation of why he should sing for Lycidas, the second time it is an explanation of why both Lycidas and himself merit the same consideration. They are both poets: the reason is the same in each case. The description, in the following verse-paragraph, is not so much an account in pastoral imagery of their life together as students in Cambridge; it is an account of their joint self-dedication as poets, and the pastoral imagery is employed in order to link their function as poets with the tradition of Western literature. This continuous linking of the theme with classical mythology is not decorative but functional: it keeps the poem rooted in an elevated conception on the nature, scope and historical significance of the poet's art.

One notes in this third paragraph a genuine emotion about Nature, which blends effectively with the purely conventional characteristics of the pastoral imagery and which reminds the reader of such earlier images as 'mellowing yeare':

> Together both, ere the high lawns appear'd
> Under the glimmering eye-lids of the morn,[1]
> We drove a-field, and both together heard
> What time the gray-fly winds her sultry horn,
> Batt'ning our flocks with the fresh dews of night,
> Oft till the ev'n-starre bright[2]
> Toward heav'ns descent had slop'd his burnisht[3] wheel.
> Meanwhile the rural ditties were not mute
> Temper'd to th'oaten flute:
> Rough Satyres danc'd, and Fauns with cloven heel
> From the glad sound would not be absent long,
> And old Dametas lov'd to heare our song.

In the first part of this paragraph we get a sense of community in an elemental activity. Such a phrase as 'the opening [*earlier,* "glimmering"] eye-lids of the morn' (a literal rendering of a Hebrew phrase used in the third chapter of Job, though also common in Elizabethan poetry) or the revised line 'Oft till the Star that rose, at Ev'ning, bright' introduces that favourite attitude to Nature regarded with a sense of the passing of time already hinted at in the fifth line of the poem and to be used at the end of the poem in a single great phrase suggesting the dawn of a new day unobtrusively yet with immense promise:

> To morrow to fresh woods and pastures new.

The two poets are thus described pursuing their activities together against a background of changing nature, which culminates with the rising of the evening star. And so our gaze is shifted from earth to heaven ('Toward heav'ns descent had slop'd his burnisht wheel'), and so a whole sense of cosmic implication, before the images suggesting poetry ('rural ditties', 'oaten flute') are introduced. There is almost a suggestion of dance rhythms about the two lines ending 'mute' and 'flute', the second, short, line rhyming with the immediately preceding longer one. We do

---

[1] This is the reading of the 1638 ed. Milton later changed 'glimmering' to 'opening'.

[2] So 1638. Milton altered the line to

> Oft till the Star that rose, at Ev'ning, bright

[3] So 1638. Later, 'westering'.

not need to speculate on the identity of 'old Dametas' (later spelt 'Damætas') in order to see in him a symbol of the approval of the properly constituted judges of poetry or at least of poetic ambition.

> And old Dametas lov'd to heare our song

ends the paragraph on a note of self-satisfaction: they were both recognized as promising young poets. They pleased both those who judge merely by instinct (the rough satyrs and the fauns with cloven heel) and the cultivated critic. They were, in fact, both on their way to literary fame.

No sooner has he suggested this than Milton realizes afresh that one of them is no longer there, that poetic promise is not enough to guarantee immortality:

> But oh the heavy change, now thou art gone,
> Now thou art gone, and never must return!

The images of Nature which have previously suggested growth and maturity (i.e. change implying progress and hope) are replaced by images of Nature suggesting decay and death:

> Thee shepherd, thee the woods, and desert caves
> With wild thyme and the gadding vine oregrown,
> And all their echoes mourn.
> The willows and the hasil-copses green
> Shall now no more be seen
> Fanning their joyous leaves to thy soft layes.
> As killing as the canker to the rose,
> Or taint-worm to the weanling herds that graze,
> Or frost to flowers that their gay wardrobe wear,
> When first the white-thorn blowes;
> Such, Lycidas, thy losse to shepherds eare.

One does not need to emphasize the emotional effect of such repetitions as 'now thou art gone, and never must return' or 'thee shepherd, thee the woods ...' or the sharpening of the meaning by the inversion in the latter of these. And here again it is Lycidas as poet who is mourned: it is the loss of his song, his loss to

shepherd's *ear*, that matters. Even the songster cannot be saved—
even the Muses cannot protect their own, as the succeeding verse-
paragraph immediately points out:

> Where were ye Nimphs when the remorselesse deep
> Clos'd ore the head of your lov'd Lycidas?

This is the second reference in the poem to the fact that Lycidas
had met his death by drowning, and it is introduced here in order
that Milton may avail himself of appropriate mythological references. The water nymphs could not save him, nor could the
tutelary spirits of that region near which the ship went down:

> For neither were ye playing on the steep,
> Where the old Bards the famous Druids lie,
> Nor on the shaggie top of Mona high,
> Nor yet where Deva spreads her wisard stream:
> Ah me, I fondly dream!
> Had ye been there—for what could that have done?
> What could the Muse her self that Orpheus bore,
> The Muse her self, for her inchanting sonne?
> Whom universall nature did lament,
> When by the rout that made the hideous rore
> His goary visage down the stream was sent,
> Down the swift Hebrus to the Lesbian shore.

King had been drowned off the north coast of Wales, a fact
which allows Milton to exploit the old Celtic traditions of England
(in which he had always been interested) and enrich the classical
pastoral conception of the poet with references to the ancient
Druids (who were poet-priests), associated especially with the
island of Mona or Anglesey, and to the whole Celtic conception
of the bard with its implications. 'Deva' is the River Dee, which
forms part of the boundary between England and Wales, and is
rich in Celtic folk traditions (hence 'wisard stream'). Milton has
here deftly widened his conception of the poet to include both the
classical and the Celtic; and to clinch this paragraph he returns
to a classical image, picturing the frightful death of Orpheus,
himself the son of Calliope, one of the Muses, and the very em-
bodiment of poetic genius. Orpheus, the founder and symbol of

poetry and a son of the Muse, could not be saved from a more frightful death than that which befell Lycidas; and Milton briefly but effectively touches on the gruesome story (told both by Virgil and Ovid) of his being torn to pieces by the frenzied Thracian women, his head being cast into the River Hebrus and carried out to the island of Lesbos. The emotion reaches its height with that final, terrible image:

> His goary visage down the stream was sent,
> Down the swift Hebrus to the Lesbian shore.

This passage is much worked over in the Trinity manuscript, and the sustained power of the final version is the result of several careful revisions. Milton always found the death of Orpheus a peculiarly moving and somehow a very personal story: in the opening of the seventh book of *Paradise Lost* he asks his divine muse to drive far off the royalist revellers whom the restoration of Charles II had brought back to London and compares them to the bacchanalian mob that murdered Orpheus:

> But drive farr off the barbarous dissonance
> Of *Bacchus* and his Revellers, thc Race
> Of that wilde Rout that tore the *Thracian* Bard
> In *Rhodope*, where Woods and Rocks had Eares
> To capture, till the savage clamor dround
> Both Harp and Voice; nor could the Muse defend
> Her Son.

'Nor could the Muse defend her Son.' 'What could the Muse her self that Orpheus bore/The Muse her self, for her inchanting sonne?...' To be a poet was no guarantee against sudden death.

The concept of the poet has by now been completely universalized; it is no longer Milton and his friend but the poet in both his classical and Celtic aspects: yet this is the fate he may expect. Why, then, he asks in the paragraph that follows, should one bother to dedicate oneself to a life of preparation for great poetry?

> Alas! what boots it with uncessant care
> To tend the homely slighted shepherds trade,
> And strictly meditate the thanklesse Muse?

Is it worth trying to be a poet? One pursues fame, but before one has won it one is liable to be cut off. This is the theme of this well-known passage in which Milton effectively contrasts images of self-dedication with images of self-indulgence. Can man as Christian humanist achieve anything more than man as mere sensualist? This is one of the main questions posed by the poem and its answer emerges implicitly only at the poem's end. For the moment, the poet finds a tentative answer, but it clearly does not satisfy him any more than it provides a satisfactory conclusion to the poem.

> Fame is no plant that growes on mortall soil,
> Nor in the glistring foil
> Set off to th'world, nor in broad rumour lies;
> But lives, and spreads aloft by those pure eyes
> And perfect witnesse of all-judging Jove:
> As he pronounces lastly on each deed,
> Of so much fame in heav'n expect thy meed.

This reply, given to the poet by Phoebus (Apollo, the god of song and music), is not convincing even in purely formal terms. An explicit reply of this kind would have to be given by a more inclusive representative of poetry than Apollo, for the poem includes non-classical (e.g. Celtic and Christian) concepts of the poet as well. And the pat aphoristic nature of that final couplet—

> As he pronounces lastly on each deed,
> Of so much fame in heav'n expect thy meed . . .

—could not possibly be a solution to such a complex poem as 'Lycidas'. There is almost a note of irony in the copy-book lesson. It is a deliberately false climax, and Milton returns to his pastoral imagery to contemplate his theme again.

In the next verse-paragraph Milton develops his earlier question—What were the responsible authorities doing to allow such a disaster to befall Lycidas?—in traditional pastoral terms. This fact is in itself sufficient indication that he is not satisfied with the solution he has just brought forward. The god of the sea, the god of the winds and the Nereids are each interrogated or considered, and each is acquitted of having caused Lycidas' death. The poet has here given up for the moment any attempt at a larger solution to the whole problem posed by his friend's death and is trying to find out only who is immediately responsible. But he can find no answer to the question, except the baffling one that it was destiny:

> It was the fatall and perfidious bark,
> Built in th' eclipse, and rigg'd with curses dark,
> That sunk so low that sacred head of thine.

The section thus ends on a note of frustration and even despair. Dark images of superstition and fatalism provide the only response to Milton's questions. This seventh verse-paragraph, which moves from cheerful pastoral imagery to the suggestion of man's helplessness against fate, is worth careful consideration: in structure, movement and balance it shows a remarkable craftsmanship. Note, for example, the sense of muttering frustration to which the poet is reduced at the end:

> That sunk so low that sacred head of thine.

But with the adjective 'sacred' a new thought emerges: Lycidas, like Milton, had been a dedicated man (Edward King had, in fact, been destined for the Church). His university could ill spare such a student and the Church could ill spare such a recruit. The hero as poet is now enlarged to encompass the hero as Christian champion, and as such his loss is deplored both by Cambridge (represented by Camus, the River Cam) and St. Peter. (It is worth noting that Milton uses biographical facts about King only when they help him to expand his meaning at the proper point in the poem; otherwise he ignores or even distorts them.)

The point now becomes not the loss suffered by the poet himself by dying young and being unable to fulfil his potentialities, but the loss to society when the poet (who is now spiritual leader as well as singer) dies before he can serve it. And so we have the famous statement of St. Peter:

Last came, and last did go,
The Pilot of the Galilean lake,
Two massie keyes he bore of metalls twain,
(The golden opes, the iron shuts amain).
He shook his mitred locks, and stern bespake,
How well could I have spar'd for thee, young swain,
Enough of such as for their bellies sake
Creep and intrude and climb into the fold?
Of other care they little reckoning make,
Then how to scramble at the shearers feast,
And shove away the worthy bidden guest.
Blind mouthes! that scarce themselves know how to hold
A sheephook, or have learn'd ought else the least
That to the faithfull herdmans art belongs!
What recks it them? what need they? they are sped;
And when they list their lean and flashie songs
Grate on their scrannel pipes of wretched straw,
The hungry sheep look up, and are not fed,
But swoln with wind, and the rank mist they draw,
Rot inwardly, and foul contagion spread:
Besides what the grimme wolf with privy paw
Daily devoures apace, and little said.
But that two-handed engine at the doore,
Stands ready to smite once, and smite no more.

This passage is, of course, an attack on the Anglican clergy,
but it is not the digression that critics have generally assumed it
to be. Milton has been developing the theme that the good are
destroyed while the bad remain—a theme which in turn emerges
from his earlier point that there is no sense in choosing a life of
self-dedication to great art if the dedicated man is given no
preferential treatment by fate over that accorded to mere sensual-
ists and opportunists. Not only is the potential poet-priest no
more likely to survive and fulfil his promise, he seems actually
less likely to survive than the evil men who do harm to society
where the poet-priest would have done good. Granted that the
poet must take his chance of survival along with everybody else,
is it fair to *society* to cut him off and let the drones and the
parasites remain? The theme of 'Lycidas' is the fate of the poet-
priest in all his aspects, both as individual and as social figure.

Even this bitter passage retains the pastoral imagery. The

shepherd as the symbol of the spiritual leader is of course an old Christian usage, and goes right back to the Bible. But in the classical tradition the shepherd also sings and pipes. So by combining Christian and classical pastoral traditions Milton can use the shepherd as a symbol for the combination of priest and poet which was such an important concept to him. (With reference to the biblical element in the imagery of this passage, it is worth noting that the first verse of the twenty-third Psalm in the English Psalter of 1530 reads: 'The lorde is my pastore and feader: wherfore I shal not wante.') The association of classical and biblical imagery in the passage is further emphasized in the lines

> Of other care they little reckoning make,
> Then how to scramble at the shearers feast,
> And shove away the worthy bidden guest,

with the reference to the parable in the twenty-second chapter of Matthew.

The technical devices employed in this passage to indicate the poet's contempt for those he is attacking have often been noted and scarcely need elaboration here. Once again we have the gesture, the clearly seen movement, presented in terms which associate it with an attitude of contempt:

> Creep and intrude and climb into the fold.

This is a very precise line, with three verbs each possessing an exact, different but complementary meaning. One might note also the effect in their contexts of such phrases as 'shove away', 'scramble' and 'swoln with wind'. And one need hardly catalogue the effective qualities of such lines as:

> What recks it them? what need they? they are sped;
> And when they list their lean and flashie songs
> Grate on their scrannel pipes of wretched straw.

Mr. Prince sees in these lines an echo of 'rustic raillery' found in the Italian pastorals of Sannazaro, where, in humorous passages with double rhyme, he presents exchanges of abuse between two

rival shepherds. But, though Milton might have learned something technically from this sort of Italian verse, the tone here is
his own and far from humorous.

The conclusion of St. Peter's outburst suggests, with deliberate
and effective vagueness, that something will be done about those
who abuse society's trust:

> But that two-handed engine at the doore,
> Stands ready to smite once, and smite no more.

There is no need to follow generations of editors in their speculations on what Milton really meant by the 'two-handed engine':
all that is really necessary for an understanding of the poem is to
note that retribution is certain through a device which suggests
purposive activity on the part of society. The implication of 'two-
handed' is that men will use it with their own two hands, and this
suggestion of purposive activity anticipates and prepares the way
for the final resolution of the problem posed by the poem—which
is that man as poet and moralist should, so long as he remains
alive, keep on working and striving, continuing to proceed from
task to task until he is no longer able. Thus, though the poem
opens on a note of regret that the poet is forced once again to
write before his talent is mature, it ends by his turning with
renewed zeal to fresh poetic activity:

> To morrow to fresh woods and pastures new.

Having suggested the lines on which the resolution of the
poem is to be achieved, Milton returns to the dead Lycidas, aware
of the fact that the only answer to the problem posed by his
premature death is for those who survive to carry on more
zealously than ever. Such an answer implies an abandonment of
sorrow and a leaving behind of thoughts of the dead potential
poet, and before he can bring himself to do this he must try to
transmute the dead Lycidas into something beautiful and fragrant. And so, as a sort of apology to Lycidas before leaving him
for ever, he turns passionately to his dead body and attempts to
smother it with flowers:

> Bring the rathe primerose that forsaken dies,
> The tufted crow-toe, and pale gessamine,
> The white pink, and the pansie freakt with jeat,
> The glowing violet, . . .
> To strew the laureat herse where Lycid lies.

Milton apparently added this passage later; the Trinity manuscript shows it as an insertion, in two versions, the first longer and more elaborate than the one finally worked out. Perhaps the idea of making some sort of amends to Lycidas, as it were, for having to forsake him at the last, occurred to Milton on reading over a first draft of the poem, and he therefore inserted the passage as a transition from the attack on the clergy to the picture of Lycidas' body washed out to sea. Yet he is still reluctant to leave him:

> Ay me! whil'st thee the shores and sounding seas
> Wash farre away, where ere thy bones are hurl'd,
> Whether beyond the stormy Hebrides,
> Where thou perhaps under the humming tide[1]
> Visit'st the bottom of the monstrous world;
> Or whether thou to our moist vowes deni'd,
> Sleep'st by the fable of Bellerus old,
> Where the great vision of the guarded mount
> Looks toward Namancos and Bayona's hold;
> Look homeward Angel now, and melt with ruth,
> And, O ye dolphins, waft the haplesse youth.

The body of the dead Lycidas refuses to be smothered with flowers, refuses to allow the poet to 'interpose a little ease' and 'dally with false surmise'. He is indeed drowned—but no sooner has Milton accepted this fact anew than, with a deliberate echo of the references to Mona and Deva in the fifth verse-paragraph, he exploits geography with tremendous effect. Lycidas lies drowned off the coast of Wales. Perhaps his body has been washed northwards up to the romantic Hebrides; perhaps he is exploring the monstrous depths of the ocean; perhaps—and here the emotion rises—he has made his peace with the great Celtic guardians of pre-Anglo-Saxon Britain (Celtic Britain always had

---

[1] So 1638. Later changed by Milton to 'whelming tide'.

an immense fascination for Milton) and sleeps with 'the fable of Bellerus old', i.e. with the fabled Cornish giant from whose name the Roman name for Land's End, Bellerium, was supposed to have been derived. Milton here suddenly projects an image of the south-west corner of England (Wales and Cornwall, with their associations with the Celtic heritage of Britain) and infuses into this projection a passionate sense of English history and English patriotism. 'The guarded mount' is St. Michael's Mount, near Penzance. Following the imagined drifting of Lycidas' body, Milton is led to associate it with that part of England, so rich in history and folklore, which projects into the sea and looks towards Spain (Nemancos and Bayona's hold, i.e. stronghold, were districts in northern Spain, so marked in several seventeenth-century maps; Nemancos was mis-spelled 'Namancos' in Ojea's map of Galicia and in subsequent maps, including Mercator's atlas). England looking towards Spain suggests the whole challenge of Anglo-Spanish relations of the late sixteenth century, culminating in the defeat of the Spanish Armada in 1588. Catholic Spain remained the enemy for the very Protestant Milton, and this passage has its links with the earlier reference to the 'grimme wolf with privy paw', which refers to the proselytizing Roman Catholic Church. To see Lycidas in this context is to see him in conjunction with English history and with the guardian angel of England, St. Michael, who looks out over the sea towards the long-since-defeated Spanish enemy. He has thus at last managed to associate Lycidas with a sense of triumph, and he can now afford to leave the dead for a moment and interpose a great cry for his country:

> Look homeward Angel now, and melt with ruth,
> And, O ye dolphins, waft the haplesse youth.

He seems to be saying here: 'Look no more out towards Spain, but look instead homeward towards Lycidas.' But surely there is a strong implication here of a plea that England's guardian angel should cease to look away from home but look homeward at the state of the country, ministered to by a clergy whose corruption and inefficiency he has already so vividly described. 'Look homeward Angel now' rings out like a passionate cry for his country and for himself. The dolphins can take care of the dead man; England and England's potential great poet John Milton require your present aid.

Lycidas can now be disposed of conventionally. The problem has moved beyond him, so Milton can let himself picture his reception in Heaven with all the triumphant resources of Christian imagery. And that is the function of the penultimate verse-paragraph beginning:

Weep no more, wofull shepherds, weep no more.

There is a content here, a restrained passion, a controlled happiness. Milton has prepared the way for the emergence of the attitude in the light of which the question posed by the poem can be answered—What shall the Christian humanist do in the face of imminent death, what shall man the creator do in the prospect of extinction?—and having done so he can at last accept the conventional Christian answer to the question of Lycidas' own fate. The note of acquiescence emerges clearly here, as it did not in the answer provided earlier by Phoebus. Yet the picture of Lycidas' triumph in Heaven is not altogether conventionally Christian. Lycidas hears 'the unexpressive nuptiall song', and this is another echo of Milton's passionate belief in the special reward waiting in Heaven for those who kept themselves chaste on earth. We have seen how that belief combines Pythagorean, Platonic and Christian elements and is related both to his view of the music of the spheres and his interpretation of the first five verses of the fourteenth chapter of Revelation. He is more explicit and detailed about the mystic joys of heavenly nuptials reserved for those who were chaste on earth in the conclusion of another elegy, the Latin *Epitaphium Damonis* he was to write two years later for his friend Diodati.

But this cannot be the end of the poem, as it should have been if Milton were writing a conventional Christian elegy. He has to return to himself, to man as poet and creator, and give his final statement on the question posed by the poem. What shall the creator do when he knows he may die at any time? The answer, already prepared for in several passages, emerges at the end firmly and with conviction. We return to Milton, to the poet who has been mourning his dead friend. And as we return to him, a new day dawns, and he sets out on new tasks. The answer is not dissimilar to that given in the sonnets on his twenty-third birthday and on his blindness: man can only do what in him lies as best he can.

> Thus sang the uncouth swain to th' oaks and rills,
> While the still morn went out with sandals gray;
> He touch'd the tender stops of various quills,
> With eager thought warbling his Dorick lay:
> And now the sunne had stretch'd out all the hills,
> And now was dropt into the western bay;
> At last he rose, and twitch'd his mantle blew,
> To morrow to fresh woods and pastures new.

He returns at the end to those pastoral images most suggestive of the poet. He pays his respects to the Greek pastoral poets ('Dorick lay') and to the Latin (the fifth line is Virgil's *Majoresque cadunt altis de montibus umbrae*) and thus associates himself firmly with the Western literary tradition. And the last line suggests a determination to proceed to yet greater poetic achievements. Lycidas is forgotten: the world remains in the hands of the living and is shaped by their purposes. Keats, in his sonnet 'When I have fears that I may cease to be', faced the same problem Milton faced in 'Lycidas'. Suppose he died 'before my pen has gleaned my teeming brain'? Keats' answer was to lose himself in a mood of sad-sweet contemplation:

> then on the shore
> Of the wide world I stand alone, and think
> Till love and fame to nothingness do sink.

Milton's answer is very different. His poem ends by his stepping out of himself, as it were, instead of losing himself in introspection. He sees himself humbly, as an 'uncouth swain' singing as a new dawn comes up and brings new work to do.

'Lycidas' is dated in the Trinity manuscript November 1637. He must have already been planning his tour abroad at this time, and perhaps 'pastures new' is a reference to it. At any rate, he left in April 1638, on what was presumably intended to be the last great phase of his self-preparation as a poet—a visit to the

Mediterranean centre of European culture. It turned out to be largely an Italian visit, for events at home recalled him as he was about to proceed to Sicily and Greece. But even so it was, in Professor Hanford's words, 'one of the great *Wanderjahre* of literary history, a moment of contact between cultures comparable with the Italian journeys of Erasmus and of Goethe'. Here is Milton's own account, as he later gave it in the *Defensio Secunda* :

Taking ship at Nice, I arrived at Genoa, and afterwards visited Leghorn, Pisa and Florence. In the latter city, which I have always more particularly esteemed for the elegance of its dialect, its genius and its taste, I stopped about two months; when I contracted an intimacy with many persons of rank and learning; and was a constant attendant at their literary parties; a practice which prevails there, and tends so much to the diffusion of knowledge, and preservation of friendship. No time will ever abolish the agreeable recollections which I cherish of Jacob Gaddi, Carolo Dati, Frescobaldo, Coltellino, Bonomatthei, Clementillo, Francini, and many others. From Florence I went to Siena, thence to Rome, where, after I had spent about two months in viewing the antiquities of that renowned city, where I experienced the most friendly attentions from Lucas Holstein and other learned and ingenious men, I continued my route to Naples. There I was introduced by a certain recluse, with whom I had travelled from Rome, to John Baptista Manso, marquis of Villa, a nobleman of distinguished rank and authority, to whom Torquato Tasso, the illustrious poet, inscribed his book on friendship. During my stay, he gave me singular proofs of his regard : he himself conducted me round the city, and to the palace of the viceroy; and more than once paid me a visit to my lodgings. On my departure he gravely apologized for not having shown me more civility, which he said he had been restrained from doing, because I had spoken with so little reserve on matters of religion. When I was preparing to pass over into Sicily and Greece, the melancholy intelligence which I received of the civil commotions in England made me alter my purpose; for I thought it base to be travelling for amusement abroad while my fellow citizens were fighting for liberty at home. While I was on my way back to Rome, some merchants informed me that the English Jesuits had formed a plot against me if I returned to Rome, because I had spoken too freely on religion; for it was a rule which I laid down to myself in those places, never to be the first to begin any conversation on religion; but if any questions were put to me

concerning my faith, to declare it without any reserve or fear.
I, nevertheless, returned to Rome. I took no steps to conceal either
my person or my character; and for about the space of two
months I again openly defended, as I had done before, the reformed
religion in the very metropolis of popery. By the favour of God,
I got safe back to Florence, where I was received with as much
affection as if I had returned to my native country. There I stopped
as many months as I had done before, except that I made an
excursion for a few days to Lucca; and, crossing the Apennines,
passed through Bologna and Ferrara to Venice. After I had spent
a month in surveying the curiosities of this city, and had put on
board a ship the books which I had collected in Italy, I proceeded
through Verona and Milan, and along the Leman lake to Geneva.
. . . At Geneva I held daily conferences with John Diodati, the
learned professor of Theology. Then pursuing my former route
through France, I returned to my native country after an absence
of one year and about three months.

Milton seems to have had a particularly good time at Florence.
We find him writing on 10 September, 1638, to Benedetto Bono-
mattei of Florence congratulating and encouraging him on his
work, now almost finished, on the Italian language and urging
him to add an appendix on pronunciation for the use of foreigners.
The tone of the letter is one of affectionate friendship in spite of
its formality. It is in Latin, and he apologizes for not writing in
Italian: 'It is precisely because I want to have this Italian tongue
of yours cleared up in precepts by yourself that I employ Latin
openly in my confession of poverty and want of skill.' It was as
a Latin poet that Milton was received and acclaimed by literary
circles in Italy. The Italian literary societies ('private academies',
as Milton called them), which were largely discussion groups at
which members read and discussed each other's work, flourished
in Italy at this time, and Milton soon came to know many of them.
He read a Latin poem at one of the Florentine societies on
16 September, as we know from the society's minutes. 'In the
privat Academies of *Italy*,' wrote Milton of this phase in his
career, in *The Reason of Church-Government*, 'whither I was
favor'd to resort, perceiving that some trifles which I had in
memory, compos'd at under twenty or thereabout (for the manner
is that every one must give some proof of his wit and reading
there) met with acceptance above what was lookt for, and other

things which I had shifted in scarcity of books and conveniences to patch up amongst them, were receiv'd with written Encomiums, which the Italian is not forward to bestow on men of this side the *Alps*.'

Milton seems to have formed a real friendship with Carlo Dati, then a young man of eighteen, later to become a distinguished literary figure; Dati contributed a Latin eulogy of Milton which was prefixed to Milton's Latin poems published in 1645. Of the other Italian friends Milton mentions, Antonio Francini, also younger than Milton and a poet, contributed an Italian ode to the 1645 volume. But it was not only with the young literary figures that Milton made friends; the venerable Giovanni Battista Manso, Marquis of Villa, for whom Tasso had written his treatise *De Amicitia*, became a warm friend. Milton's pride in Manso's friendship is shown not only by the way he refers to him in the account of his Italian visit in the *Defensio Secunda*, but also in the Latin poem *Mansus*, addressed to Manso and written and sent to him by Milton before he left Naples. Manso contributed a Latin compliment to the 1645 volume:

> Ut mens, forma, decor, facies, mos, si pietas sic,
> Non Anglus, verum hercle Angelus ipse fores.

> If your religion were only like your mind, form, grace, morals and face, you would indeed be not an Englishman [Anglus] but an Angel [Angelus].

This epigram reminds us of the charm of manner and personal attractiveness which all the testimony indicates that the young Milton possessed; it shows, too, that Manso had not forgotten that Milton in Italy could not always restrain himself from arguing against the religion of his hosts.

It is interesting that it was his friendship with Manso that Milton regarded as the high point of his Italian journey. His visit to Galileo he mentioned only in *Areopagitica* when he was warning against censorship and licensing:

> I could recount what I have seen and heard in other Countries, where this kind of inquisition tyrannizes; when I have sat among their lerned men, for that honor I had, and bin counted happy

to be born in such a place of *Philosophic* freedom, as they suppos'd
England was, while themselves did nothing but bemoan the servil
condition into which lerning amongst them was brought ; . . . There
it was that I found and visited the famous *Galileo* grown old, a
prisner to the Inquisition, for thinking in Astronomy otherwise
then the Franciscan and Dominican licencers thought.

This passage bears out the impression one gets from other sources
that Milton, while he charmed the Italians with his learning, his
poetic skill and his gift for friendship, was often aggressively
patriotic in his attitude to foreign ideas and institutions. At
Geneva on his way home from Italy Milton visited the Neapolitan
nobleman Cerdogni, and wrote in his album the concluding lines
from *Comus*, with his name and nationality : it is on both counts
a highly significant pronouncement :

> —if Vertue feeble were
> Heaven it selfe would stoope to her
> Johannes Miltonius
> Anglus
> Junii 10° 1639.

Yet Milton controlled his anti-Catholicism sufficiently to dine
at the English Jesuit College in Rome on 30 October, 1639. Nor
did religious views keep him from forming a friendship with
Lucas Holstein, the Vatican librarian, to whom he wrote from
Florence on 30 March, 1639, thanking him in the warmest terms
for his 'courteous and most friendly actes' and his hospitality.
The letter to Holstein refers to Holstein's having introduced him
to Cardinal Francesco Barberini with the result that Milton was
cordially invited by the Cardinal to a 'public musical entertainment' which he gave 'with truly Roman magnificence'. This
musical entertainment was in fact a historic occasion—the performance in Rome, amid great splendour, of one of the first
Italian comic operas. Milton's interest in music led him to
welcome such contacts with the lively musical life of Italy. That
there were others is indicated by the three Latin epigrams, full of
admiration and praise, which he wrote to the celebrated Neapolitan singer, Leonora Baroni. How Milton conducted himself
amid the gaiety and luxury of the Casa Barberini can only be

guessed ; but when we think of the older Milton growing steadily sterner in his view of the good life we must not forget that he had this experience behind him.

Milton took his time about coming home after his decision to return ; he took nearly eight months over the journey, stopping again at Rome and Florence and spending a month in Venice. At Geneva he met Giovanni Diodati, émigré Protestant theologian from Italy and uncle of Milton's friend Charles Diodati. He arrived back in England about the beginning of August 1639, in that uneasy period between the settlement of the so-called First Bishops' War and the outbreak of the second in 1640

The Latin poem which Milton sent to Manso before he left Naples shows that Milton's ambitions as an epic poet were rising steadily. The poem begins with stately compliments to Manso in Ovidian elegiacs, but less than half-way through he turns the subject to himself. 'You who are so good will not despise a foreign muse,' he tells Manso, and goes on to talk of the prospects for poetry in Britain and his own poetic ambitions. Manso, he says, has been a great friend and patron of poets ; would that he, Milton, might be given such a friend :

> O mihi si mea sors talem concedat amicum
> Phoebaeos decorasse viros qui tam bene norit,
> Si quando indigenas revocabo in carmina reges
> Arturumque etiam sub terris bella moventem;
> Aut dicam invictae sociali foedere mensae,
> Magnanimos Heroas, et (O modo spiritus adsit)
> Frangam Saxonicas Britonum sub Marte phalanges.

O, if my fate would grant me such a friend, who knows so well how to honour the devotees of Apollo; if ever I shall call back our native kings into our songs, and Arthur waging war even under the earth, or celebrate the great-hearted heroes of the round table, unconquered because of their mutual loyalty and—O, let only the spirit be with me—shall shatter the Saxon phalanxes beneath the British Mars.

And he ends by painting a picture of his posthumous poetic fame and eternal reward.

He was saving everything up to tell his friend Charles Diodati when he returned home. But Diodati died in late August 1638 and when Milton arrived home he found no one with whom he could talk intimately about his Italian successes or to whom he could confide his poetic plans. The elegy he wrote for Diodati, the Latin *Epitaphium Damonis*, is an altogether more directly personal affair than 'Lycidas', even though both poems use the convention of the pastoral elegy. The sense of personal loss rises plangently from the repeated refrain

> Ite domum impasti, domino iam non vacat, agni.
>
> Go home unfed, my lambs; your master has now no time for you.

The real point of the poem lies in the question asked in the forty-fifth line: 'Pectora cui credam?' 'To whom shall I confide my heart?' Milton works into the poem the confidences he had looked forward to telling Diodati:

> Ipse ego Dardanias Rutupina per aequora puppes
> Dicam, et Pandrasidos regnum vetus Inogeniae,
> Brennumque Arviragumque duces, piscumque Belinum,
> Et tandem Armoricos Britonum sub lege colonos;
> Tum gravidam Arturo fatali fraude Iögernen,
> Mendaces vultus, assumptaque Gorlöis arma,
> Merlini dolus. O mihi tum si vita supersit,
> Tu procul annosa pendebis fistula pinu
> Multim oblita mihi, aut patriis mutata camoenis
> Brittonicum strides, quid enim? omnia non licet uni
> Non sperasse uni licet omnia.

For my part, I shall tell of the Dardanian ships in the Rutupian sea, and of the ancient kingdom of Inogen, daughter of Pandrasus, and of the chiefs, Brennus and Arviragus, and old Belinus, and of the Armorican settler who at last came under British law; then of Igraine pregnant with Arthur by a fatal trick, the features of Gorlois and his arms falsely assumed by Merlin's trickery. O then, my pipe, if further life remains to me, you shall hang far away on some old pine tree, wholly forgotten by me, or else sound forth in harsher tones a British theme to your native muses. What then? One man cannot do everything, nor can one man hope for everything.

These were themes from early British history, which Milton was revolving in his mind as possible subjects for a national epic.

III

PROSE AND THE SONNETS

ON his return to England in the summer of 1639 Milton did not immediately enter into the political and religious controversies that were dividing the nation. He moved to 'a pretty garden-house' in Aldersgate Street, where he undertook the education of his two nephews, his widowed sister's sons, and after a while he took in other boarders who likewise became his pupils. Milton never refers directly to his activities as a teacher in any of the many autobiographical passages in his prose works; teaching never seemed to have claimed a major part of his attention, though his pamphlet *Of Education* (not to mention his Latin Grammar and his text-book on logic) shows that he had thought seriously about both its theory and practice. Edward Phillips later listed the Latin and Greek authors 'which, through his excellent judgment and way of teaching, far above the pedantry of common public schools, . . . were run over within no greater compass of time, than from ten to fifteen or sixteen years of age'. These included 'the four grand authors *De Re Rustica*, Cato, Varro, Columella and Palladius'; Pliny's *Natural History*, Vitruvius' *Architecture*, Frontinus' *Stratagem*, Lucretius and Manilius. The Greek authors studied included Hesiod ('a poet equal with Homer') and a great number of often obscure works on astronomy, geometry, warfare, education and history, including books by Oppian, Apollonius Rhodius, Plutarch and Xenophon. The Pentateuch was read in the original Hebrew and also in the Aramaic or 'Chaldee' version, and Milton's pupils got 'besides an introduction into several arts and sciences, by reading Urstisius his *Arithmetic*, Riff's *Geometry*, Joannes de Sacro Bosco *De Sphaera*, and into the Italian and French tongues, by reading in Italian Giovan Villani's *History of the Transactions between several petty states of Italy*, and in French a great part of Pierre Davity, the famous geographer of France in his time'. On Sundays they read the Greek Testament and heard 'his learned exposition upon the same'. Meanwhile, Milton was also meditating topics for an epic and plans for a drama on the subject of the Fall. And he was watching the development of the political situation.

King Charles had summoned the Short Parliament in 1640 in the hope of getting a money vote, but Parliament insisted on redress of grievances first, and Charles dissolved Parliament in disgust after three weeks. The Second Bishops' War ended in October after the defeat of Charles' army by a Scottish force, and Charles had to summon Parliament again. This, the Long Parliament, turned at once to the punishment of those who had advised the King in his absolute course—the Earl of Strafford and Archbishop Laud—and then proceeded to legislate for the regularizing of parliamentary procedure and the curbing of the royal authority. For the Presbyterians in the Long Parliament, however—and they were in the majority, though but narrowly— the main problem was ecclesiastical rather than political; it was, in Professor Haller's words, 'the problem of delimiting and coordinating the civil and spiritual authorities in the nation'. The 'root and branch' petition, presented to Parliament in December 1640 with fifteen thousand names attached to it, was an attempt by the citizens of London 'and other Inhabitants thereabouts' to put pressure on Parliament to legislate in favour of 'Reformation in Church-government, as also for the abolishment of Episcopacie'. Puritan preachers throughout the country argued with eloquence and learning in favour of a more thorough reformation of the Church in accordance with God's Word. Exactly what this implied was not made clear. The preachers, like the 'root and branch' petitioners, agreed that the form of ecclesiastical government as at present set up, 'with all its dependencies, rootes and branches,' should be abolished in favour of 'the government, according to Gods word', but nobody specified what new forms of ecclesiastical government this would involve. The more the Puritans pressed the matter of church government the graver grew the political crisis and the nearer came the final break between King and Parliament, for ecclesiastical and political government were too much bound up with each other in the system that had developed from the time of the Elizabethan settlement to allow one to be radically altered without immediate repercussions on the other.

Throughout 1641 the voice of the Puritan preachers was heard throughout England in impassioned pleas for 'a godly preaching ministry' free from episcopal control. At the same time the censorship of the Press, which Archbishop Laud had exercised in the interests of the establishment, lapsed abruptly on Laud's overthrow, and a fierce pamphlet war raged. Outpreached by the eloquence and endurance of the Puritan godly preaching ministry, the bishops and their supporters turned to the Press, which was now free for both sides, to urge their point of view. And the books and pamphlets which they produced were duly answered by spokesmen for the other side. Joseph Hall, Bishop of Norwich, poet, satirist and miscellaneous man of letters, had already produced, under Laud's direction, a blast against the Scottish anti-prelatical arguments in his *Episcopacy by Divine Right*, 1640. Now he entered the fray again and in January 1641 published his *Humble Remonstrance to the High Court of Parliament*, defending episcopacy and the establishment with the conventional arguments of his party—the continuity of the episcopal tradition from apostolic times and the central importance of the liturgy as opposed to the infinite number of erratic individual interpretations of the Bible. A group of Puritan preachers undertook a reply to Hall; they included Thomas Young, who had been Milton's tutor, and others, the first letters of whose names together made up the word 'Smectymnuus', under which name the pamphlet appeared. Its full title is significant: *An Answer to a Book entituled An Humble Remonstrance. In which the original of Liturgy and Episcopacy is discussed and Quaeres propounded Concerning both; the parity of Bishops to Presbyters in Scripture demonstrated; The occasion of their Imparities in Antiquitie discovered. The Disparitie of the Ancient and Modern Bishops manifested. The Antiquitie of Ruling Elders in the Church, The Prelaticall Church Bounded. Written by Smectymnuus.* This appeared in February 1641 and it was answered in April by Bishop Hall with *A Defence of the Humble Remonstrance, Against the frivolous and false exceptions of Smectymnuus.* To this the Smectymnuans duly replied in June, and in that month, too, John Milton entered the dispute with an anonymous pamphlet in defence of his old tutor, *Of Reformation touching Church-Discipline in England: and the Causes that hitherto have hindred it.* About the same time a small pamphlet, arguing in favour of the hierarchical principle in church government, appeared with the title *The Judgement of Doctor Rainoldes*

*touching the Originall of Episcopacy. More largely confirmed out
of Antiquity by James Archbishop of Armagh.* Reynolds was a
distinguished Elizabethan Puritan divine and scholar, and Archbishop James Ussher's name also carried great weight, so Milton
replied with a short pamphlet, *Of Prelatical Episcopacy, and
Whether it may be deduc'd from the Apostolic times by vertue of
those Testimonies which are alledg'd to that purpose in some late
Treatises: One whereof goes under the Name of James Archbishop
of Armagh.* He then turned again to Bishop Hall and in July
published a pamphlet in which he answered Hall's attacks on the
Smectymnuans; it was entitled *Animadversions upon the Remonstrant's Defence, against Smectymnuus.* At the same time Hall
replied to the second Smectymnuan tract with *A Short Answer to
the Tedious Vindication of Smectymnuus,* while early in 1642 either
Hall or his son replied to Milton's *Animadversions* with a sharp
attack on Milton in *A Modest Confutation of a Slanderous and
Scurrilous Libell, entituled, Animadversions upon the Remonstrants
Defence against Smectymnuus.* To this Milton in turn replied in
March 1642 with *An Apology Against a Pamphlet call'd A Modest
Confutation of the Animadversions upon the Remonstrant against
Smectymnuus.* The ponderous house-that-Jack-built titles give
some idea of the ding-dong nature of the argument. Meanwhile,
in February 1642 Milton followed up his earlier short answer to
Hall's moderate arguments in favour of a limited episcopacy with
a much longer and more deeply pondered and elaborately reasoned
work, *The Reason of Church-Government Urg'd against Prelaty.*

The main thought in Milton's anti-prelatical pamphlets was
that the English Reformation had not been completed in Tudor
times, and now was the time to complete it. He has the true
Protestant view of the Reformation, rejoicing to recall 'how the
bright and blissful Reformation (by divine power) struck through
the black and settled night of ignorance and antichristian tyranny'.
He asks himself, in his first pamphlet, how it should come to pass
that England, which had, by the grace of God, led the nations in
'the recovery of lost truth', should now be behindhand 'in the
injoyment of that peace, whereof she taught the way to others'.
He replies by interpreting the ecclesiastical history of England
from the time of Henry VIII. *Of Reformation in England* is a
vigorously argued pamphlet, marshalling evidence from history

and literature (he cites Dante, Petrarch, Chaucer and Ariosto, as well as ecclesiastical writers) and pressing its points forcefully and with a certain dignity in a prose whose long sentences are managed with considerable rhetorical skill. *Of Prelatical Episcopacy* turns to the arguments of the other side, and refutes them point by point in what to the modern reader is tedious detail, though here, as in the former pamphlet, there comes through clearly Milton's view of the lamentable gap between the Gospel injunctions and the elaborate paraphernalia of ecclesiastical systems. *Animadversions* deals in a more satirical way with Hall, whose arguments Milton sets out and replies to in question-and-answer form, often turning the argument *ad hominem* in what Milton considered a sportive manner. *The Reason of Church-Government* (the first to appear with the author's name) is an elaborately reasoned defence of the presbyterian form of church government against the episcopal; there is no sportiveness here, only earnest and scholarly argument. *An Apology* shows how the debate had deteriorated into personalities. Milton had himself been personally attacked by this time, and he replied in kind, showing his characteristic ability to identify himself with a cause and to regard autobiography as defence of the cause. This pamphlet is full of picturesque abuse, and parts are in a style of colloquial flippancy which, while popular in controversial literature of the time, does not wear well. This manner, which the progress of the debate forced on Milton, led to a pettiness and lack of generosity that are found all too often in Milton's controversial prose. It is worth noting, however, that in *An Apology* Milton interrupts his point-by-point reply to his opponent with an eloquent address to Parliament in the manner of Isocrates.

It is the controlled personal feeling expressed through deliberate rhetorical devices that gives Milton's polemical prose its characteristic eloquence. 'O Sir, if we could but see the shape of our deare Mother *England*, as Poets are wont to give a personal form to what they please, how would she appeare, think ye, but in a mourning weed, with ashes upon her head, and teares abundantly flowing from her eyes, to behold so many of her children expos'd at once, and thrust from things of dearest necessity, because their conscience could not assent to things which the Bishops thought *indifferent*.' This sentence, from *Of Reformation in England*, shows how skilfully Milton could exploit the elegiac note when he wished. But he could also sound the patriotic note most eloquently, as in this passage from the same pamphlet:

> O thou that after the impetuous rage of five bloody Inundations, and the succeeding Sword of intestine *Warre*, soaking the Land in her owne gore, didst pitty the sad and ceasles revolution of our swift and thick-coming sorrowes when wee were quite breathlesse, and of thy *free grace* didst motion *Peace*, and termes of Cov'nant with us, and having first wel-nigh freed us from *Antichristian* thraldome, didst build up this *Britannick Empire* to a glorious and enviable heighth with all her Daughter Ilands about her, stay us in this felicitie, . . . That we may still remember in our *solemne Thanksgivings*, how for us the *Northern Ocean* even to the frozen *Thule* was scatter'd with the proud Ship-wracks of the *Spanish Armado*, and the very maw of Hell ransack't, and made to give up her conceal'd destruction, ere shee could vent it in that horrible and damned blast.
>
> O how much more glorious will those former Deliverances appeare, when we shall know them not onely to have sav'd us from greatest miseries past, but to have reserv'd us for greatest happinesse to come. Hitherto thou has but freed us, and that not fully, from the unjust and Tyrannous Claime of thy Foe, now unite us intirely, and appropriate us to thy selfe, tie us everlastingly in willing Homage to the *Prerogative* of thy eternall *Throne*.

This is eloquence, and eloquence of a different kind from the sportive and satirical reference to the bishops and their arguments only a couple of pages earlier in the same pamphlet:

> They intreate us that we would not be weary of those insupportable greevances that our shoulders have hitherto crackt under, they beseech us that we should think 'em fit to be our Justices of peace, our Lords, our highest officers of State, though they come furnish't with no more experience then they learnt betweene the *Cook*, and the *manciple*, or more profoundly at the Colledge *audit*, or the *regent house*, or to come to their deepest insight, at their *Patrons Table*; they would request us to indure still the russling of their Silken Cassocks, and that we would burst our *mid-riffes* rather then laugh to see them under Sayl in all their Lawn, and Sarcanet, their shrouds, and tackle, with a *geometricall rhomboides* upon their heads: . . .

There is something else, however, which is found in these anti-prelatical pamphlets which is purely Miltonic and which throws much light on Milton's state of mind at this time. He was still the dedicated poet, though the necessities of the time might take him temporarily into other kinds of writing. On his return from Italy he had been full of poetic plans, and was desolated, as we have seen, to find that his friend Charles Diodati was no longer alive to hear them. In the *Epitaphium Damonis* he had listed some of the themes from early British history which he had been meditating. With the kindling of his imagination at the prospect of a new and regenerate England arising out of the completion of the Reformation for which he was pleading in his anti-prelatical pamphlets, he thought of himself more and more as the poet of that brave new world, waiting for the completion of God's deliverance to utter forth his mighty harmonies. He thinks now more of divine than of secular subjects. But he does still think of poetry, and his poetic ambitions are higher than ever. Who else but Milton could end a pamphlet on church government as Milton ended *Of Reformation in England*, with a passionate outburst expressing his faith in a reformed and greater England of which he will be the poet?

Then amidst the *Hymns*, and *Halleluiahs* of *Saints* some one may perhaps bee heard offring at high *strains* in new and lofty *Measures* to sing and celebrate thy *divine Mercies*, and *marvelous Judgements* in this Land throughout all AGES; whereby this great and Warlike Nation instructed and inur'd to the fervent and continuall practice of *Truth* and *Righteousnesse*, and casting farre from her the rags of her old *vices* may presse on hard to that *high* and *happy* emulation to be found the *soberest*, *wisest*, and *most Christian People* at that day when thou the Eternall and shortly-expected King shalt open the Clouds to judge the severall King-domes of the World, and distributing *Nationall Honours* and *Rewards* to Religious and just *Common-wealths*, shalt put an end to all Earthly *Tyrannies*, proclaiming thy universal and milde *Monarchy* through Heaven and Earth. Where they undoubtedly that by their *Labours*, *Counsels*, and *Prayers* have been earnest for the *Common good* of *Religion* and their *Countrey*, shall receive, above the inferiour *Orders* of the *Blessed*, the *Regall* addition of *Principalities*, *Legions*, and *Thrones* into their glorious Titles, and in supereminence of *beatifick Vision* progressing the *datelesse* and *irrevoluble* Circle of *Eternity* shall clasp inseparable Hands with *joy*, and *blisse* in over measure for ever.

This is a most remarkable outburst to find in a pamphlet on episcopacy. It is the true voice of the young Milton, but it is also the voice of his time, combining with the immense ambition of the poet the patriotic utopianism of the English Puritan reformer. We must remember this tone of boundless optimism when we come to assess the nature of Milton's disillusion at the failure of the Commonwealth and the restoration of Charles II.

The personal note emerges in the most unexpected places in his prose pamphlets. In the *Animadversions* he turns suddenly from a contemptuous dismissal of one of the Remonstrant's arguments to contemplate with almost mystical fervour the coming Heaven on earth. The prose is tremulous with excitement as he addresses God:

> O perfect, and accomplish thy glorious acts; for men may leave their works unfinisht, but thou art a God, thy nature is perfection; shouldst thou bring us thus far onward from *Egypt* to destroy us in this Wildernesse though wee deserve; yet thy great name would suffer in the rejoycing of thine enemies, and the deluded hope of all thy servants. When thou hast settl'd peace in the Church, and righteous judgement in the Kingdome, then shall all thy Saints addresse their voyces of joy, and triumph to thee, standing on the shoare of that red Sea into which our enemies had almost driven us. And he that now for haste snatches up a plain ungarnish't present as a thanke-offering to thee, which could not be deferr'd in regard of thy so many late deliverances wrought for us one upon another, may then perhaps take up a Harp, and sing to thee an elaborate Song to Generations. . . . Come forth out of thy Royall Chambers, O Prince of all the Kings of the earth, put on the visible roabes of thy imperiall Majesty, take up that unlimited Scepter which thy Almighty Father hath bequeath'd thee; for now the voice of thy Bride calls thee, and all creatures sigh to bee renew'd.

After this it is not surprising that in the *Apology for Smectymnuus*, having rebutted charges of unchastity made against him by his opponents, he goes on to elaborate his theory of chastity, explaining how he came to hold it and the Platonic and Christian authorities for it in a well-known passage, quoted in Chapter I.

Even in the serious and scholarly argument of *The Reason of Church-Government* Milton manages to become autobiographical, beginning the second book by expressing regret that the advancement of knowledge should require controversy, which was not naturally his task. 'But when God commands to take the trumpet and blow a dolorous or a jarring blast, it lies not in mans will what he shall say, or what he shall conceal.' He explains that his 'sharp, but saving words' are, unfortunately, necessary. This leads him into a long autobiographical digression, where he addresses the 'elegant and learned reader':

> To him it will be no new thing though I tell him that if I hunted after praise by the ostentation of wit and learning, I should not write thus out of mine own season, when I have neither yet compleated to my minde the full circle of my private studies, although I complain not of any insufficiency to the matter in hand, or were I ready to my wishes, it were a folly to commit any thing elaborately compos'd to the carelesse and interrupted listening of these tumultuous times. Next if I were wise only to mine own ends, I would certainly take such a subject as of it self might catch applause, whereas this hath all the disadvantages on the contrary, and such a subject as the publishing whereof might be delayed at pleasure, and time enough to pencill it over with all the curious touches of art, even to the perfection of a faultlesse picture, whenas in this argument the not deferring is of great moment to the good speeding, that if solidity have leisure to doe her office, art cannot have much. Lastly, I should not chuse this manner of writing wherin knowing my self inferior to my self, led by the genial power of nature to another task, I have the use, as I may account it, but of my left hand. And though I shall be foolish in saying more to this purpose, yet since it will be such a folly as wisest men going about to commit, have only confest and so committed, I may trust with more reason, because with more folly to have courteous pardon. For although a Poet soaring in the high region of his fancies with his garland and singing robes about him might without apology speak more of himself then I mean to do, yet for me sitting here below in the cool element of prose, a mortall thing among many readers of no Empyreall conceit, to venture and divulge unusual things of my selfe, I shall petition to the gentler sort, it may not be envy to me. . . .

And on he goes, to talk about his early education, his visit to Italy and the praises he received there, and his growing conviction that 'I might perhaps leave something so written to after-times, as they should not willingly let it die'. He continues:

> These thoughts at once possest me, and these other. That if I were certain to write as men buy Leases, for three lives and downward, there ought no regard be sooner had, then to Gods glory by the honour and instruction of my country. For which cause, and not only for that I knew it would be hard to arrive at the second rank among the Latines, I apply'd my selfe to that resolution which *Ariosto* follow'd against the perswasions of *Bembo*, to fix all the industry and art I could unite to the adorning of my native tongue; not to make verbal curiosities the end, that were a toylsom vanity, but to be an interpreter and relater of the best and sagest things among mine own Citizens throughout this Iland in the mother dialect. That what the greatest and choycest wits of *Athens*, *Rome*, or modern *Italy*, and those Hebrews of old did for their country, I in my proportion with this over and above of being a Christian, might doe for mine: not caring to be once nam'd abroad, though perhaps I could attaine to that, but content with these British Ilands as my world, whose fortune hath hitherto bin, that if the Athenians, as some say, made their small deeds great and renowned by their eloquent writers, *England* hath had her noble atchievments made small by the unskilfull handling of monks and mechanicks.

This is a most interesting development of the theme he first announced before his fellow-students at Cambridge in his 'Vacation Exercise'. His personal ambitions as a poet in English are bound up with his ardent patriotism. Milton then goes on to discuss with his readers the kinds of poetry he contemplates writing:

> Time servs not now, and perhaps I might seem too profuse to give any certain account of what the mind at home in the spacious circuits of her musing hath liberty to propose to her self, though of highest hope, and hardest attempting, whether that Epick form whereof the two poems of *Homer*, and those other two of *Virgil* and *Tasso* are a diffuse, and the book of *Job* a brief model: or whether the rules of *Aristotle* herein are strictly to be kept, or

nature to be follow'd, which in them that know art, and use judgement is no transgression, but an inriching of art. And lastly what K. or Knight before the conquest might be chosen in whom to lay the pattern of a Christian *Heroe*. And as *Tasso* gave to a Prince of *Italy* his chois whether he would command him to write of *Godfreys* expedition against the infidels, or *Belisarius* against the Gothes, or *Charlemain* against the Lombards; if to the instinct of nature and the imboldning of art ought may be trusted, and that there be nothing advers in our climat, or the fate of this age, it haply would be no rashnesse from an equal diligence and inclination to present the like offer in our own ancient stories. Or whether those Dramatick constitutions, wherein *Sophocles* and *Euripides* raigne shall be found more doctrinal and exemplary to a Nation, the Scripture also affords us a divine pastoral Drama in the Song of *Salomon* consisting of two persons and a double *Chorus*, as *Origen* rightly judges. And the Apocalypse of Saint *John* is the majestick image of a high and stately Tragedy, shutting up and intermingling her solemn Scenes and Acts with a sevenfold *Chorus* of halleluja's and harping symphonies: . . . Or if occasion shall lead to imitat those magnifick Odes and Hymns wherein *Pindarus* and *Callimachus* are in most things worthy, some others in their frame judicious, in their matter most at end faulty: But those frequent songs throughout the law and prophets beyond all these, not in their divine argument alone, but in the very critical art of composition may be easily made appear over all the kinds of Lyrick poesy, to be incomparable. These abilities . . . are the inspired guift of God, rarely bestow'd, but yet to some (though most abuse) in every Nation: and are of power beside the office of a pulpit, to inbreed and cherish in a great people the seeds of vertu, and publick civility, to allay the perturbations of the mind, and set the affections in right tune, to celebrate in glorious and lofty Hymns the throne and equipage of Gods Almightinesse, and what he works, and what he suffers to be wrought with high providence in his Church, to sing the victorious agonies of Martyrs and Saints, the deeds and triumphs of just and pious Nations doing valiantly through faith against the enemies of Christ, to deplore the general relapses of Kingdoms and States from justice and Gods true worship. Lastly, whatsoever in religion is holy and sublime, in vertu amiable, or grave, whatsoever hath passion or admiration in all the changes of that which is call'd fortune from without, or the wily suttleties and refluxes of mans thoughts from within, all these things with a solid and treatable smoothnesse to paint out and describe. . . .

This is a remarkable literary programme, and shows not only Milton's Christian humanist awareness of the claims of both classical and biblical literature and his own high conception of the moral function of literature, but also his awareness of and interest in the technical literary forms in the Bible. It shows, too, that he has digested Renaissance critical theory and applied it in his own way to his Christian view of the function of art. He has a clear idea of the place of craftsmanship, of *technique*, in the production of great art, and he realizes that, while the ultimate purpose of great art is moral, this purpose can be achieved directly or indirectly in a great variety of ways. And it is worth noting that already in this early phase of his poetic career, when he was still looking to early British history for a subject for his epic, he conceded that, even on the grounds of purely literary merit, the biblical writers exceeded the classical; so that when he makes this point more emphatically in *Paradise Regained* it does not represent the change of mind that some critics have seen it to be.

The Protestant patriotism which flashes forth from Milton's anti-prelatical pamphlets was not peculiar to himself: though Milton expressed it more eloquently and with more personal feeling than other Protestant writers, it was a popular point of view. The Protestant view of ecclesiastical history was that the true, primitive Church had flourished in Palestine and in Rome until Antichrist usurped the chair of Peter at Rome and the true Church was driven into exile. The English Protestant view was that, in spite of the designs of Antichrist, some vestige of the true Church had continued to flourish in England, that with Wycliffe the Reformation had begun in England, and that England was destined to lead the nations in effecting final reformation and destroying Antichrist. The seventeenth-century Puritan believed strongly in this tradition of continuous English Protestantism and thus looked to his own country to lead the way to the final triumph of the kingdom of the saints. The political and religious controversies of his own day he saw in this context, and interpreted them (in the light of Daniel and Revelation) as part of an unfolding divine purpose for England and so for the world.

In citing Church Fathers, early historians, chroniclers and poets, Milton kept a firm distinction between the saving truth that is to be found only in the Bible and the historical and personal circumstances which could make human testimony fallible. An authority is only an authority if he proves himself to be so by his arguments; a man is not necessarily in possession of the truth because he died a martyr or had a great name or lived a long time ago. In holding scriptural truth to be the only fundamental source of Christian knowledge and understanding Milton was in complete agreement with the Puritans of his time; but there were anti-clerical implications in Milton's arguments for the equality of all true Christians which already indicated that he was not going to find it easy to go along with the programme of any Puritan sect. He made clear, in *The Reason of Church-Government*, that no special kind of sanctity or authority belonged to the priestly function, expressing a deep-rooted suspicion of a professional, paid clergy that was to emerge even more clearly in his later career. But it was already evident that, while he might support the Presbyterians because the system of church government by presbytery, synod and assembly seemed more democratic than an episcopal hierarchy, he would have his own objections to the presbyterian form when he came to look into the matter more closely. As things turned out, the actions of the Presbyterians, rather than his own further examination of their system, led to his rapid disillusion with them.

The poet turned pamphleteer sometimes forgot that he was not now writing poems 'doctrinal and exemplary to a nation' but polemical pamphlets against specific opponents. Every now and again he tried to reconcile his poetic with his polemic activities by assimilating arguing, preaching and writing poetry as an ideal activity of the poet-priest (we have seen a suggestion of this ideal in 'Lycidas'). There is an interesting passage in *The Reason of Church-Government* where Milton reflects on the relation between teaching and entertainment:

> But because the spirit of man cannot demean it selfe lively in this body without some recreating intermission of labour, and serious things, it were happy for the Common wealth, if our Magistrates . . . would take into their care . . . the managing of our publick sports, and festival pastimes, that they might be, not such as were autoriz'd a while since, the provocations of drunkennesse and lust, but such as may inure and harden our bodies by

martial exercises to all warlike skil and performance, and may
civilize, adorn and make discreet our minds by the learned and
affable meeting of frequent Academies, and the procurement of
wise and artfull recitations sweetned with eloquent and gracefull
inticements to the love and practice of justice, temperance and
fortitude, instructing and bettering the Nation at all opportunities, that the call of wisdom and vertu may be heard every
where, . . . Whether this may be not only in Pulpits, but after
another persuasive method, at set and solemn Paneguries, in
Theaters, porches, or what other place, or way may win most
upon the people to receiv at once both recreation, and instruction,
let them in autority consult.

The suggestion that public dramatic performances on suitable
themes could supplement preaching is characteristically Miltonic.
The list of subjects for poems and plays found in the Trinity
manuscript was probably made in connection with this suggestion. There are plays with such characters as Michael, Heavenly
Love, Chorus of Angels, Lucifer, Adam, Eve, Conscience, Death
and others, including Faith, Hope and Charity. Another list of
characters includes Moses, Justice, Mercy, Wisdom, Heavenly
Love, 'Hesperus the Evening Starre', Chorus of Angels, and many
more. Titles of suggested tragedies are 'Adam in Banishment',
'The Flood', 'Abram in Ægypt', 'The Deluge', 'Sodom' and
scores of others from biblical story (including 'Salomon Gynae-
cocratumenus'—'Solomon Ruled by Women'—a nice example of
his oddly classicized biblical titles, of which there are many), as
well as a long list from early British history. There are outlines of
plots of a play, *Paradise Lost*, and of other biblical plays—*Abram
from Morea, or Isack Redeemd, Baptistes*, and (another treatment
of the *Paradise Lost* theme) *Adam unparadiz'd*. He also lists a
number of 'Scotch stories, or rather Brittish of the north parts'.
  It was Milton's precipitate marriage, probably in the spring
of 1642, that helped to move him towards a more independent
position in ecclesiastical as in other matters. After years of
dedicated chastity, he suddenly turned all his passionate idealistic
thought about a perfect mate on to a flighty young girl of royalist
family, imagining that her dumbness in his presence was a sign
of modest thoughtfulness and looking forward to an intellectual
as well as a physical companionship which he felt he had fully

earned. Mary Powell, the wife he chose, was the daughter of an Oxfordshire justice of the peace; she was but sixteen, and Milton was thirty-three. Both were rapidly disillusioned; and Mary soon returned to her parents' home on a visit from which she did not come back until a reconciliation was patched up in the summer of 1645. The emotional shock to Milton was enormous and, with his usual gift for deriving general conclusions from a personal situation, he immediately set himself to discover and to proclaim publicly the legal and other problems involved, and their solution. Marriage was meant to be a perfect companionship, spiritual, intellectual and physical, and if through well-meaning misjudgment it turned out to be something very different, release should be made possible. This was the position he argued in *The Doctrine and Discipline of Divorce*, published in August 1643. It was because his ideal of marriage was so high, not because he took a low view of it, that he pleaded for liberty of divorce. The personal note rings out with sad naïveté in Chapter III:

The sobrest and best govern'd men are least practiz'd in these affairs; and who knowes not that the bashfull muteness of a virgin may oft-times hide all the unliveliness and naturall sloth which is really unfit for conversation; nor is there that freedom of accesse granted or presum'd, as may suffice to a perfect discerning till too late: and where any disposition is suspected, what more usuall then the perswasion of friends, that acquaintance, as it increases, will amend all. And lastly, it is not strange though many who have spent their youth chastly, are in some things not so quick-sighted, while they hast so eagerly to light the nuptiall torch; nor is it therefore that for a modest error a man should forfeit so great a happines, and no charitable means to release him. Since they who have liv'd most loosely by reason of their bold accustoming, prove most successfull in their matches, because their wild affections unsettling at will, have been as so many divorces to teach them experience. When as the sober man honouring the appearance of modesty, and hoping well of every sociall vertue under that veile, may easily chance to meet, if not with a body impenetrable, yet often with a mind to all other due conversation inaccessible, and to all the more estimable and superior purposes of matrimony uselesse and almost liveles: and what a solace, what a fit helpe such a consort would be through the whole life of a man, is lesse pain to conjecture then to have experience.

It is the virtuous man, with no experience of women, who is most likely to make a fatal error of judgment in marriage, while the rakes, having sown their wild oats, have learned from experience and choose more wisely when they come to marry. Alas, what boots it with uncessant care . . .

Milton addressed the second edition of *The Doctrine and Discipline of Divorce* (published early in 1644) 'To the Parlament of England, with the Assembly'. (The 'Assembly' was the Westminster Assembly of divines convened on 1 July to decide on the new form of government of the English Church.) He was making a practical proposition with a view to legislation. His views, it need hardly be said, were not popular and aroused much opposition, which led him to write, in 1644 and 1645, three further pamphlets in more controversial vein, one (*The Judgement of Martin Bucer concerning Divorce*) citing the opinions of an earlier divine who had favoured divorce, another (*Tetrachordon*) reinforcing his arguments with a great play of scriptural texts, and a third (*Colasterion*) replying, with a wealth of sportive abuse, to an opponent who had attacked his first divorce pamphlet.

Though Milton's interest in divorce sprang from a personal experience and though his views found no support among the Puritan leaders of the day, his arguments about the nature of marriage were in the tradition of Protestant thought on the subject. Luther and subsequent reformers had denied that marriage was a sacrament and allowed, under specific conditions, separation followed by re-marriage. The main cause the reformers allowed for divorce was adultery, and sometimes also desertion. The Anglican Church under Archbishop Laud granted divorce on the grounds of adultery, but not re-marriage, though re-marriage often took place. Canon law still prevailed in England, and under it Milton could have sought an annulment of his marriage. But Milton had no use for Anglican canon law: he wanted Parliament to grant the justness of his arguments and embody them in appropriate legislation. For all his juggling to reconcile New Testament forbidding of re-marriage by a divorced partner with Old Testament allowing of such re-marriage, Milton was moved by a clear and strong Protestant view of marriage as spiritual companionship. He is driven at the end to appeal from the biblical text to 'the law of nature and of equity imprinted in us', to which the Bible *must* correspond if it is really the word of God, which it certainly is. Fallen man needed companionship even more desperately than unfallen Adam had needed it; yet did not God give Adam a companion in prelapsarian Eden? If the aim of marriage is companionship, marriage which does not yield companionship must be dissolved to make possible one that does. A contract that fails of its objective as understood in the light of natural law and the good of man should be dissolved in favour of one which achieves this objective. This was exactly the same argument that the opponents of King Charles were using in urging the claims of Parliament against absolute monarchy, and it was an argument that Milton himself was to use later in his political pamphlets: government is a social contract for the good of the governed, and if it fails to secure that good the contract becomes null and void. So marriage is a social contract for the good of the partners.

Meanwhile, the breach between Presbyterians and Independents was growing in Parliament and throughout the country. The Westminster Assembly, struggling to define the structure of the newly purified English Church, was finding it increasingly difficult to reconcile the demand for Presbyterian order (voiced especially by the delegates from Scotland) with the liberty of preaching which even under Laud the Puritans had enjoyed and which in fact had made possible their rise and influence within the Anglican Church. The Assembly had accepted the principle, laid down for its guidance by Parliament, that 'No Man [should] be denied to enter his Dissent from the Assembly, and his Reasons for it, in any Point', and any dissenting minority was allowed to harangue the majority indefinitely even after the majority had reached a decision. More serious was the fact that pamphlets and books were appearing—such as Roger Williams' *Bloudy Tenant of Persecution*—in which it was argued that under God's law freedom should be granted in all countries for 'the most *Paganish, Jewish, Turkish,* or *Antichristian consciences* and *worships*'. The appeal to the individual conscience was as much a part of the Protestant heritage as the search for a godly discipline, but many Puritans became thoroughly alarmed when they realized to what proliferation of sects and to what extreme demands for total freedom of conscience one side of the Protestant tradition had led. The Presbyterians were determined to secure order and discipline in God's Church; unlike the Independents, they were acutely conscious of the political problems involved in ecclesiastical freedom, and they saw the danger to their cause of rampant individualism. Parliament established control of the Press by ordinance in June 1643, thus filling the vacuum left by the collapse of the censorship which had resulted from the Long Parliament's abolition of Star Chamber and sending Laud to the Tower. The new licensing authorities found themselves even less able to enforce their control over printing than the old had been; the flood of religious and political pamphleteering which the great debate on the reorganizing of Church and state had let loose could not be stemmed. Milton himself seems at first to have treated the whole business with genial contempt. He did not bother to secure a licence for *The Doctrine and Discipline of Divorce*, and cheerfully put his name to the second edition, the one which was addressed to Parliament. (He did, however, obtain a licence for *The Judgement of Martin Bucer*.) But the hostility aroused by Milton's views on divorce led to the invoking of the ordinance of June 1643 against him for *The Doctrine and Discipline of Divorce*. Nothing seems to have happened as a result, except that three months later, in November 1644, Milton was moved to address Parliament, in a grand, classical, written oration, on the whole question of freedom of speech and publication. *Areopagitica*, modelled on the speeches of Isocrates in whose tradition of rhetoric in the public service Milton had been trained at St. Paul's, argued a position which was a unique blend of Protestant individualism, patrotic utopianism and humanist idealism. And it showed him moving steadily further away from the presbyterian parliamentary majority towards the minority of Independents.

Although much in *Areopagitica* was familiar to left-wing Protestant thought of the period, both the tone of the argument and the way it was developed were peculiarly Miltonic, and in some ways more familiar to nineteenth-century liberal thought than to his own time. Truth, Milton maintains, will prevail over error only in open conflict; and in any case (and this may seem an unexpected argument from a passionate Puritan Christian) truth is not in its single wholeness capable of being grasped by men, each of whom may only discover a single, and different, fragment:

Truth indeed came once into the world with her divine Master, and was a perfect shape most glorious to look on: but when he ascended, and his Apostles after him were laid asleep, then strait arose a wicked race of deceivers, who as that story goes of the *Ægyptian Typhon* with his conspirators, how they dealt with the good *Osiris*, took the Virgin Truth, hewd her lovely form into a thousand peeces, and scatter'd them to the four winds. From that time ever since, the sad friends of Truth, such as durst appear, imitating the carefull search that Isis made for the mangl'd body of *Osiris*, went up and down gathering up limb by limb still as they could find them. We have not yet found them all, Lords and Commons, nor ever shall doe, till her Masters second comming; . . .

He is not afraid of the multiplying of sects:

There be who perpetually complain of schisms and sects, and make it such a calamity that any man dissents from their maxims. 'Tis their own pride and ignorance which causes the disturbing, who neither will hear with meeknes, nor can convince, yet all must be supprest which is not found in their *Syntagma*. . . . To be still searching what we know not, by what we know, still closing up truth to truth as we find it (for all her body is *homogeneal*, and proportionall) this is the golden rule in *Theology* as well as in Arithmetick, and makes up the best harmony in a Church; not the forc't and outward union of cold, and neutrall, and inwardly divided minds.

Truth is strong, but not single:

For who knows not that Truth is strong next to the Almighty; she needs no policies, nor stratagems, nor licencings to make her victorious, those are the shifts and the defences that error uses against her power: give her but room, and do not bind her when she sleeps, for then she speaks not true, . . . Yet it is not impossible that she may have more shapes than one. What else is all that rank of things indifferent, wherein Truth may be on this side, or on the other, without being unlike her self.

There is the indignity, too, of being subject to the ferula like a schoolboy. 'When a man writes to the world, he summons up all his reason and deliberation to assist him; he searches, meditats, is industrious, and likely consults and conferrs with his judicious friends; after all which done he takes himself to be

inform'd in what he writes, as well as any that writ before him ; . . .'
Who is any licenser to challenge John Milton ? In any case, controversy strengthens truth, and to believe things merely on authority is no real belief. Good can only be known by evil, truth by falsehood, virtue by trial against the temptations of the world. 'Since therefore the knowledge and survay of vice is in this world so necessary to the constituting of human vertue, and the scanning of error to the confirmation of truth, how can we more safely, and with less danger scout into the regions of sin and falsity then by reading all manner of tractats, and hearing all manner of reason ?' Again : 'To sequester out of the world into *Atlantick* and *Eutopian* polities, which never can be drawn into use, will not mend our condition ; but to ordain wisely as in this world of evill, in the midd'st whereof God hath plac't us unavoidably.' And again : 'I cannot praise a fugitive and cloister'd vertue, unexercis'd and unbreath'd, that never sallies out and sees her adversary, but slinks out of the race, where that immortall garland is to be run for, not without dust and heat.'

The note of patriotic optimism also sounds strongly in *Areopagitica*, with expectation of great things to come from England :

> Lords and Commons of England, consider what Nation it is wherof ye are, and wherof ye are the governours : a Nation not slow and dull, but of a quick, ingenious, and piercing spirit, acute to invent, suttle and sinewy to discours, not beneath the reach of any point the highest that human capacity can soar to. . . . Now once again by all concurrence of signs, and by the generall instinct of holy and devout men, as they daily and solemnly expresse their thoughts, God is decreeing to begin some new and great period in his Church, ev'n to the reforming of Reformation it self : what does he then but reveal Himself to his servants, and as his manner is, first to his English-men ; . . .

This passage has often been quoted to illustrate the naïve egotism of Milton's patriotism, but the sentiments here expressed are far from being uniquely Miltonic : the view that God had vouchsafed special mercies to England in preserving the true apostolic faith in some degree from the beginning and in first beginning the Reformation there was a commonplace in Puritan preaching as was the application of the Apocalypse of St. John in order to prophesy new divine manifestations in English history.

Milton goes on to paint a vivid picture of beleaguered London —'this vast City; a City of refuge, the mansion house of liberty'— thirsting after knowledge and understanding. In the midst of civil war the citizens are 'wholly tak'n up with the study of highest and most important matters to be reform'd, . . . disputing, reasoning, reading, inventing, discoursing, ev'n to a rarity, and admiration, things not before discourst or writt'n of'. He flatters Parliament by attributing this to 'a singular good will, contentednesse and confidence in your prudent foresight, and safe government'. It is the very best of omens, 'a lively and cherfull presage of our happy successe and victory'. He goes on with rising eloquence:

Methinks I see in my mind a noble and puissant Nation rousing herself like a strong man after sleep, and shaking her invincible locks: Methinks I see her as an Eagle muing her mighty youth, and kindling her undazl'd eyes at the full midday beam; purging and unscaling her long abused sight at the fountain it self of heav'nly radiance; while the whole noise of timorous and flocking birds, with those also that love the twilight, flutter about, amaz'd at what she means, and in their envious gabble would prognosticat a year of sects and schisms.

The opening of *Areopagitica* cites precedents from Athens and Republican Rome and then goes on to sneer at Roman Catholic censorship, with scornful citing of examples of the *imprimatur*. But the real burden of his argument concerns free-will, liberty of choice, the testing of character by struggling to attain virtue in an imperfect world, the importance of the un-hindered search for the fragments of truth scattered all over a fallen world, and the prospect of a new and regenerate England arising as a result of the passionate debates now going on. There are, of course, limits to Milton's toleration. After declaring, 'Yet if all cannot be of one mind, as who looks they should be? this doubtless is more wholsome, more prudent and more Christian that many be tolerated, rather then all compell'd', he goes on to add: 'I mean not tolerated Popery, and open superstition, which as it extirpats all religious and civill supremacies, so it self should be extirpat, provided first that all charitable and compassionate

means be us'd to win and regain the weak and misled : that also
which is impious or evil absolutely either against faith or maners
no law can possibly permit, that intends not to unlaw it self.' At
the same time he cannot think well 'of every light separation' and
remarks significantly that 'it is not possible for man to sever the
wheat from the tares, the good fish from the other frie ; that must
be the Angels Ministry at the end of mortall things'.

In June 1644, between his first and second divorce pamphlets
and five months before the publication of *Areopagitica*, Milton
published his little treatise *Of Education*, in the form of a letter
to Samuel Hartlib, whose known interest in educational reform
and in the ideas of John Comenius made him an obvious recipient
of such a communication. Milton is here concerned with the
training of an *élite* in regional academies containing about a
hundred and thirty pupils and a staff of about twenty. His
educational ideal is a Christian humanist one ; he defines the end
of learning as 'to repair the ruines of our first Parents by regaining
to know God aright, and out of that knowledge to love him, to
imitate him, to be like him, as we may the neerest by possessing
our souls of true vertue, which being united to the heavenly grace
of faith makes up the highest perfection'. Shortly afterwards he
states : 'I call therefore a compleat and generous Education that
which fits a man to perform justly, skilfully and magnanimously
all the offices both private and publick of Peace and War', a
declaration made in the true spirit of Renaissance humanism. He
attacks 'the Scholastick grossness of barbarous ages', and opposes early emphasis on such 'abstract' studies as logic and meta-
physics, insisting on a substantial amount of varied reading in
Latin and Greek, from the point of view of the usefulness of their
content (including agriculture, geometry, astronomy, geography,
medicine and natural history) and not merely of their stylistic
elegance. Thence the students proceed to classical writers on
ethics and economics, 'and either now, or before this, they may
have easily learnt at any odd hour the *Italian* Tongue'. Politics
comes next, and then (Hebrew, together with 'the *Chaldey*, and
the *Syrian* Dialect' now having been learned) biblical studies and
Church history, and only after that come 'choice Histories, *Heroic
Poems*, and *Attic* Tragedies of stateliest and most regal argument', and rhetoric and logic follow at a still later stage. Regular

exercise, walks in the country, fencing and recreation 'with the solemn and divine harmonies of Musick' are also prescribed. The curriculum is of course impossibly large by modern standards, but it must be remembered that Milton is concerned (though he never explicitly says so) with training a ruling class of specially gifted people, and that, with characteristic optimism, he was developing to new and ideal heights some common Renaissance notions of aristocratic education.

Looking back afterwards on his earlier writings, Milton wrote in the *Defensio Secunda* that he came to write on marriage, education and freedom of the Press by a simple logical process:

> When the bishops could no longer resist the multitude of their assailants, I had leisure to turn my thoughts to . . . the promotion of real and substantial liberty, which is rather to be sought from within than from without, and whose existence depends, not so much on the terror of the sword as on sobriety of conduct and the integrity of life. When, therefore, I perceived that there were three species of liberty which are essential to the happiness of social life—religious, domestic and civil; and as I had already written concerning the first, and the magistrates were strenuously active in obtaining the third, I determined to turn my attention to the second, or the domestic species. As this seemed to involve three material questions, the conditions of the conjugal tie, the education of children, and the free publication of thoughts, I made them objects of distinct consideration.

One cannot help thinking, however, that this is in some degree a rationalization after the event, and that it was Milton's personal circumstances and interests that impelled him to write on these subjects at this time. Nevertheless, the traditional view that Milton was impelled wholly by personal circumstances rather than by general principles cannot be maintained; as always with him, public and private motives were inextricably intermingled, and if he was the last to be able to disentangle them this was less because of his egotism than because much in his personal thinking at this time was in the tradition of the patriotic Puritan utopianism of the age.

Meanwhile, Milton was moving steadily away from the Presbyterians, whom he saw now as narrow and intolerant, towards

the Independents, who eventually gained control of Parliament
and began to think more and more in radical anti-monarchist
terms. Between 1645 and 1649 Charles was defeated and imprisoned, escaped to renew the Civil War, and was finally defeated
again. Milton was writing no pamphlets at this time. Reflecting
on the implications of his quarrel with the Presbyterians and the
arguments he had developed in *Areopagitica*, he turned to an
analysis of Christian doctrine that would make clear that man was
created by God with free-will, the ability to choose between
good and evil, that by Adam's disobedience in Eden this free-
will was abused and man therefore brought punishment and
thraldom to the law justly on himself until the implementing of
the Christian scheme of redemption freed man again to discern
truth from falsehood. In elaborating these points in great detail
with reference to the biblical text, Milton stressed again and again
that the true issue was between man and God, that man had to
fight the battle for himself, exercise his own choice for truth and
good and against falsehood and evil, which fought within him.
He wrote in Latin, and entitled the work *De Doctrina Christiana*.
It was begun in the middle 1640's but not finished until more than
ten years later and not published until 1825. The work is of great
interest to students of Milton's mind as giving a detailed account
of his interpretation of Christian doctrine, in the light of which
some obscurities of intention in *Paradise Lost* can be cleared up.

Milton also turned to history at this time, intending at first
to celebrate God's mercies to England from the beginning. But
he found as he looked into Celtic, Roman and Anglo-Saxon
England nothing but confusion, superstition and lack of 'civility',
and as he wrote he was reminded of parallels in the confusions
and preposterous claims of Presbyterian divines who seemed to
Milton to be throwing away the fruits of victory by their narrow
and selfish behaviour. The result was that the *History of Britain*,
on which he worked from 1645 to 1649, turned from a celebration to a denunciation and at length he put it aside unfinished
in order to put his pen at the service of the army leaders who
were challenging Presbyterian rigidity. These leaders, with
Cromwell at their head, were responsible for the trial and execution of Charles in January 1649. This action had been preceded
by an enormous amount of debating and pamphleteering by all

sections of public opinion on the question of the nature of civil and religious government, the proper source of authority in civil and religious affairs, and kindred questions. As the army prepared to bring the King to trial Milton collected his thoughts on the whole question of political power, its origins and its limits, and in February 1649 published the first of his political pamphlets, *The Tenure of Kings and Magistrates*.

The execution of the King was the work of a determined minority who had decided to end the *mystique* of kingship once and for all. It is probable that by this time Milton had moved very close to the position of this minority. At any rate, barely a fortnight had passed after the execution when the first of his political pamphlets appeared, concerned with constitutional questions and the rights of the people against tyrants. Its full title is illuminating: *The Tenure of Kings and Magistrates: Proving, That it is Lawfull, and hath been held so through all Ages, for any, who have the Power, to call to account a Tyrant, or wicked King, and after due consideration, to depose, and put him to death; if the ordinary Magistrate have neglected, or deny'd to doe it. And that they, who of late, so much blame Deposing, are the Men that did it themselves.* It is a carefully reasoned argument in favour of the revocability of the supreme civil power. All men, Milton argued, were naturally born free, and lived free until Adam's transgression led them to mutually destructive actions and made necessary 'a common league to bind each other from mutual injury'. That was the origin of cities, towns and commonwealths. A civil authority was necessary because men could not be trusted to keep their covenants without an external force to compel them. But the kings and magistrates thus put in authority over others are also fallen men, and could be tempted to 'injustice and partiality', and therefore laws, 'either framed or consented to by all', were invented to confine and limit their authority. Law and reason were to be set above the ruler, just as the ruler was to be set above the people. The power of kings and magistrates 'is only derivative, transferred, and committed to them in trust from the people to the common good of them all'. Several things follow from this, among them that a king or magistrate, who holds office for the people's good and not his own, can be either chosen or rejected, retained or deposed, 'though no tyrant', by the people as they judge best. A tyrant is someone who regards neither law nor the common good, but 'reigns onely for himself and his faction'. And as a just king causes great good and happiness so a tyrant causes enormous misery and wrong; the former is the public father of his country, the latter the common enemy against whom the people may lawfully proceed 'as against a common pest and destroyer of mankind'. It emerges, however, that the decision as to who is a tyrant should be left not to vague public opinion but 'to Magistrates, at least to the uprighter sort of them, and of the people, though in number less by many, in whom faction least hath prevaild above the Law of nature and right reason'. This vague qualification (it seems to mean here simply Milton and his friends) reminds us, if reminder were needed, that Milton was a Christian humanist, and neither John Locke nor Rousseau. Milton's arguments go behind Stuart theories of divine right and Tudor theories of absolutism to a liberal political tradition common to mediaeval and Renaissance thought; there is also much in the *Tenure* which was common to the revolutionary movement of the time; and there are notions that point forward to Locke's *Second Treatise on Civil Government*.

From now on Milton was the official apologist of the regicides before Europe as well as an important servant of the new government. In March 1649 he was appointed Latin Secretary to the Council of State (the post was also called Secretary of State for Foreign Tongues). He had postponed writing his greatest poetry until he was sure that his period of self-preparation was complete, and now history had caught up with him and he had to postpone it further.

The execution of Charles had shocked Europe, and in England there was still a great deal of personal feeling for the dead King, a feeling exploited by the publication in February 1649 of *Eikon Basilike*, the 'Portraicture of His Sacred Majesty in his Solitudes and Sufferings', in the form of a record of his supposed self-communings during his last years (though actually invented by Bishop Gauden). Milton undertook to destroy the effect of this dangerously popular work, with its sentimental idealizing picture of the King, and in *Eikonoklastes* ('the Image-Breaker'), published in October 1649, he produced a stinging attack on the royal character as revealed in *Eikon Basilike*. Though he begins by saying with some dignity that it is not commendable, nor is it his intention, to descant on the misfortunes of a man fallen from so high a dignity, who has paid his final debt both to nature and his faults, he soon becomes carping in tone, ingeniously pressing every point that can be made against the King's character and behaviour, tracing his actions in political and ecclesiastical matters in considerable detail. His purpose is to destroy the image of the saint and martyr built up by Bishop Gauden and replace it by that of a vain and hypocritical tyrant. In the very first chapter he seizes with glee on the fact that Charles had 'so little care of truth in his last words, or honour to himself, or to his friends, òr sense of his afflictions, or of that sad hour that was upon him, as immediately before his death to pop into the hand of that grave bishop who attended him, for a special relique of his saintly exercises, a prayer stolen word for word from the mouth of a heathen fiction praying to a heathen god; and that in no serious book, but the vain amatorious poem of Sir Philip Sidneys *Arcadia*; a book in that kind full of worth and wit, but among religious thoughts and duties not to be nam'd; . . .' That Milton was the first to recognize the plagiarism testified to his own intimate knowledge of *Arcadia*, a work which in other circumstances he would have been glad to praise.

The next stage of Milton's official pamphleteering for Cromwell's Government involved a European rather than a purely English audience. The French scholar Claude Saumaise, generally known as Salmasius and now living in Holland, had been commissioned by the exiled Charles II to write a public attack in Latin on those who were responsible for the execution of Charles I, and the result was his *Defensio Regia pro Carolo I*. This appeal to Europe by a distinguished scholar was dangerous for the Commonwealth Government, and Milton replied with a long Latin work, *Ioannis Miltoni Angli pro Populo Anglicano Defensio contra Claudii Anonymi, alias Salmasii, Defensionem Regiam*. This *Defence of the English People* is a detailed and scornful reply to Salmasius, mingling legal, historical and moral arguments with fierce personal attacks on his character, scholarship and grammar. The defence seems to have been effective; Salmasius, now living at the court of Queen Christina of Sweden, left in disgrace and died soon afterwards. But other champions took up the fight against the regicides. A powerful anonymous work appeared in 1652, with the rhetorical title *Regii Sanguinis Clamor ad Coelum, adversus Parricidas Anglicanos*, 'The Cry of the Royal Blood to Heaven against the English Parricides'. To this Milton replied with *Joannis Miltoni Angli pro Populo Anglicano Defensio Secunda*, the *Second Defence of the English People*, which appeared in May 1654. This, too, contains much personal abuse, directed against Alexander More, whom Milton wrongly took to be the author of the *Regii Sanguinis Clamor*; Milton had received personal abuse in the *Clamor* and gave at least as good as he got. But there is also a note of high patriotic eloquence in the work, and in addition those revealing autobiographical passages in which he countered abuse by talking of his own education and ambitions. He talks of his youth, his friendships, his studies, his Italian visit, his feelings when the Civil War broke out, in a long passage which is of the first importance for the student of Milton's mind. He explains and defends his entry into controversial pamphleteering:

> I saw that a way was opening for the establishment of real liberty; that the foundation was laying for the deliverance of man from the yoke of slavery and superstition; that the principles of religion, which were the first objects of our care, would exert a salutary influence of the manners and constitution of the republic; and as I had from my youth studied the distinctions between religious and civil rights, I perceived that if ever I wished to be of use, I ought at least not to be wanting to my country, to the church, and to so many of my fellow-Christians in a crisis of so much danger; I therefore determined to relinquish the other pursuits in which I was engaged, and to transfer the whole force of my talents and my industry to this one important object.

Milton's identification of himself with the cause he championed was never clearer. The *Defensio Secunda* ends with praise of Cromwell and an eloquent appeal to him to continue 'with the same unrivalled magnanimity'.

The personalities into which the controversial habits of the age pushed Milton led him at last to a work devoted wholly to a defence of himself. More, not unnaturally resenting Milton's violent attack on himself for a work which he had not written, replied with a fierce attack on Milton, in which he sneered particularly at his crude vanity in taking it upon himself to lay down the law to Cromwell (who became Lord Protector in 1653). Milton's reply, *Joannis Miltoni Angli pro se Defensio contra Alexandrum Morum*, the *Defence of Himself against More*, appeared in 1655 : it is personal and abusive and of little interest to the modern reader. It is interesting, however, that Milton shows himself sensitive to More's charge that he employed 'language of unwashed foulness, naked words and indelicate', and he replied not only by returning the charge ('No shade could veil your filthiness, not even that notable fig-tree') but also by citing illustrious precedents for the use of plain, naked words—Sallust, Herodotus, Seneca, Plutarch, 'the gravest of authors'. Further, if it is to be considered indecent to speak frankly about 'subjects abundantly gross', 'how often will you have to charge with indecency and obscenity Erasmus, . . . Thomas More, . . . the ancient fathers of the church, Clement of Alexandria, Arnobius, Lactantius, Eusebius, when they uncover and cast derision upon the obscene mysteries of the old religions !'

After this there was a pause in Milton's pamphleteering until after Cromwell's death in 1658, when he addressed himself to the question of the relation between the civil and the ecclesiastical power in a pamphlet entitled *A Treatise of Civil Power in Ecclesiastical Causes*, published in 1659. The sub-title, 'Shewing that it is not lawfull for any power on Earth to compell in matters of Religion', indicates Milton's main theme. He had become increasingly dissatisfied with the whole idea of Church establishment, his highly individualistic temperament reinforcing the Protestant conception of every man with his Bible finding his own path to God (though C. S. Lewis has shown that the insistence on spiritual leaders and followers was also a Protestant characteristic in the sixteenth and seventeenth centuries). He argued that no man or synod or assembly could judge definitively the sense of Scripture to another man's conscience (he called this 'a general maxim of the Protestant religion'), and that no man who genuinely interprets Scripture according to his own conscience and his utmost understanding could be censured as a heretic, no matter how erroneous he might appear to others. It is the same argument that he had urged in *Areopagitica* : man can only embrace the truth as he sees it. (He does not, however, push his principle so far as to wish toleration for those whose view of the truth forbids them to accept Scripture as a divinely authoritative work at all; he was Milton after all, not John Stuart Mill.) The *Treatise* was addressed to Parliament in the vain hope of producing a practical effect. A second pamphlet on the same subject, *Considerations touching the likeliest Means to remove Hirelings out of the Church*, appeared later in the same year, after Cromwell's son, Richard, had given up the attempt to carry on his father's position and the Rump Parliament had been recalled by the army to consider the position. Hopeful as ever, Milton saw in this turn of events a chance of moving nearer his ideal commonwealth, and sketched out a plan for a virtually un-salaried clergy drawn only from those truly eager for spiritual services, instead of 'a distinct order in the Commonwealth' educated in the 'babbling schools' and maintained as parasites at the public cost.

With the political situation fluid again, and the question of what form of government England should have once more under discussion, Milton with an almost pathetic hopefulness published his *Readie and Easie Way to establish a Free Commonwealth*. And yet the optimism is somewhat forced, as the note of foreboding in the introduction indicates. This might be the last chance to speak freely, he announces, before the 'once abjur'd and detested Thraldom of Kingship returns'. But his optimism rises as he develops his argument. At times he really seems to believe that 'few words will save us, well consider'd; few and easy things, now seasonably done'. There is a new tone of almost desperate pleading in parts of this brief tract, in which he puts forward his favourite scheme of a single Parliament 'in perpetuity of membership for life', a stable oligarchy of the best men chosen by a properly qualified electorate. Biblical and classical precedents are used equally: nowhere does Milton's Christian humanism appear so vividly. He has the humanist's admiration for 'the old *Athenian* Commonwealth, reputed the first and ancientest place of Civility in all *Greece*'. He has schemes for public education on the Athenian model, with 'Schools and Academies . . . wherein Children may be bred up . . . to all Learning and noble Education; not in Grammar only, but in all Liberal Arts and Exercises. This would soon spread much more Knowledg and Civility, yea, Religion, through all parts of the Land'. But only under a Free

Commonwealth will this and similar benefits be obtained. Spiritual and Civil Liberty (the former, liberty of conscience, being 'above all things . . . dearest and most precious') as well as education, religion, trade and all the features of a healthy state, will flourish best under the kind of Free Commonwealth he advocates. The pamphlet aroused interest and produced replies, and a second, enlarged edition appeared on the very eve of the Restoration, by which time any possibility of a new republican form of government had vanished. The conclusion of the second edition has a nostalgic eloquence, as though Milton really knew that history had overtaken him :

What I have spoken, is the Language of that which is not call'd amiss *The good Old Cause*: if it seem strange to any, it will not seem more strange, I hope, than convincing to Backsliders. Thus much I should perhaps have said, though I were sure I should have spoken only to Trees and Stones; and had none to cry to, but with the Prophet, *O Earth, Earth, Earth !* to tell the very Soil it self, what her perverse Inhabitants are deaf to. Nay, though what I have spoke, should happ'n (which Thou suffer not, who didst create Mankind free; nor Thou next, who didst redeem us from being Servants of Men!) to be the last words of our expiring Liberty.

The Restoration brought all Milton's political hopes to an end, destroying at the same time his vision of a reformed and regenerate England which had sustained him for so long. Further political pamphleteering was now useless. Only in 1673, two years before his death, he turned again to pamphleteering to argue, in *Of True Religion, Hæresie, Schism, Toleration and what best means may be us'd against the growth of Popery*, in favour of all creeds based on honest interpretation of God's word, however mutually different, and against that one species of Christianity that imposes a man-made tradition on all.

Meanwhile, he had gone blind, the left eye beginning to go in 1644 and total blindness having developed by 1652. In 1652 he was deprived of his chambers in Whitehall but was given an assistant in his government work. In the same year he moved to a house in Petty Fraunce, Westminster. His enemies saw God's judgment in his blindness, but Milton accepted his affliction with dignity and fortitude, comparing himself, in the *Defensio Secunda*, to 'those wise and ancient bards whose misfortunes the gods are said to have compensated by superior endowments'. The record of Milton's adjustment to the fact of his blindness is plain in his writings. First, the famous sonnet on his blindness, 'When I consider how my light is spent', showing momentary rebellion turning to trust in God's purpose for him—'They also serve who only stand and waite'. (So, in *Paradise Regained*, Jesus meditates on his Father's purpose for him, and concludes that he must trustfully await its manifestation.) Then the dignified passage in the *Defensio Secunda*, comparing himself to blind heroes and sages of old. Then the lines at the beginning of Book III and of Book IV of *ParadiseLost* (they are quoted and discussed in the following chapter). And in the end he makes a tragic hero of the blind Samson.

It was while he was engaged in writing his divorce pamphlets that Milton published his first volume of poems, which appeared in January 1646. (It is usually referred to as the 1645 edition, as the date on the title page is 1645, 'old style'.) The title was simply : *Poems of Mr. John Milton, both English and Latin, Compos'd at several times. Printed by his true Copies.* It contained most of the poems already discussed, including paraphrases of Psalms 114 and 136, the Italian sonnets and (with a separate title page) the Latin poems. The poem 'On the Death of a fair Infant dying of a Cough' was not included, and first appears in the second enlarged edition of 1673. Four English sonnets were also included, placed with the Italian sonnets. They are : 'O Nightingale', 'How Soon hath Time', 'Captain or Colonel, or Knight in Arms', 'Lady that in the prime of earliest youth' and 'Daughter to that good Earl, once President'. The sonnets are arranged in what appears to be their order of composition. Later sonnets appear in the 1673 edition.

Milton wrote sonnets at intervals throughout the period of his pamphleteering and his work for the Commonwealth. They were mostly 'occasional' poems, about his own circumstances or some contemporary event or poems of compliment to friends or public figures. While some of his sonnets show us Milton in undress, and the utterance is personal and even intimate, these are all formal poems in which for the most part a deliberate dignity of tone is sought and achieved through a careful handling of devices he had largely learned from the Italian sonneteers, especially Della Casa. F. T. Prince—whose study of the Italian element in Milton's verse supplements and elaborates J. S. Smart's pioneer work on the sonnets—has called Milton's sonnets 'essays, on a small scale, in the "magnificent" style', and he has convincingly shown how, by manipulation of word order as well as by cunning counterpointing of the pattern of sense and the pattern of quatrains and tercets of which the sonnet form is composed, he manages to 'transform occasional verse into singular and vivid poetry'. It was Della Casa who taught Milton to pattern his sonnets this way, rather than to fit the thought neatly into the quatrains and tercets, which had hitherto been the way of English sonneteers, who had thus made the sonnet something of an epigrammatic form. Milton's sonnets are far from epigrams; they are complexly balanced and steadily flowing utterances. In the control of the cadence, the handling of the pauses, and drawing the sense out variously from line to line, Milton in his sonnets was developing a kind of skill which was to stand him in good stead in his epic blank verse.

'Captain or Colonel, or Knight in Arms' (entitled in the Trinity manuscript 'When the Assault was intended to the city', or alternatively, 'On his door when the city expected an assault') was written in November 1642, when it looked as though the Royalists were about to take London. (They were in fact repulsed by Essex at Turnham Green.) The tone is both highly formal and half-humorous. In appealing to the officer 'whose chance on these defenceless dores may sease', he asks protection for himself as a poet who can 'call Fame on such gentle acts as these' and reminds the officer of Alexander's sparing Pindar and the sparing of Athens by the Spartans as a result of the singing of a chorus from Euripides' *Electra*. The poem moves gradually further and further away from the officer addressed and from Milton himself, to end quietly in the absorbed recollection of Greek history:

> Lift not thy spear against the Muses Bowre,
>   The great *Emathian* Conqueror bid spare
>   The house of *Pindarus*, when Temple and Towre
> Went to the ground: And the repeated air
>   Of sad *Electra's* Poet had the power
>   To save th'*Athenian* Walls from ruine bare.

The Latinism of 'repeated air' (for 'repetition of the air') helps the formality of the poem; but the most interesting feature of the concluding pair of tercets in this sonnet is the placing of the pauses and the effect this has on the tone of the poem. We begin, in 'Captain or Colonel, or Knight in Arms', face to face with the anticipated Royalist officer; we end far away in time and place, listening to 'the repeated air of sad *Electra*'s Poet'. That phrase itself, 'sad *Electra*'s Poet', with its quiet retrospective melancholy, helps the withdrawal from seventeenth-century London to ancient Athens, and the withdrawal is part of the design and intention of the poem.

Milton's next sonnet (in the order in which he arranged them for publication), 'Lady that in the prime of earliest youth', was addressed to a girl who, Smart plausibly conjectured, 'had been the subject of reproof or asperity and had made Milton the confidant of her distress'. The manipulation of the word order is particularly in evidence here; this and the placing of the pauses help to achieve a calm formality of utterance that is very striking. Next comes a complimentary sonnet addressed to the Lady Margaret Ley, daughter of James Ley, Earl of Marlborough, successively Lord Chief Justice, Lord High Treasurer and Lord President of the Council under first James I and then Charles I. A note of high courtesy is sustained throughout the poem, which with its reference to ancient Greek politics and to Isocrates builds up an atmopshere of noble public service in which context the lady and her late father are gravely complimented. This was the last of the ten sonnets in the 1645 volume. The others discussed below appeared in the 1673 edition, except for those to Fairfax, Cromwell, Sir Henry Vane, and 'To Mr Cyriack Skinner upon his Blindness', all of which were first printed later.

The next sonnet, written to vent Milton's annoyance at the hostile reception accorded to his third divorce pamphlet, *Tetra-chordon*, shows an ironic humour deriving in part from Latin epigram and in part from his own view of 'sportiveness'. He pours scorn on the casual reader who dipped into the work on the book-stall and then laid it down, mystified. The placing of the pauses here is most adroitly done to heighten the effect of scorn:

A Book was writ of late call'd *Tetrachordon*;
　　And woven close, both matter, form and stile;
　　The Subject new: it walkd the Town a while,
　　Numbring good intellects; now seldom por'd on.
Cried the stall-reader, bless us! what a word on
　　A title page is this! and some in file
　　Stand spelling false, while one might walk to Mile-
　　End Green. Why is it harder Sirs than Gordon,
Colkitto, or Macdonnel, or Galasp?
　　Those rugged names to our like mouths grow sleek
　　That would have made *Quintilian* stare and gasp.
Thy age, like ours, O Soul of Sir *John Cheek*,
　　Hated not Learning worse than Toad or Asp;
　　When thou taughtst *Cambridge* and King *Edward* Greek

'Colkitto, or Macdonnel, or Galasp' were the names of Scots made familiar to Londoners by the Civil War: it is interesting that they are chosen for their outlandish sound (to Milton's ears) rather than for the eminence or the views of their possessors: Colkitto was one of Montrose's lieutenants, and Galasp was probably the Covenanting divine, George Gillespie. Milton was thinking of Quintilian's attack on foreign names and words in his *Institutes*. As the poem proceeds, its tone of contempt growing through the use of comic rhymes and startling pauses, a contrast between the barbarian present and the civilized classical past emerges. The final tercet shifts attention altogether away from the present to dwell on thoughts of Sir John Cheke, sixteenth-century English humanist and Greek scholar, and on his age. This is followed by another sonnet on the same theme, 'I did but prompt the age to quit their cloggs', where the note of personal irritation sounds more clearly and drives out the ironic humour of the previous sonnet:

I did but prompt the age to quit their cloggs
　　By the known rules of ancient libertie,
　　When straight a barbarous noise environs me
　　Of Owls and Cuckoos, Asses, Apes and Doggs. . . .

This is mere abuse, forceful rather than subtle, and its tone is not changed when Milton goes on to refer to Ovid's story of Jove turning the tormentors of Latona into frogs. It ends (with the thought deliberately crossing the pattern of the two final tercets) with anger changing suddenly and effectively into sadness: the first sign in Milton of disillusion with the results of the Civil War from which he expected so much for England:

> Licence they mean when they cry libertie;
> For who loves that, must first be wise and good;
> But from that mark how far they roave we see
> For all this wast of wealth, and loss of blood.

The last line rings out sadly as a comment on the waste and futility of war. Milton, though he often wrote in terms of martial struggle between good and evil and though he defended the execution of Charles I, was essentially a man of peace, as his sonnet to Cromwell in May 1652 so clearly shows. 'Peace hath her victories no less renownd than warr', he told Cromwell, and it was with those victories that Milton was really concerned. It is a measure of Milton's bitter disillusion later that in Book XI of *Paradise Lost* he should make Adam speak for him with:

> But I was farr deceiv'd; for now I see
> Peace to corrupt no less than Warr to waste.

The third of Milton's angry sonnets directed against those on the Parliament side with whom he was in growing disagreement (they were principally the Presbyterians) is entitled 'On the new forcers of Conscience under the Long Parlament'. It is a *sonetto caudato*, as the Italians called it, a sonnet with a *coda* or tail, a type used for humorous or satiric verse by such Italian poets as Francisco Berni. He accuses the Presbyterians of having thrown off prelacy only 'to seise the widow'd whore Pluralitie / From them whose sin ye envi'd, not abhor'd', and continues with magnificent scorn:

> Dare ye for this adjure the Civill Sword
>> To force our Consciences that Christ set free,
>> And ride us with a classic Hierarchy
>> Taught ye by mere *A.S.* and *Rotherford*?

'Mere *A.S.* and *Rotherford*' is finely contemptuous. A. S. was Alan
Steuart, a Scottish divine active in London, and 'Rotherford' was
Samuel Rutherford, one of the four Scottish commissioners at the
Westminster Assembly; both were active pamphleteers against
the Independents, and Rutherford's vast and learned treatise,
Due Right of Presbyteries, provided much ammunition for those
who preferred Presbyterian order and discipline to Independent
individualism. What was worst of all to Milton was that

> Men whose Life, Learning, Faith and pure intent
>   Would have been held in high esteem with *Paul*
> Must now be nam'd and printed Hereticks
>   By shallow *Edwards* and Scotch what d'ye call.

Thomas Edwards was a violent Presbyterian opponent of the
Independents, who had attacked Milton's views on divorce and
whose *Gangraena : or A Catalogue and Discovery of many of the
Errours, Heresies, Blasphemies and pernicious Practices of the
Sectaries of this time, vented and acted in England in these four
last years*, published early in 1646, was only one of his many
fierce attacks on independency. (One of his later tracts was
entitled *The Casting Down of the last and strongest hold of Satan,
or, A Treatise against Toleration And pretended Liberty of Conscience*.) The last eight lines of Milton's twenty-line tailed sonnet
are cunningly linked by the rhyme scheme to the preceding tercet,
whose pattern is again deliberately crossed by the pattern of
meaning and the pauses :

> But we do hope to find out all your tricks,
> Your plots and packings wors than those of *Trent*
>   That so the Parlament
> May with their wholsom and preventive Shears
> Clip your Phylacteries, though bauk your Ears,
>   And succour our just Fears,
> When they shall read this clearly in your charge
> *New Presbyter* is but *Old Priest* writ Large.

The last line rings out, a grim epigram summing up the whole
sonnet.

Very different in tone and purpose is the graceful complimentary sonnet 'To Mr H. Lawes, on his Aires', a beautifully balanced, well turned piece of verse, perfectly suited to its purpose of friendly but formal compliment:

> *Harry* whose tuneful and well measur'd Song
>   First taught our English Musick how to span
>   Words with just note and accent, ...

It ends, as so often with this type of Miltonic sonnet, with a comparison, a reference to the past, which brings the poem gently to rest in a distant land and time:

> *Dante* shall give Fame leave to set thee higher
>   Than his *Casella*, whom he woo'd to sing
>   Met in the milder shades of Purgatory.

A sonnet to the memory of Mrs. Catharine Thomason is a more conventional piece of compliment, deftly enough turned, but couched throughout in distant generalities:

> When Faith and Love, which parted from thee never,
>   Had ripen'd thy just soul to dwell with God,
>   Meekly thou didst resign this earthly load
> Of Death, call'd Life; which us from Life doth sever.

The phrase 'which us from Life doth sever' sounds suspiciously like padding put in to fill out the rhythm and preserve the rhyme. The whole poem is written at rather low pressure. Much more interesting is the group of three complimentary poems written to Fairfax, Cromwell and Sir Henry Vane. Milton had learned from Tasso's heroical sonnets and other Italian sources that the sonnet is not devoted solely to love (as it had been in England before Milton's time), and here he brings a new kind of what might be called public emotion into the English sonnet. These poems give both praise and advice to their subjects: Milton is speaking for England:

> *Fairfax*, whose name in armes through *Europe* rings
>   Filling each mouth with envy, or with praise,
>   And all her jealous monarchs with amaze
>   And rumors loud, that daunt remotest kings,

Thy firm unshak'n vertue ever brings
   Victory home, though new rebellions raise
   Thir Hydra heads, and the fals North displaies
   Her brok'n league, to imp thir serpent wings,
O yet a nobler task awaites thy hand;
   For what can Warr but endless warr still breed,
   Till Truth and Right from Violence be freed,
And Public Faith clear'd from the shamefull brand
   Of Public Fraud. In vain doth Valour bleed
   While Avarice and Rapine share the land.

Here again we have the external form of the sonnet crossed by
the pattern of pauses and the rise and fall of the emotion, yet not
so as to destroy the external form, but so as to achieve an effective complex counterpointing of the metrical and rhyme scheme
on the one hand and the movement of thought on the other. And
again we note Milton's dislike of war and his concern with civil
reforms.

The sonnet 'To the Lord Generall Cromwell May 1652' is
similarly constructed, beginning with compliment—

Cromwell, our chief of men, who through a cloud
   Not of warr onely, but detractions rude,
   Guided by faith and matchless Fortitude
   To peace and truth thy glorious way hast plough'd
And on the neck of crowned Fortune proud
   Hast rear'd Gods Trophies,

—and ending with advice:

                     yet much remaines
   To conquer still; peace hath her victories
   No less renownd than warr; new foes arise
Threatning to bind our soules with secular chaines:
   Help us to save free Conscience from the paw
   Of hireling wolves whose Gospel is thir maw.

The sonnet to Vane, comparing him to a noble and patriotic
Roman senator, is more conventional in general tone and imagery,
but the manipulation of pauses and word-order is as skilful as in

the other two. The advice here is more general, and is part of the
compliment :

> Therfore on thy firme hand religion leanes
> In peace, and reckons thee her eldest son.

Very different in tone and subject is the sonnet 'On the late
Massacher in *Piemont*'. The massacre of the Protestant Waldensians by the Piedmontese subjects of the Duke of Savoy on
24 April, 1655, aroused great indignation in England. Letters,
probably drafted by Milton as Latin Secretary, were despatched
to the heads of different European states voicing this indignation,
and an eloquent Latin protest, also probably Milton's, was sent
to the Duke of Savoy. The Waldensians or Vaudois were regarded
by Protestants as the earliest Protestants, who had kept the true
flame alight during the darkest mediaeval period ; thus to the
natural horror at the cruelty of the massacre was added a deep
religious feeling, which Milton shared. But his sonnet is not a
mere overflow of anger : the emotion, which is profound, is perfectly controlled, and the poem moves out at the conclusion to
contemplate hoped-for beneficial results from this martyrdom :

> Avenge O Lord thy slaughter'd Saints, whose bones
>   Lie scatter'd on the Alpine mountains cold,
>   Ev'n them who kept thy truth so pure of old
> When all our Fathers worship't Stocks and Stones,
> Forget not : in thy book record their groanes
>   Who were thy Sheep and in their antient Fold
>   Slayn by the bloody Piemontese that roll'd
>   Mother with Infant down the Rocks. Their moans
> The Vales redoubl'd to the Hills, and they
>   To Heav'n. Their martyr'd blood and ashes sow
>   O're all th'*Italian* fields where still doth sway
> The triple Tyrant : that from these may grow
>   A hunderd-fold, who having learnt thy way
>   Early may fly the *Babylonian* wo.

The strong invocation of the opening, 'Avenge O Lord thy
slaughter'd Saints', is followed by a pause, deliberately counter-
ing the metrical run of the line, before the thought is developed

to give a picture of the scattered dead; then, with only a slight pause, Milton comes back to the saints and their claim to glory with an effective repetition of the object of the opening verb— '*ev'n them*'—and the sentence runs on to the emphatic 'Forget not' at the beginning of the fifth line. It now becomes clear that 'ev'n them' is not the object of 'Avenge' but of 'Forget not'. The shift is surely deliberate and results in the reader taking 'ev'n them' first as the object of 'Avenge' and later as the object of 'Forget not', so that in fact it is the object of both. 'Avenge thy slaughter'd Saints, ev'n them who kept thy truth so pure' is how we read it first, and then, having come to the emphatic opening of the fifth line, our view of the structure of the sentence shifts and we read: 'Ev'n them who kept thy truth so pure . . . forget not'. This sort of device is in perfect keeping with the deliberate weaving of the thought throughout the poem so characteristic of Milton's handling of the sonnet form; he was to use similar devices in *Paradise Lost*, and for the same purpose, to have 'the sense variously drawn out from one Verse into another'. Once again the placing of the pauses within the line shows Milton's counterpointing of the basic metrical and rhyme scheme with the pattern of thought and emotion, and the result here is peculiarly effective, as here:

> Their moans
> The Vales redoubl'd to the Hills, and they
> To Heav'n. Their martyr'd blood and ashes sow
> O're all th'*Italian* fields where still doth sway
> The triple Tyrant: . . .

The '*Babylonian* wo' of the conclusion refers to the Papal Court (just as 'the triple Tyrant' is the Pope): Milton is here echoing a reference by Petrarch in his 138th sonnet (or 108th as Milton numbered it when he quoted part of it in translation in Book I of *Of Reformation in England*) to the Papal Court as a modern Babylon and a fountain of woe.

The next sonnet is the famous one on his blindness. Here the weaving of the thought in and out of the *octave* and *sestet* is masterly. The first major thought of the poem moves on restlessly, refusing to be held by the end of a line or other normal division of the sonnet form:

> When I consider how my light is spent,
>   Ere half my days, in this dark world and wide,
>   And that one Talent which is death to hide,
>   Lodg'd with me useless, though my Soul more bent
> To serve therewith my Maker, and present
>   My true account, least he returning chide,
>   Doth God exact day-labour, light deny'd,
>   I fondly ask; . . .

The adverbs and conjunctions *when, ere, and, though, and, least,* wind through the lines, prolonging the cadence and maintaining continuity of thought and steady rise of emotion. The second movement of the sonnet begins in the middle of the last line of the *octave*:

>   But patience to prevent
> That murmur, soon replies, God doth not need
>   Either man's work or his own gifts, who best
>   Bear his milde yoak, they serve him best, his State
> Is Kingly. Thousands at his bidding speed
>   And post o're Land and Ocean without rest:
>   They also serve who only stand and waite.

Milton's punctuation clearly indicates the complex movement of the sonnet—nothing but commas until the semi-colon after 'I fondly ask', then commas again until the full stop after 'Kingly'. A colon after 'without rest' sets off the confident declaration of the last line.

There follows the charming sonnet to the young Edward Lawrence, 'of vertuous Father vertuous Son', justly popular for the light formality in which Milton invites his friend to dinner and for its reminder that Milton was not the dour Puritan of legend but an attractive and sociable man with a gift for friendship. (One is reminded that Edward Phillips, in his biography of his uncle, recorded that Milton 'would drop into the society of some young sparks of his acquaintance' and with them would make so bold 'as now and then to keep a gawdy-day'.) There is a perfect classical poise about the manner in which Milton expresses his invitation to temperate feasting:

> What neat repast shall feast us, light and choice,
>> Of Attick taste, with Wine, whence we may rise
>> To hear the Lute well toucht, or artfull voice
> Warble immortal Notes and *Tuskan* Ayre?
>> He who of those delights can judge, and spare
>> To interpose them oft, is not unwise.

This is the Horatian note with a difference; even in this slight poem the blending of Christian, classical and Renaissance idealism can be seen.

A similar note is sounded in the sonnet to Cyriack Skinner, another young friend of distinguished descent. This is likewise an invitation to temperate festivity, 'to drench / In mirth, that after no repenting drawes'. The quietly formal mingling of invitation and moralizing is most evident in the *sestet*:

> To measure life, learn thou betimes, and know
>> Toward solid good what leads the nearest way;
>> For other things mild Heav'n a time ordains,
> And disapproves that care, though wise in show,
>> That with superfluous burden loads the day,
>> And when God sends a cheerful hour, refrains.

The second sonnet to Skinner is on his blindness, and it has the same winding structure and artfully balanced pauses as 'When I consider how my light is spent'. Again the note sounded is one of resignation and self-confidence:

>   Yet I argue not
> Against heavns hand or will, nor bate a jot
> Of heart or hope; but still bear up and steer
> Right onward. What supports me, dost thou ask?
>> The conscience, Friend, to have lost them overply'd
>> In Liberties defence, my noble task,
> Of which all Europe talks from side to side.
>> This thought might lead me through the worlds vain mask
>> Content though blind, had I no better guide.

This sonnet is one among many pieces of evidence of the immense pride and satisfaction Milton took in having defended Cromwell's government before Europe.

Finally, we have the sonnet on his second wife after her death in February 1658. Milton had become reconciled to Mary Powell in 1645: Edward Phillips describes how she suddenly appeared 'making submission and begging pardon on her knees before him'. 'An act of oblivion, and a firm league of peace for the future' was the result, and when Milton shortly afterwards moved to his new house in the Barbican his wife joined him. (To keep the biographical record straight, it should be added that on the death of his father in 1647 Milton gave up his pupils and moved to a smaller house in High Holborn.) His daughter Anne was born in 1646 and another daughter, Mary, in 1648. A son, John, born in March 1651, survived only until June of the following year. Milton's wife died about the same time as the infant John, shortly after giving birth to a third daughter, Deborah. In November 1656 Milton married Katharine Woodcock, and it seems to have been a deeply happy marriage during the short time that Katharine survived. She died in February 1658, together with a daughter who had been born the previous October. It was about Katharine Woodcock (whom he had never seen, for he married her after he had become totally blind) that he wrote the sonnet:

> Methought I saw my late espoused Saint
>   Brought to me like *Alcestis* from the grave,
>   Whom *Joves* great Son to her glad Husband gave,
>   Rescu'd from death by force though pale and faint.
> Mine as whom washt from spot of child-bed taint,
>   Purification in the old Law did save,
>   And such, as yet once more I trust to have
>   Full sight of her in Heaven without restraint,
> Came vested all in white, pure as her mind:
>   Her face was vail'd, yet to my fancied sight,
>   Love, sweetness, goodness, in her person shin'd
> So clear, as in no face with more delight.
>   But O as to embrace me she enclin'd,
>   I wak'd, she fled, and day brought back my night.

This handling of the familiar experience of dreaming that some-one whose loss one has mourned is really alive after all is marked by the restraint and quiet gravity of its tone. We know from the beginning that the vision is a phantom—the opening word 'methought' makes it clear, and the analogy from classical mythology makes it clearer. Even the pedantic reference to the 'old Law' (*see* Leviticus, xii) is subdued to the gently plangent note which sounds throughout the sonnet, and rises to a fuller realization of loss with the cry, 'But O . . .'. 'Her face was vail'd', because Milton had never seen her, but also to mark the sense of frustration at the deepest level that always accompanies such wish-fulfilment dreams. There is less experiment in the placing of pauses than in most of Milton's sonnets; the emotion moves steadily along with the movement of the lines and for the most part Milton is content to let pauses demanded by the sense and those demanded by the metre coincide—though the emphatic run-over in lines 11–12 'in her person shin'd / So clear' is a striking exception. The swift and uncompromising utterance of the final line

> I wak'd, she fled, and day brought back my night

is remarkable for its vivid expression of loss without self-pity. (Neither Tennyson nor Matthew Arnold could have written a line like this.)

Milton produced a number of verse translations of Psalms in the late 1640's and early 1650's. They are exercises merely, showing Milton more interested in literal accuracy than in poetic effectiveness. Nine of them have all the words not actually in the original Hebrew printed in italics; the result is merely a curiosity. But all this time Milton was also meditating on his great epic, which, though published in 1667, was complete in 1665 if not earlier and must have been begun well before the Restoration.

IV

PARADISE LOST

THAT Milton, who had defended the execution of Charles I before Europe, survived the Restoration is said by Edward Phillips to have been due to the intervention of some of his friends in Parliament, particularly Andrew Marvell. There is also a tradition that Sir William Davenant obtained Milton's release, repaying a similar favour Milton had done for him in 1650. The details remain obscure. He does seem to have been imprisoned for a brief while; there exists the order for his release, dated 15 December, 1660. Thus Milton was abruptly returned to private life, permanently disillusioned with public affairs, to resume his career as a poet and to work on his great epic of the Fall of Man, begun under the Commonwealth. This was in many respects a very different Milton from the optimistic young poet who had looked forward to being the bard of a new and regenerate England. As he sat in darkness and heard the bells ring out the death of all his political hopes he must have needed all his faith in God's ultimate purpose for him to avoid bitterness and despair. But, though he was thrown back on himself as he had been more than once in his career, he never lost confidence or that 'self-esteem, grounded on just and right', which Raphael recommended to Adam. He had come to terms with his loss of sight and with domestic misfortune; he would adjust himself also to the life of a lonely Christian poet in a naughty world. Yet he was not left really lonely. He married again in February 1663, and his twenty-four-year-old wife was devoted and loyal, though the same cannot be said for his daughters, whose patience he had sorely tried by training them to read to him foreign languages which they could not understand. He had friends, too, and many visitors who, as Edward Phillips records, included noblemen and 'many persons of eminent quality' as well as curious foreigners.

The notes in the Trinity MS. make it clear that at one time he considered writing of the Fall of Man in dramatic form. But, though he may well have begun *Paradise Lost* as a tragedy (as

Edward Phillips maintained, quoting ten lines of Satan's address to the sun at the beginning of Book IV 'as designed for the very beginning of the said tragedy'), he cannot have worked long at it before deciding that the epic was the appropriate form for a great poetic work on a theme of such universal implications. How much of *Paradise Lost* he had written before the Restoration we cannot say. Some parts would appear to have been written between the writing of the *Second Defence* and his last pamphlets written just before the Restoration, while most of the latter part of the poem must have been written after the period of confusion and danger which Milton went through in 1660. Professor Hanford suggests that the second half of *Paradise Lost* was written between Milton's third marriage and his giving his young friend and pupil Thomas Ellwood the completed manuscript to read in September 1665. It was published in 1667, divided into ten books ; a second, revised, edition, with the poem divided into twelve books, represents Milton's final text.

At long last Milton had written that poem 'doctrinal and exemplary to a nation' that he had been determined to write from his earliest years. It was inevitably a very different poem from the one whose Platonic idea haunted him in his Cambridge and Horton days, and different, too, from the poem he would have written had he not lived to see the wreck of all his hopes for England. In the invocation at the beginning of Book VII he notes the change in his circumstances while claiming that his voice remains 'unchang'd / To hoarce or mute'. But it was changed in subtler ways. *Paradise Lost* was a richer, profounder and maturer epic because of what Milton had gone through before he completed it. A decorative poetic treatment of the Christian story of the Fall was no novelty in European literature. A younger Milton might have added another, probably the most workman-like as well as the most deeply felt, to the number of naïve poems of this kind, modelling himself on Sylvester's translation of Du Bartas whose superficial influence is so clearly seen in *Paradise Lost* as we have it although its tone and texture is so utterly different from Milton's poem. Milton's *Paradise Lost* is a poetic rendering of the story of the Fall in such a way as to illuminate some of the central paradoxes of the human situation and the tragic ambiguity of man as a moral being.

Paradise Lost was a heroic poem, but its theme was to be far above the themes of conventional heroic poems. To narrate the story of the Fall of Man was

> Sad task, yet argument
> Not less but more Heroic than the wrauth
> Of stern *Achilles* on his Foe persu'd
> Thrice Fugitive about *Troy* Wall; or rage
> Of *Turnus* for *Lavinia* disespous'd,
> Or *Neptun's* ire or *Juno's*, that so long
> Perplexd the *Greek* and *Cytherea's* Son;
> If answerable stile I can obtaine
> Of my Celestial Patroness, who deignes
> Her nightly visitation unimplor'd,
> And dictates to me slumbring, or inspires
> Easie my unpremeditated Verse:
> Since first this Subject for Heroic Song
> Pleas'd me long choosing, and beginning late;
> Not sedulous by Nature to indite
> Warrs, hitherto the onely Argument
> Heroic deemd, . . .

The 'answerable stile' demanded a verse which allowed of both a dignity and a flexibility, an ability to rise to the most sublime heights and at the same time to indicate through changes in movement shifts in moral attitude, differences in cosmic status, and the relationship between the four great theatres of action—Heaven, Eden, Hell, and (by suggestion and implication only, yet most strongly and significantly) the ordinary, familiar postlapsarian world. The popular view that Milton in *Paradise Lost* has but one voice, and that an organ one, is wholly unjustified. No epic poet was a master of such a variety of styles as Milton, and the variety with which he could use 'English Heroic Verse without Rime' (as he called it in his preliminary note, in which he unnecessarily attacks rhyme and sees himself as recovering ancient liberty to English heroic poetry) will, it is hoped, emerge clearly from the discussion that follows.

Milton's development of English blank verse as an epic style owes much—as Dr. Johnson first suggested and as Mr. F. T. Prince has conclusively shown—to the Italians, whose tradition of epic blank verse in the sixteenth century Milton knew well and adapted to his own purposes. In his manipulation of nouns and adjectives, suspending, interrupting, prolonging or balancing a statement so as to enable it to take its proper place in the unfolding texture of the poetic narrative, Milton borrowed and developed devices from Tasso, Della Casa and others. The violation of the normal English word-order and other elements in Milton's epic blank verse, which have upset some purists, are carefully and systematically employed in order to achieve different kinds of emotional pitch, to effect continuity and integration in the weaving of the epic design and above all to sustain the poem as a poem and to keep it from disintegrating into isolated fragments of high rhetoric. Rhyme would clearly be an interference in this kind of carefully woven poetic narrative, and while we may be impatient with Milton's dismissal of rhyme, in his introductory note, as 'the Invention of a barbarous Age, to set off wretched matter and lame Meeter', we can understand why he goes on to insist that 'true musical delight' consists not in rhyme but in 'apt Numbers, fit quantity of Syllables, and the sense variously drawn out from one Verse into another'. But any discussion of Milton's handling of verse is more profitably carried on by means of examination of specific passages than by any attempt to formulate general metrical laws. The flexibility and variety of Milton's poetic idiom cannot be properly demonstrated by description in terms of an iambic pentameter varied by different kinds of 'equivalence'. Milton's metrical unit (though not his rhetorical unit) is the line, not the foot, and we must see him as working with a ten-syllable line capable of much variation in the placing of the pause and the balancing of the elements of which it is composed but always moving, whether violently or in the most subdued manner, to a stressed final syllable, with another stress on the fourth or sixth syllable of the line. This line provides what might be called the basic physical element in his poetic utterance, and however much one line may run over to the next, to pause on the sixth syllable or elsewhere, the ear remains conscious of it. Lines are lines, but they must also be linked, and the reader must both hear the lines and be carried forward by the links. As for Milton's vocabulary, something of its nature, variety and kinds of effectiveness will emerge from the discussion of individual passages which follows.

Milton's statement of his theme at the beginning of Book I not only follows epic precedent in making such an opening statement; it also, in a remarkably sustained verse-paragraph, indicates the ambitious and comprehensive nature of his task and establishes his status as an epic poet on a higher moral plane than the Latin and Greek classics.

> Of Mans First Disobedience, and the Fruit
> Of that Forbidden Tree, whose mortal taste
> Brought Death into the World, and all our woe,
> With loss of *Eden*, till one greater Man
> Restore us, and regain the blissful Seat,
> Sing Heav'nly Muse, that on the secret top
> Of *Oreb*, or of *Sinai*, didst inspire
> That Shepherd, who first taught the chosen Seed,
> In the Beginning how the Heav'ns and Earth
> Rose out of *Chaos*: Or if *Sion* Hill
> Delight thee more, and *Siloa's* Brook that flowd
> Fast by the Oracle of God; I thence
> Invoke thy aid to my adventrous Song,
> That with no middle flight intends to soar
> Above th' *Aonian* Mount, while it persues
> Things unattempted yet in Prose or Rime.
> And chiefly Thou O Spirit, that dost preferr
> Before all Temples th' upright heart and pure,
> Instruct me, for Thou knowst; Thou from the first
> Wast present, and with mighty wings outspred
> Dove-like satst brooding on the vast Abyss
> And mad'st it pregnant: What in me is dark
> Illumin, what is low raise and support;
> That to the highth of this great Argument
> I may assert Eternal Providence,
> And justifie the wayes of God to men.

The placing of the pauses, the rise and fall of the emotion, the high emotional charge in which the poet's sense of dedication and of communion with the great biblical figures of the Old Testament is communicated, the supplicatory cadence of the appeal to have his darkness illumined and his mind elevated, and the final powerful simplicity of the concluding statement of his purpose—all this represents poetic art of a high order. As we have seen,

Milton had experimented much with the verse-paragraph in his earlier poems, and in *Paradise Lost* he was able to handle it with a variety and a structural cunning that go beyond anything else of the kind in English poetry. Classical echoes mingle with stark English simplicities and with overtones of meaning derived from Milton's awareness of the precise sense of relevant words in the Hebrew Bible. Sometimes much accurate scholarship is distilled in one word or phrase. 'Dove-like satst brooding on the vast Abyss', for example, is Milton's rendering of the Hebrew word *merachepheth* in Genesis i, 2, translated by the Authorized Version as 'moved'—'And the Spirit of God moved upon the face of the water'—but explained by both Jewish and Christian commentators as implying brooding and hatching. 'This is that gentle heat that brooded on the waters, and in six days hatched the world,' wrote Sir Thomas Browne in *Religio Medici*, and Henry Vaughan, in his poem 'The Water-fall', wrote:

> . . . Unless that Spirit lead his minde,
> Which first upon thy face did move,
> And hatch'd all with his quickning love.

The eleventh-century Jewish biblical commentator Solomon ben Isaac, generally known as Rashi, whose work Milton knew, explains that the Throne of Glory was suspended in the air and hovered over the face of the waters, sustained by the breath (the Hebrew *ruach* means both 'breath' and 'spirit') of God and God's command, like a dove hovering over a nest. Basil and other patristic commentators render *incubabat*, which again has the sense of brooding and hatching. Milton, in choosing the expression he does, is appealing as the poet, the *poetes* or maker, to God the creator and quickener of all things. He is also in the literal Latin sense appealing for *inspiration*, and the breath or spirit he wishes breathed into him is the *ruach* or spirit of God.

All this may sound pedantic; but it is worth pointing out that Milton could use scholarship poetically. That he is the most learned of English poets is neither an original nor an important observation; but that he was continually exploring new and effective ways of letting his learning give scope and suggestiveness to his poetic utterance is an important fact about him as a poet.

There are scores of examples of this in *Paradise Lost*. To consider one more: in Book XI, describing the murder of Abel by Cain, he tells how Abel

> Groand out his Soul with gushing blood effus'd.

Genesis iv tells how, after Cain had risen up against his brother and slain him, God asked Cain where Abel was and added: 'The voice of thy brother's blood crieth unto Me from the ground'. In the Hebrew the word for blood is, oddly, in the plural, 'the voice of thy brother's *bloods*' (*kol d'mei achicha*), which Rashi explains as meaning that Abel was wounded in many places, from all of which the blood gushed forth, for Cain did not know which place would be fatal. That is where Milton got the idea of 'with gushing blood effus'd'. One could go through *Paradise Lost* demonstrating this sort of thing again and again.

The devices which Milton uses for sustaining the flow of his great opening passage are worth careful examination. It begins emphatically with simplicity and amplitude: 'Of Mans First Disobedience'. The sense is then developed, extended, modified, qualified, reconsidered, in a great variety of ways, by the subordination of clauses and the adroit use of conjunctions, prepositions and relative pronouns—*and, whose, and, with, till,* ... The reversal of the normal English word-order enables him to place the object of the opening sentence—and it is the object, the theme of the poem, which is most important—at the beginning; the first main verb does not come until the sixth line, and when it does come it rings out with tremendous emphasis: 'Sing Heav'nly Muse'. But Milton does not pause here, sustaining the flow with a relative pronoun in 'who first taught ...' and weaving on again with 'or ... and ... that ...' The theme as he states it is both Paradise Lost and Paradise Regained; his balanced concatenation of clauses enables him to take in, by the way, as it were, the Christian scheme of redemption that was to follow the Fall: 'till one greater Man / Restore us, and regain the blissful Seat'. And in calling Christ 'one greater Man' he reveals a preference for considering Christ as Man rather than as God which is part of the implicit Arianism we find through Milton and which is made explicit only in the *De Doctrina Christiana*. But this is incidental. He goes on to explain that the Muse he invokes is not the classical Muse but the one who spoke to Moses on Mount Horeb and on Sinai and inspired him to write the story of the Creation. And the water which refreshes him is not the spring of Aganippe on Mount Helicon but '*Siloa*'s Brook', 'the waters of Shiloah that go softly', mentioned in the eighth chapter of Isaiah. And he, with no middle flight, will soar 'above th' *Aonian* Mount', that is, above Mount Helicon; he will excel the classical epic to achieve 'Things unattempted yet in Prose or Rime'. Ambition and humility are mingled in the sense and movement of the verse. When we think he has concluded his opening statement with the line

> Things unattempted yet in Prose or Rime

he moves on, with another 'and', to modify the self-confidence of that bold statement with an appeal for divine inspiration, and the rocking motion of

> What in me is dark
> Illumin, what is low raise and support

balances the tone between modesty and self-confidence until the verse soars up to the conclusion of the opening statement:

> That to the highth of this great Argument
> I may assert Eternal Providence,
> And justifie the wayes of God to men.

Here the lines move steadily onwards without any internal pause to come to rest with a grand, elemental statement. Milton can use complex Latin forms when he wishes, but the climax of this invocation could hardly be more simply English: except for the one word 'justifie' the words in the line are all monosyllables and of Anglo-Saxon origin. He writes 'the wayes of God to men', not something like 'designs of Deity to all mankind' nor even the abstract general 'man'.

Paradise Lost shows Milton as Christian humanist using all the resources of the European literary tradition that had come down to him—biblical, classical, mediaeval, renaissance; pagan, Jewish and Christian. Imagery from classical fable and mediaeval

romance, allusion to myths, legends and stories of all kinds, geographical imagery deriving from Milton's own fascination with
books of travel and echoes of the Elizabethan excitement at the
new discoveries, biblical history and doctrine, rabbinical and
patristic learning—all these and more are found in this great
synthesis of all that the Western mind was stored with by the
middle of the seventeenth century. Like *The Faerie Queene*,
Milton's epic is a great synthesizing poem, but Milton's synthesis
is more successful than Spenser's because he places his different
kinds of knowledge—biblical, classical, mediaeval, modern—in a
logical hierarchy, and never mingles, as Spenser often does,
classical myth and biblical story on equal terms. If all the resources of classical mythology are employed in order to build up
an overwhelming picture of the beauty of Eden before the Fall,
that is because Milton is saying that here, and here only, were all
the yearnings of men for ideal gardens fully realized. The description of Eden in Book IV is indeed one of the finest examples of
Milton's use of pagan classical imagery for a clearly defined
Christian purpose:

> The Birds thir quire apply; airs, vernal airs,
> Breathing the smell of field and grove, attune
> The trembling leaves, while Universal *Pan*
> Knit with the *Graces* and the *Hours* in dance
> Led on th' Eternal Spring. Not that fair field
> Of *Enna*, where *Proserpin* gathring flowrs
> Her self a fairer Flowre by gloomie *Dis*
> Was gatherd, which cost *Ceres* all that pain
> To seek her through the world; nor that sweet Grove
> Of *Daphne* by *Orontes*, and th' inspir'd
> *Castalian* Spring, might with this Paradise
> Of *Eden* strive; . . .

There is a tremulous glory in this description of ideal Nature
fully realized, and repetitions such as 'airs, vernal airs', and
'Proserpin gathring flowrs / Her self a fairer Flowre' help to give
the proper emotional quality to the verse. The classical imagery
is neither purely decorative nor as solidly grounded in reality as
the biblical groundwork of the story: Milton uses myth for what
it is, the imaginative projection of all man's deepest hopes and

fears. Matthew Arnold cited the lines about Proserpine and Ceres as a touchstone of great poetry, but did not pause to inquire why. It is in the combined suggestion of infinite beauty and of foreboding and loss that Milton manages to capture the plangent sense of transience which accompanies all postlapsarian response to beauty, and thus even while describing a prelapsarian scene he introduces overtones of the Fall. And more than that—these overtones emphasize a paradox that lies at the very heart of *Paradise Lost*, namely that only after one has lost something ideally lovely can its true worth be known, so that the Fall is necessary that we may pursue the ideal, in the teeth of all the obstacles that now confront us, with a deeper sense of its desirability.

Book I is devoted to the fallen angels in Hell beginning to recover from the numbing shock of defeat and expulsion. They represent the different aspects of the evil principle which is to tempt man to his Fall; the nature of this principle must thus be clearly shown if we are to understand how Adam and Eve voluntarily abused their reason by making the wrong choice, so fatal to themselves and their descendants. Why and under what circumstances did the first man of his own free will surrender the bliss of the unfallen state?

> Say first, for Heav'n hides nothing from thy view
> Nor the Deep Tract of Hell, say first what cause
> Mov'd our Grand Parents in that happy State,
> Favour'd of Heav'n so highly, to fall off
> From thir Creator, and transgress his Will
> For one restraint, Lords of the World besides?

A good question. In order to answer it, we must take a good look at the fallen angels. And so we turn to Satan, rolling with his horrid crew in the fiery gulf. Satan is a great figure, and he is meant to be: evil is not slight or trivial—nor, unfortunately, is it always unattractive. If evil were always obviously ugly, there would be no problem for men, and the task of recognizing and resisting it would be easy. The speeches of Satan and his followers in Books I and II are magnificent in their way, 'Miltonic' in the popular sense of the word; they represent the attractiveness of plausible evil. And it is just because high-sounding rhetoric can so easily make the worse appear the better reason, and that man so easily thrills to grandiose rantings about honour and revenge uttered with all the mock passion and the theatricality of a Nuremberg rally, that Satan is so great a danger. To see Satan as a hero because Milton goes out of his way to show the superficial seductiveness of this kind of evil is to show an extraordinary naïveté. In his portrait of Satan Milton is in some degree exposing and castigating all those false romantic notions, rampant in history and even more so in literature, of heroism as egotistical magnificence, the view that heroic energy in a bad cause is admirable, the dressing up of spite and vanity in grandiose language. He is quite explicit about his intention of presenting a theme 'not less but more Heroic' than those of classical epics; he is celebrating

> the better fortitude
> Of Patience and Heroic Martyrdom

and not the traditional fortitude of swagger, ambition and grandiloquence. As we have already noted, Milton grew more and more suspicious of rhetoric as he grew disillusioned with politics and the public life which rhetoric served. The devils have the grandiloquence in *Paradise Lost*, just as Satan has all the rhetoric in *Paradise Regained*. This does not mean that Milton was 'unconsciously' on Satan's side: it means that he was deliberately drawing attention to the traps which public life lays for vanity and to the difficulty of not deceiving oneself when one indulges in rhetorical public utterance. When, in Book IV, Satan has entered Eden and observes the innocent love of Adam and Eve, he justifies his spiteful and self-defeating plan for their ruin in the language of public policy:

> public reason just,
> Honour and Empire with revenge enlarg'd,
> By conquering this new World, compells me now
> To do what else though damned I should abhorr.

This is high-sounding nonsense. There is no 'public reason' why Satan should want to ruin Adam and Eve, and terms such as

Honour,' 'Empire', 'revenge', ring hollow in this context. Satan has now got to the stage of talking to *himself* in public rhetorical terms, concealing from himself the fact that all he is about to do is to cut off his nose to spite his face.

The first reference to Satan in *Paradise Lost* projects his moral situation with an almost brutal clarity:

> Who first seduc'd them to that foul revolt?
> Th' infernal Serpent; he it was, whose guile
> Stird up with Envy and Revenge, deceiv'd
> The Mother of Mankind, what time his Pride
> Had cast him out from Heav'n, . . .

Satan here is already the serpent—not simply a character who utilizes the serpent's body, as he does in Eden, but the serpent he became later. The tone of the phrase 'Th' infernal Serpent' is both nasty and contemptuous. The preceding line ends emphatically with the strong words 'foul revolt' and the next three lines end respectively with 'guile', 'deceiv'd, 'Pride'. The stress falls heavily on these words. The story of his casting out from Heaven is here told briefly and sternly:

> Him the Almighty Power
> Hurld headlong flaming from th' Ethereal Skie
> To bottomless perdition, there to dwell
> In Adamantine Chains and penal Fire,
> Who durst defie th' Omnipotent to Arms.

The ordering of the phrases here, so unlike the normal order of spoken English, reflects that concern with emphasis, continuity and balance which Milton first shows in the sonnets and which he learned in some degree from the Italians. The relative clause, 'Who durst defie th' Omnipotent to Arms', coming at the end, almost as an afterthought, reminds us of the reason for Satan's fall. First Satan, then the Almighty Power whom he had defied, then the hurling to bottomless perdition, then the recapitulation of why he was hurled—the pattern is most deliberately woven. As for the 'abstractness' of the phrase 'bottomless perdition', nothing could be more appropriate, for it both suggests a physical punishment and at the same time symbolizes a moral punishment.

Too precise a localization and visualization of Hell would have
introduced a kind of interest not proper to a poem which is about
moral states; it would have distracted the reader and also reduced
the possibilities of expansion of meaning by suggestion and sym-
bolization. The deliberate use of general adjectives which provide
sufficient physical suggestion while building up an atmosphere of
despair and damnation can be seen in the following lines:

> for now the thought
> Both of lost happiness and lasting pain
> Torments him; round he throws his baleful eyes
> That witnessed huge affliction and dismay
> Mixt with obdurat pride and stedfast hate:
> At once as far as Angels kenn he views
> The dismal Situation waste and wild;
> A Dungeon horrible, on all sides round
> As one great Furnace flam'd, yet from those flames
> No light, but rather darkness visible
> Serv'd only to discover sights of woe,
> Regions of sorrow, doleful shades, where peace
> And rest can never dwell, hope never comes
> That comes to all; but torture without end
> Still urges, and a fiery Deluge, fed
> With ever-burning Sulphur unconsum'd:
> Such place Eternal Justice had prepar'd
> For those rebellious, . . .

A note of elegy rises in the midst of the horror. 'At once as far as
Angels kenn he views / The di. .al Situation waste and wild' rises
almost in hope to fall back in despair at the prospect. The emotional impact of

> No light, but rather darkness visible
> Serv'd only to discover sights of woe

comes from the cunning use of abstractions. And when, with the
plangent lines, so carefully balanced, about hope that comes to
all not coming to these, we are led to the brink of pity (but no
further in that direction), sympathy is nipped off with the grim
reminder of why they were there:

> Such place Eternal Justice had prepar'd
> For those rebellious.

This first description of Hell comes to an end with a rising line which, without any internal pause, sums up the whole situation with moving simplicity:

> O how unlike the place from whence they fell!

Every word here, except the second, is a monosyllable, and all are common words of Anglo-Saxon origin.

We next see Satan's second in command, introduced to us by name in a startling beat at the opening of a line:

>   ... and weltering by his side
> One next himself in power, and next in crime,
> Long after known in *Palestine*, nam'd
> *Beëlzebub*.

The full horror of the name—Baal-zebub, lord of flies, as Milton knew—comes out in that emphatic position. We are held in suspense while we are told about him, and he is named at last in a violent and ugly explosion of 'b's'.

Satan's opening speech to Beëlzebub is a magnificent set-piece, beginning with the broken cadences of elegy—

> If thou beest he; But O how fall'n! how chang'd

—and rising to vainglorious defiance. But what romantic critics of Milton have failed to notice is that there is irony throughout, which continually reduces Satan's stature even when it superficially seems that it is being built up. Satan exclaims:

>   yet not for those
> Nor what the Potent Victor in his rage
> Can else inflict do I repent or change,
> Though chang'd in outward lustre, that fixt mind
> And high disdain, from sense of injurd merit, ...

He will not 'repent or change', he boasts, associating repentance

with change and proud of his constancy. But he has already
changed and is changing before our eyes. We saw him first as
'th' infernal Serpent', so that we already know him in a changed
form. Indeed, in order to accomplish his purpose with Eve he had
to change. The whole poem is, among other things, the story of
his inevitable degeneracy, the result of obstinacy in evil. His state
of mind, which he is so sure will remain the same, will move from
rebellion to defiance to spite to stupid and petty self-frustration,
and the process is going on even as he speaks. Further, the
histrionics of 'high disdain' and 'sense of injurd merit' have a
faint overtone of the ludicrous. There is something weak and
childish in a character's asserting to others that he is full of high
disdain and has a sense of injured merit. And indeed what does
that fine-sounding phrase 'sense of injurd merit' mean but simply
'Not fair!', which nobody has ever considered to be a heroic cry?
But the speech rises to something more impressive:

> What though the field be lost?
> All is not lost; th'unconquerable Will,
> And study of revenge, immortal hate,
> And courage never to submit or yield:
> And what is else not to be overcome?

This is high rhetoric, and it goes with a swing. We do not at first
notice the barrenness, the sheer negative quality, of the line

> And study of revenge, immortal hate,

which suggests no action at all but simply brooding on revenge
and hate. Revenge will be eternally 'studied', hate will be sustained for ever. Quite apart from the fact that on no valid moral
criteria are these things admirable, and that to a Christian the
courage to repent represents a finer, and a more difficult, heroism
than mere stubbornness, the line of behaviour sketched out by
Satan here leads nowhere at all. Yet it is grandly expressed, and
we thrill to the implied suggestion of continuing a fight against
hopeless odds, about which there *is* something admirable.

After this speech by Satan and Beëlzebub's reply Milton shifts
his perspective somewhat and gives us a view of the monstrous
creatures lying prone on the flood

> in bulk as huge
> As whom the Fables name of monstrous size,
> *Titanian* or *Earth-born*, that warrd on *Jove*,
> *Briarios* or *Typhon*, whom the Den
> By ancient Tarsus held, or that Sea-beast
> *Leviathan*, . . .

Wonder takes control, and the image momentarily fades into
other strange and monstrous images, from classical mythology
and other sources. In comparing Satan to the sea-beast Leviathan
Milton remembers the quaint old story of sailors mistaking a
whale for an island and goes on with an interesting modulation of
tone :

> Him haply slumbring on the *Norway* foam
> The Pilot of som small night-founderd Skiff,
> Deeming som Iland, oft, as Sea-men tell,
> With fixed Anchor in his scaly rinde
> Moors by his side under the Lee, while Night
> Invests the Sea, and wished Morn delays.

Milton moves from the enormous and strange to the familiar and
back again. 'The Pilot of som small night-founderd Skiff' is
a pleasing and almost a familiar figure after the picture of Satan and
Beëlzebub; there is something intimate and friendly about the
description. Yet the notion of the pilot anchoring on a huge sea-
beast thinking it an island is anything but familiar and intimate.
The pilot is deluded, and so, for a moment, are we. Satan, after all,
is the master of delusion, and in mediaeval bestiaries where the
story of sailors anchoring on whales can be found we sometimes
find the treacherous whale referred to as a type of Satan. Milton
is not, however, concerned with the allegorical quality of a
deceptive whale so much as with shifts in tone between the familiar
and the monstrous. The picture of the pilot waiting patiently by
what he thinks is an island

> while Night
> Invests the Sea, and wished Morn delays

is curiously human and touching. The impression of a quiet

nocturnal seascape rises from the line. The pilot is waiting for
dawn and light, and for a brief moment all our interest is with him.
Then comes the sudden and deliberate change of tone:

> So stretcht out huge in length the Arch-fiend lay
> Chaind on the burning Lake.

Satan rises (with God's permission, Milton hastens to assure us,
in order that he might damn himself further and that his malice
might bring forth more goodness in God—an argument that
leaves much unexplained), and continues his speech to Beëlzebub.
It is full of ringing phrases, expressed with a deliberate sonority.
A brief elegiac note rises again, to give way almost at once to
rhetorical assertions of self-confidence:

> Farewel happy Fields
> Where Joy for ever dwells: Hail horrors, hail
> Infernal World, and thou profoundest Hell
> Receive thy new Possessor: One who brings
> A mind not to be chang'd by Place or Time.
> The mind is its own place, and in it self
> Can make a Heav'n of Hell, a Hell of Heav'n.

Here, again, irony underlies the rhetoric. The mind is indeed its
own place and can make a Heaven of Hell or a Hell of Heaven.
This does not mean, however, what Satan thinks it means: it
means that Satan can never escape from Hell but is doomed to
carry it around with him for ever. Milton is surely remembering
the scene in Marlowe's *Doctor Faustus* where Faustus asks Mephistophilis how it comes that he is out of Hell and Mephistophilis
replies:

> Why this is hel, nor am I out of it:
> Thinkst thou that I who saw the face of God,
> And tasted the eternal joyes of heaven,
> Am not tormented with ten thousand hels,
> In being depriv'd of everlasting blisse?

As for the ringing line

> Better to reign in Hell, than serve in Heav'n,

though it has a certain Byronic appeal, its melodramatic tone scarcely conceals the mixture of pride and spite which it expresses. If Hell is evil and Heaven is good, then it is quite simply *not* better to reign in Hell than serve in Heaven in any proper sense of the word 'better'. What Satan is really saying is that so long as he is boss he does not care what he is boss of. These splendid public utterances do not stand up to scrutiny. They represent a combination of vanity, self-deception, whistling in the dark and rabble-rousing, something very different from that rhetoric as public service which the younger Milton had so firmly believed in.

Milton continually shifts the perspective from which he looks at the scene in Hell, now coming close to watch a character's features, now moving away to see the whole group as a great host scattered over a vast distance. Though the main purpose of these shifts is to sustain interest—they are part of the many devices for achieving variety with continuity that Milton employs so conspicuously in the poem—they also help to convey the author's attitude to his subject. The famous simile in which the mass of fallen angels are seen

> Thick as Autumnal Leaves that strow the Brooks
> In *Vallombrosa*

suddenly reduces the size and significance of the host and at the same time brings a breath of fresh air into the poem. The perspective, as well as the atmosphere, shifts again when Milton goes on to compare them to Pharaoh's horsemen drowned in the Red Sea:

> . . . or scatterd sedge
> Afloat, when with fierce Winds *Orion* armd
> Hath vext the Red-Sea Coast, whose waves orethrew
> *Busiris* and his *Memphian* Chivalrie,
> While with perfidious hatred they persu'd
> The Sojourners of *Goshen,* who beheld
> From the safe shore thir floating Carcasses
> And broken Chariot Wheels: so thick bestrown
> Abject and lost lay these, covering the Flood,
> Under amazement of thir hideous change.

Milton here begins by comparing the fallen angels to the 'scatterd

sedge afloat' on the Red Sea, and then, with a characteristic concatenation of clauses ('when . . . whose . . . while . . .') he reminds
us that the Red Sea was the scene of the overthrow of Pharaoh's
host, and *this* defeated host is in a similar state. Pharaoh and his
defeated army become (erroneously, as a matter of fact, but the
best scholarship of Milton's day identified this biblical Pharaoh
with Busiris) '*Busiris* and his *Memphian* Chivalrie', a transforma-
tion which plays down the biblical overtones and suggests instead
a mediaeval romance. Throughout *Paradise Lost* Milton makes
oblique ironic digs at chivalric ideals of heroism and at the ideal
of courtly love: true heroism and true love are different from
these. Pharaoh's horsemen are thus '*Memphian* Chivalrie'. It is
also worth noting that Milton refers to the sedge on the Red Sea
because he knew that it was reputed to be sedgy and that the
Hebrew for the Red Sea, *Yam Suph*, meant literally 'Sea of sedge'
or 'Sea of weeds'. He begins by seizing on this fact and then works
his way deftly round to the picture of the abject and lost host.

Satan's speech rousing his followers echoes the imagery of the
preceding description. He tries to shame them out of their abject
state:

> . . . in this abject posture have ye sworn
> To adore the Conqueror? who now beholds
> Cherube and Seraph rouling in the Flood
> With scattered Arms and Ensigns, . . .

He concludes with a trumpet call:

> Awake, arise, or be for ever fall'n.

They *are* for ever fallen, however, in a profounder sense than they
or Satan realizes, and they rise physically only in order to fall
more deeply into utter damnation.

The lively and varied way in which Milton describes the risen
host, with rapid shifts of perspective and changing similes, each
with its own moral suggestions, is worth the closest study. At one
point they are like the locusts brought over Egypt by Moses as one
of the ten plagues, at another like the huge barbarian hordes who
came from the frozen north to destroy the sunny Mediterranean
civilization of Rome. He gives the whole feel of the barbarian

invasions and the end of the Roman world before a new and cruder way of life:

> A multitude, like which the populous North
> Pourd never from her frozen loins, to pass
> *Rhene* or the *Danaw*, when her barbarous Sons
> Came like a Deluge on the South, and spred
> Beneath *Gibraltar* to the *Lybian* sands.

Finally they are described as the false gods they were to become, seducing men into evil ways, trapping, deluding, perverting, leading men into monstrous cruelties and unspeakable horrors. The grim roll is called, beginning with Moloch, 'horrid King besmear'd with blood of human sacrifice', and going on to other gods who led the people of Israel and Judah astray of old. The shift in tone between the description of Thammuz and that of the Philistine fish-god is striking:

> Next came one
> Who mournd in earnest, when the Captive Ark
> Maimd his brute Image, head and hands lopt off
> In his own Temple, on the grunsel edge,
> Where he fell flat, and sham'd his Worshippers:
> Dagon his Name, Sea Monster, upward Man
> And downward Fish.

This reference to the story in 1 Samuel v, 1–5 is made with grim contempt and a deliberate roughness of language. When it came to a straight contest between a Philistine god and the God of Israel Milton could never describe the situation objectively: he was deeply involved, and he speaks strongly from the point of view of a contemporary Israelite. The menace of the Egyptian gods—and this we have also seen in the Nativity Ode—is subtler: there is a horrid magic at work there:

> After these appear'd
> A crew who under Names of old Renown,
> *Osiris, Isis, Orus*, and thir Train
> With monstrous shapes and sorceries abus'd
> Fanatic *Egypt* and her Priests, to seek
> Thir wandering Gods disguis'd in brutish forms
> Rather than human.

The whole amazing catalogue of gods moves through history from Mesopotamia, Canaan, Egypt, on to Greece and Italy, progressing both chronologically and geographically. But it is more than history and geography: it is a map of all the major moral aberrations of man, all the different kinds of delusion, superstition and cruelty to which men have been led by false religions. It is only after having been shown this woeful picture of the horrors the fallen angels were to bring into the world in their later guise of pagan gods that we are allowed to look again at the satanic host and to hear them debating. Our recollection of this picture provides an ironic undercurrent to the debate as well as a warning against taking it at its face value.

These are fallen angels at the beginning of their long process of degeneration; they still bear traces of their former glory, and there is much to admire in their superficial behaviour if not in their deepest moral nature. *Corruptio optimi pessima*, the corruption of the best becomes the worst; and this is particularly clear in the case of Satan. His clarion call rouses the fallen host, and order, discipline and confidence replace despair:

> Anon they move
> In perfet *Phalanx* to the *Dorian* mood
> Of Flutes and soft Recorders; such as rais'd
> To highth of noblest temper Heroes old
> Arming to Battel, and in stead of rage
> Deliberat valour breath'd, firm and unmov'd . . .

The carefully ordered verse, its balance and stability, the echoing of 'Anon they *move*' by 'firm and *unmov'd*' five lines later, suggesting with deliberate paradox that they both move and stand firm (the very essence of military discipline), the chiming of similar vowels at the end of lines, 'move', 'mood', 'unmov'd', and 'rais'd', 'rage'—all this represents routine craftsmanship in Milton, a craftsmanship that is found so continuously throughout the poem that one can overlook it or at least take it for granted.

Satan, watching his disciplined host, swells with pride. We see them more numerous than the teeming pygmy race mentioned in the Iliad or than Greek heroes and gods joined together,

> and what resounds
> In Fable or Romance of *Uthers* Son
> Begirt with *Brittish* and *Armoric* Knights;
> And all who since, Baptiz'd or Infidel
> Jousted in *Aspramont* or *Montalban*,
> *Damasco*, or *Marocco*, or *Trebisond*,
> Or whom *Biserta* sent from *Afric* shore
> When *Charlemain* with all his Peerage fell
> By *Fontarabbia*.

This famous recollection of Arthurian legend and the *Chanson de Roland* distils the very essence of heroic romance. Ariosto is here too (in canto XVII of *Orlando Furioso* a tournament is held in Damascus between Christian and pagan champions), and the story, well known in romance, of the capture of Trebizond by the Turks in 1461. But this is not mere romantic suggestiveness. Milton is pointing up the conflict between Christian and Moslem civilization so central in mediaeval European history, and even in that wonderful phrase where he captures the very mood and meaning of the death of Roland at Roncesvalles in the *Chanson de Roland*—

> When *Charlemain* with all his Peerage fell
> By *Fontarabbia*

he twists the story slightly for his own purposes. Roland, not Charlemagne, fell at Roncesvalles; and Fontarabbia, where Milton puts the event, is forty miles from Roncesvalles. But he wanted the suggestion of Christian and Arab confronting each other, the first Holy Roman Emperor and all his peerage against the Arab civilization that threatened all he stood for; so Charlemagne himself is made to fall in that desperate battle, and he calls the place by a name which suggests the Arab side in the conflict. The great simile thus ends on an elegiac note, with a brief but vivid picture of the forces of Christianity overcome by the infidel. The suggestion, made again and again in *Paradise Lost*, is that chivalry will not save; the knightly code and courtly love have their attractiveness, but in the last analysis they are not on the side of Christian good. The fancy goings-on of chivalry are common to Christian and pagan—'all who since, Baptiz'd or Infidel / Jousted in *Aspramont* or *Montalban*'—and represent something decorative and perhaps decadent. 'Jousted in *Aspramont* or *Montalban*' is a phrase full of romantic suggestion, as has been so often said, but is there not also just a suggestion of playing at war, of elaborate exhibitionist prancings, about it? Perhaps we have here one of the reasons why Milton gave up his earlier plan to write an Arthurian epic: he cannot now take chivalry seriously.

His followers roused, Satan makes them a warlike speech, full of contradictions and absurdities when closely examined but admirable public discourse, ending with an appeal to continue the conflict:

> Warr then, Warr
> Open or understood must be resolv'd.

The whole debate as it develops in Book II is a classic presentation of the abuses of democratic assembly, and one is reminded again and again of Hitler addressing one of his monster rallies, with all the trappings of banners, uniforms and insignia. Here, towards the end of Book I, we first feel this atmosphere:

> He spake: and to confirm his words, out-flew
> Millions of flaming swords, drawn from the thighs
> Of mighty Cherubim; the sudden blaze
> Far round illumind hell: highly they rag'd
> Against the Highest, and fierce with grasped Arms
> Clashed on thir sounding shields the din of war,
> Hurling defiance toward the Vault of Heav'n.

This surely is the Nuremberg rally, with the shouts of 'Sieg Heil' going up after a hysterical speech by Hitler, and military pageantry everywhere. Milton at this stage of his life had only contempt for this kind of debased romantic gesturing. His plays on words— 'highly they rag'd against the Highest'—add to the tone of contempt in a characteristically Miltonic manner.

Then comes the building of Pandemonium, designed by the fallen angel who was to become the god called by the Greeks Hephaestus and by the Romans Vulcan or, less commonly, Mulciber. The well-known passage in Milton describing his fall draws on the Greek story of the throwing out from Heaven of

Hephaestus by Zeus, changing, suddenly and deliberately, the whole tone of the narrative to project the reader into a fabled summer eve in the ancient Greek world:

> and in *Ausonian* land
> Men calld him *Mulciber*; and how he fell
> From Heav'n, they fabl'd, thrown by angry *Jove*
> Sheer ore the Crystal Battlements: from Morn
> To Noon he fell, from Noon to dewy Eve,
> A Summers day; and with the setting Sun
> Dropd from the Zenith like a falling Star
> On *Lemnos* th' *Ægæan* Ile.

We begin by watching from the battlements as Mulciber is thrown over, and we see him falling, falling, down through immense space, a whole summer's day: but with the phrase 'A Summers day' we are on earth in summer time; the camera shifts, and we now see the falling god dropping out of the sky as we look up from Lemnos. The whole episode, which Milton regards as a distorted account of the fall of Satan and his crew, is made pleasing and literary—as though in classical mythology, and only there, the devils find their one acceptable mutation. But the story, Milton hastens to remind us, is not true:

> thus they relate,
> Erring; for he with this rebellious rout
> Fell long before; nor aught avail'd him now
> To have built in Heav'n high Towrs: . . .

'Rebellious rout' restores the note of moral disgust, and the quiet incisiveness of 'nor aught avail'd him now / To have built in Heav'n high Towrs' is a comment on vain ambition which, because of the simple and elemental quality of the imagery, rings out with an infinite suggestiveness.

The mass of fallen angels are reduced to pygmy size to accommodate them all in Pandemonium, and the reduction in size also implies a comment on their plottings and plannings. Meanwhile, in an inner chamber, the leaders, 'in their own dimensions',

> In close recess and secret conclave sat.

'Conclave' to Milton and his Protestant audience suggested Jesuit plottings : it is a deliberately contemptuous use of an ecclesiastical word, an ironical allusion to Church councils and to the supposed sinister machinations of Catholic schemers. And so 'the great consult began'.

Book II opens with a description of satanic splendour which associates pride, dictatorship and oriental luxury in an imagery full of specific moral suggestion :

> High on a Throne of Royal State, which far
> Outshon the wealth of *Ormus* and of *Ind*,
> Or where the gorgeous East with richest hand
> Showrs on her Kings *Barbaric* Pearl and Gold,
> *Satan* exalted sat, by merit rais'd
> To that bad eminence ; . . .

Not only is Milton here drawing on contemporary geographies and on recent history (the city of Ormus or Hormuz, situated on an island at the entrance of the Persian Gulf, was celebrated for its wealth and its position as the gateway to India ; in 1622 the English assisted the Shah of Persia to retake it from Portugal) ; he is also recollecting Greek suspicion of Persian tyranny and Greek and Roman dislike of Persian luxury. When Milton uses the term 'barbaric' or 'barbarian' he is generally identifying himself with the temperate Greek world against the barbarian world as viewed from Athens or Sparta at the time of the Persian wars, and he is remembering, too, Horace's 'Persicos odi puer apparatus'. There are also echoes of Old Testament prophecies against the wantonness of Babylon and Egypt. Satan's world is a world of intemperance and exhibitionism, and against it Milton implicitly opposes an ideal of restraint and self-discipline partly Hebrew, partly Greek and partly Roman. The lines

> Or where the gorgeous East with richest hand
> Showrs on her Kings *Barbaric* Pearl and Gold

show a skilful manipulation of imagery, with the emphatic word '*Barbaric*' standing in a central position in relation to images of profusion and wealth. It is magnificent but barbaric. Satan was a great showman, and the splendid vigour of his achievement is acknowledged :

> *Satan* exalted sat, by merit rais'd
> To that bad eminence.

The moral ambiguities of the position are clear. Satan was 'exalted', but in a literal not a spiritual way. His exaltation is associated with his pride; it is opposed to the proper exaltation of God described in Book III. Yet it is the result of 'merit' of a kind; he represents *corruptio optimi*, not because he is the 'best' of a bad bunch but because his badness is at all points the obverse of a possible goodness. The character of Satan as drawn by Milton shows the continual misuse of potential good qualities which become first distorted, then obscured, then perverted into an evil which is at last obviously repulsive. None of the other fallen angels is shown in this light. They are more simply evil from the beginning. Professor C. S. Lewis has convincingly demonstrated the kinds and degrees of moral evil represented by the different speakers in the debate in Book II, from the simple fury of Moloch to Mammon's attempt to persuade himself and others that Hell is just as good as Heaven. These speeches are all carefully devised set-pieces of rhetorical persuasion, with the difference that the rhetoric is also self-deception, aimed at the speaker himself as well as his audience. Of all the devils except Satan (and in a much lesser degree Beëlzebub) Milton speaks as though they had been evil from the beginning; Moloch evidently was always strong and fierce, Belial false and hollow, and Mammon even in Heaven had been wont to look down and admire more 'the riches of Heav'ns pavement, trodden Gold / Than aught divine or holy'. In these characters Milton is moving at a different level of probability than in his portrait of Satan. In Satan he is documenting, with considerable psychological cunning, the gradual but inevitable destruction of personality once irrational pride is allowed to govern all moral choice; the other fallen angels are nearer simple allegory in their representation of different kinds of vice or perversion. Yet even they are not as simple as they may at first seem. When Belial is censured by Milton for counselling 'ignoble ease, and peaceful sloath' instead of prolongation of the futile war against God, it

may appear to the superficial reader that Milton is admiring Satan
and Beëlzebub for wishing to carry on the war. The romantic
view on this point is that Milton the rebel could not help admiring
Satan the rebel. But this is nonsense. Belial's views, and Milton's
comments on them, when read properly in their context, show
Milton's horror at the subtle casuistry which can attempt to persuade rational beings that their salvation lies in acclimatizing
themselves to Hell's atmosphere, in contentedly losing everything
that makes them reasoning moral creatures. The despair of
Moloch at being shut up for ever in 'this dark opprobrious Den
of shame' is not quite so morally debased as Belial's view that
angelic natures can and should deliberately induce a state of mind
in which the Den of shame is not seen to be a Den of shame at all,
just as Mammon's argument that there never really was any
difference between Heaven and Hell represents a step even lower.
Professor Lewis is surely right in his analysis of this moral descent.

These speeches, however, are episodes in an epic poem, not
stages in a theological argument or even incidents in a novel, and
it is a mistake to discuss them without attending to the various
poetic devices by which Milton succeeds in simultaneously displaying and parodying the rhetoric of public political argument.
Satan's grandiloquence in addressing the members of his council—

> Powers and Dominions, Deities of Heav'n

—and his ability to describe his objective in splendid (but
ultimately meaningless) terms—

> we now return
> To claim our just inheritance of old

—have all the marks of a Hitler at Nuremberg. And Moloch's
military obsession and vocabulary both sums up and implicitly
mocks the advice given at political councils by innumerable
generals in all periods of history:

> them let those
> Contrive who need, or when they need, not now,
> For while they sit contriving, shall the rest,
> Millions that stand in Arms, and longing wait
> The Signal to ascend, sit lingring here . . .

'The morale of the troops is splendid, and they are eagerly await-ing the order to advance on the enemy.' Moloch is the general among the politicians. He feels their recent defeat as a blow to his military prestige :

> Who but felt of late
> When the fierce Foe hung on our broken Rear
> Insulting, and persu'd us through the Deep,
> With what compulsion and laborious flight
> We sunk thus low.

And though forced to admit by the facts of the case that the enemy's citadel is impregnable, he feels that they can at least make the enemy uncomfortable by 'perpetual inroads',

> Which if not Victory is yet Revenge.

The cadence of that culminating line almost masks its silliness. That such confused and self-defeating advice should ring out at the end of a martial speech is Milton's comment on military rhetoric, just as Satan's remark about claiming 'our just inheri-tance', or his later claim that in venturing forth to attack man in Eden he seeks 'deliverance for us all' (which is absolute nonsense), is Milton's comment on political rhetoric. The specious delibera-tive note of Belial represents another kind of public discourse. Belial's speech is full of questions and answers (both supplied by himself), and every point is arranged in order and duly ticked off when dealt with. 'First, what Revenge ? . . .' The deliberative note is heightened by the broken-up movement of the verse and the to-and-fro cadence that results :

> Thus repulst, our final hope
> Is flat despair : we must exasperate
> Th' Almighty Victor to spend all his rage,
> And that must end us, that must be our cure,
> To be no more ; sad cure ; for who would lose,
> Though full of pain, this intellectual being,
> Those thoughts that wander through Eternity,
> To perish rather, swallowd up and lost
> In the wide womb of uncreated night,

> Devoid of sense and motion? and who knows,
> Let this be good, whether our angry Foe
> Can give it, or will ever? how he can
> Is doubtful; that he never will is sure.
> Will he, so wise, let loose at once his ire,
> Belike through impotence, or unaware,
> To give his Enemies thir wish, and end
> Them in his anger, whom his anger saves
> To punish endless? wherefore cease we then?
> Say they who counsel Warr, we are decreed,
> Reserv'd and destind to Eternal woe;
> Whatever doing, what can we suffer more,
> What can we suffer worse? is this then worst,
> Thus sitting, thus consulting, thus in Arms?
> What when we fled amain, persu'd and strook
> With Heav'ns afflicting Thunder, and besought
> The Deep to shelter us? this Hell then seemd
> A refuge from those wounds: or when we lay
> Chaind on the burning Lake? that sure was worse.

And so on. One requires a fairly long quotation to illustrate this kind of deliberative rhetoric, with its strings of loaded questions and artful appearance of weighing all pros and cons.

The appearance of free discussion in the debate turns out to be illusory. The assembly are persuaded by Belial and Mammon to vote for peace instead of war, but this goes against Satan's plan, so his second-in-command Beëlzebub is put up to propound as though it were his own the scheme already determined on by his master. The plan is simply to shift the attack from God, who cannot be defeated, to newly created man, who is relatively weak and vulnerable; by seducing man they will annoy God and frustrate His plans. The spiteful relish with which Beëlzebub contemplates the setting of man against God introduces a new note into the debate:

> This would surpass
> Common revenge, and interrupt his joy
> In our Confusion, and our Joy upraise
> In his disturbance; when his darling Sons
> Hurld headlong to partake with us, shall curse
> Thir frail Original, and faded bliss,
> Faded so soon.

This licking of the lips over the prospect of an injury done to an innocent third party who, unlike God, can be attacked with impunity, removes at last all vestige of heroism from the enterprise. Indeed, Beëlzebub makes no bones about it, asking plainly

> What if we find
> Some easier enterprize?

The attack on man is the 'easier enterprize'. It is (or is thought to be) war without danger, like Mussolini's attack on France in 1940. That is the end of the illusion of heroism in the actions of Satan and his minions. And when Satan proceeds to congratulate the assembly on their wise decision, the disparity between his language and the reality of what he is about to do echoes hollowly:

> Well have ye judg'd, well ended long debate,
> Synod of Gods, and like to what ye are,
> Great things resolv'd; which from the lowest deep
> Will once more lift us up, in spite of Fate,
> Nearer our ancient Seat; . . .

The device by which Satan gets himself elected to seek out man's abode and bring about his fall is in the best traditions of exhibitionist dictatorship. The decision having been publicly announced, the fallen angels prepare themselves to pass the time in the absence of their leader. A note almost of compassion emerges in Milton's description of these lost and self-deluded characters seeking in vain to put their physical and intellectual faculties to a proper use. Here the parallel between fallen angel and fallen man is very close:

> Thence more at ease thir minds and somwhat rais'd
> By false presumptuous hope, the ranged Powers
> Disband, and wandring, each his several way
> Pursues, as inclination or sad choice
> Leads him perplext, where he may likeliest find
> Truce to his restless thoughts, and entertain
> The irksom hours, till his great Chief return.

Some engage in sports and games, others in music and poetry, others again in philosophy. But without proper humility and proper acceptance of divine truth by use of right reason, philosophy is only a temporary alleviation of intellectual restlessness ; it is a game that tires, not the exciting and satisfying discovery of metaphysical reality :

> In discourse more sweet
> (For Eloquence the Soul, Song charms the Sense,)
> Others apart sat on a Hill retir'd,
> In thoughts more elevate, and reasond high
> Of Providence, Foreknowledge, Will, and Fate,
> Fixt Fate, free Will, Foreknowledge absolute,
> And found no end, in wandring mazes lost.
> Of good and evil much they argu'd then,
> Of happiness and final misery,
> Passion and Apathie, and glory and shame,
> Vain wisdom all, and false Philosophie :
> Yet with a pleasing sorcerie could charm
> Pain for a while or anguish, and excite
> Fallacious hope, or arm th' obdured brest
> With stubborn patience as with triple steel.

There is both irony and elegy here—irony at the expense of professional philosophical discussion 'Of Providence, Foreknowledge, Will, and Fate', and elegy on the misuse of talent by both man and devil and, by implication, on the position of the intellectual in a fallen world.

In describing the landscape of Hell, Milton draws on a variety of classical and other myths with an almost wanton eclecticism ; he even anticipates certain later functions which Hell is to serve, after the Fall of Man, in contributing to the tortures of the damned. The piling up of diverse images and suggestions is deliberate ; Hell is whatever the human imagination throughout the whole of history has conceived it to be. Those who explored the confines of their new territory found everything that symbolized perpetual unfulfilled search, unending grief, eternal deprivation of light and grace and satisfying rational meaning :

> Thus roving on
> In confus'd march forlorn, th' adventurous Bands
> With shuddring horror pale, and eyes agast

> Viewd first thir lamentable lot, and found
> No rest: through a dark and drearie Vale
> They passd, and many a Region dolorous,
> Ore many a Frozen, many a Fierie Alp,
> Rocks, Caves, Lakes, Fens, Bogs, Dens, and shades of death,
> A Universe of death, which God by curse
> Created evil, for evil only good,
> Where all life dies, death lives, and nature breeds,
> Perverse, all monstrous, all prodigious things,
> Abominable, inutterable, and worse
> Than Fables yet have feignd, or fear conceiv'd,
> Gorgons and Hydras, and Chimeras dire.

The marshalling of adjectives, 'forlorn', 'shuddring horror pale' (a characteristic Miltonic order, here most effectively employed), 'agast', 'lamentable', 'dark and drearie', 'dolorous', and others, gives the sense of exhausting every possible avenue of escape. The impression is general, but it is arrived at through the accumulation of particular terms which together build up the impression of a totality of deprivation, hopelessness and perversion. 'Perverse' falls strongly at the beginning of a line, before the list is summed up in a sweeping, inclusive statement:

> all monstrous, all prodigious things,
> Abominable, inutterable, and worse
> Than Fables yet have feignd, or fear conceiv'd, . . .

The three woeful adjectives, 'Abominable, inutterable, and worse', complement the line of monosyllabic nouns, 'Rocks, Caves, Lakes, Fens, . . .' The object is not to present a visual image of Hell but to suggest all that the human imagination has most recoiled from. Criticism of Milton for not employing sufficiently precise visual imagery is peculiarly stupid; in Paradise Lost images are symbolic of states of mind, and some degree of abstraction in them is absolutely necessary. Whenever Milton becomes too specific visually, as in some of the descriptions of Heaven, he distracts attention from the symbolic moral or mental state to the merely visual, with unhappy results, as in the picture of the angels bowing to God and raising their crowns to Him in Book III.

This is a point worth emphasizing. Milton was dealing in *Paradise Lost* with Heaven, Hell, and man's prelapsarian paradisial home. Precise visual description could only be in terms of the known postlapsarian world, and could never therefore be wholly appropriate. Milton's task was to use mythology and the physical world he knew in order to enable the reader's imagination to dwell in regions which were physically beyond human awareness but which in their moral and spiritual suggestiveness were part of a known world. In the greater part of *Paradise Lost*, the familiar human world we know can only come in through metaphor, simile, or oblique reference of one kind or another. Yet in its moral pattern the poem is from the beginning concerned with our world. The poem is thus a deliberate combination of the familiar and the unfamiliar, and its visual imagery must be vivid enough to compel attention yet general enough to allow the reader's imagination to reach out to abstractions beyond the concrete world he knows. In Book IV, the Tree of Life is described as bearing 'blooming Ambrosial Fruit of vegetable Gold', a description perfect in its generalized suggestion of natural beauty. The last thing wanted was a description of a particular variety of apple. The weak points in *Paradise Lost* are always where Milton is too specific either in argument or in imagery or in narrative detail.

The remainder of Book II, taken up with Satan's journey through Chaos and his encounter with Sin and Death, is a loose amalgam of incidents, images and situations partly allegorical, partly symbolic, partly suggestive. The combination of elements from the classical myth of the birth of Minerva from the head of Jupiter with the idea expressed in the fifteenth verse of the first chapter of the Epistle of James ('Then when lust hath conceived, it bringeth forth sin; and sin, when it is finished, bringeth forth death') to explain the relation between Satan, Sin and Death is characteristic of Milton's ability to bring together pagan imagery and Christian ideas; but the main point of this whole episode is its demonstration of the true ugliness of all that Satan has done and produced. Satan's 'heroism' may appear superficially attractive when we see him deceiving himself and his followers in the great debate; but here is the other side of the medal, the true meaning of his actions. What is evil is unnatural and the unnatural is profoundly ugly. At the same time the behaviour and conversation of Sin, Death and Satan represent a monstrous parody of the behaviour of God and the Son in Heaven. This unholy trinity have their own distorted and incestuous hierarchy, and when Sin looks forward to Satan's opening up new worlds for her to conquer she sees herself reigning

> At thy right hand voluptuous, as beseems
> Thy daughter and thy darling without end,

which parodies the description in Book V of the Son sitting by the Father 'in bliss imbosomd'. Indeed there is throughout the poem a sustained parallelism and contrast between life in Hell and life in Heaven, with human life oscillating between the two. As for the characters of Chaos, Night and the inhabitants of 'the wasteful Deep', it would be a mistake to inquire too literally into their place in Milton's scheme of things or to ask when and why God created them; they are part of the general atmosphere of disorder and confusion which is appropriate both to Satan's moral state and to the uncreated region between Hell and Heaven—the created universe was thought of as suspended from Heaven over Chaos, with Hell far below—through which Satan has to journey if he is to find the home of newly created man. Nor need we be detained by the classical sources—Hesiod, Herodotus and many others—which he draws on in building up his picture of this region. Book II ends with Satan coming up through Chaos to see the pendent world (that is, the earth circled by the seven planetary spheres, one sphere of fixed stars, the crystalline sphere and the outer *primum mobile*), and above it, barely glimpsed, his lost Heaven

> extended wide
> In circuit, undetermind square or round,
> With Opal Towrs and Battlements adornd
> Of living Saphire, once his native Seat.

Milton wisely will not specify Heaven's shape; it is a shining symbolic city. The earth with its surrounding sphere hangs 'fast by', and

> Thither full fraught with mischievous revenge,
> Accurst, and in a cursed hour he hies.

Book II ends on a note of dark foreboding.

Book II ends in darkness and Book III opens in light, with the famous invocation which marks Milton's turning in the poem from Hell to Heaven and shows the strong emotion with which he proceeded to the more daring part of his work, the description of God in Heaven:

> Hail holy Light, offspring of Heav'n first-born,
> Or of th' Eternal Coeternal beam
> May I express thee unblam'd? since God is Light,
> And never but in unapproached Light
> Dwelt from Eternitie, dwelt then in thee,
> Bright effluence of bright essence increate.
> Or hear'st thou rather pure Ethereal stream,
> Whose Fountain who shall tell? before the Sun,
> Before the Heav'ns thou wert, and at the voice
> Of God, as with a Mantle didst invest
> The rising world of waters dark and deep,
> Won from the void and formless infinite.
> Thee I revisit now with bolder wing,
> Escap't the *Stygian* Pool, though long detaind
> In that obscure sojourn, while in my flight
> Through utter and through middle darkness borne
> With other notes than to th' *Orphean* Lyre
> I sung of *Chaos* and *Eternal Night*,
> Taught by the heav'nly Muse to venture down
> The dark descent, and up to reascend,
> Though hard and rare: thee I revisit safe,
> And feel thy sovran vital Lamp; but thou
> Revisitst not these eyes, that roul in vain
> To find thy piercing ray, and find no dawn;
> So thick a drop serene hath quencht thir Orbs,
> Or dim suffusion veild. Yet not the more
> Cease I to wander where the Muses haunt
> Clear Spring, or shadie Grove, or Sunnie Hill,
> Smit with the love of sacred song; but chief
> Thee *Sion* and the flowrie Brooks beneath
> That wash thy hallowd feet, and warbling flow,
> Nightly I visit: nor somtimes forget
> Those other two equald with me in Fate,
> So were I equald with them in renown,
> Blind *Thamyris* and blind *Mæonides*,

And *Tiresias* and *Phineus* Prophets old.
Then feed on thoughts, that voluntarie move
Harmonious numbers; as the wakeful Bird
Sings darkling, and in shadiest Covert hid
Tunes her nocturnal Note. Thus with the Year
Seasons return, but not to me returns
Day, or the sweet approach of Ev'n or Morn,
Or sight of vernal bloom, or Summers Rose,
Or flocks, or herds, or human face divine;
But cloud in stead, and ever-during dark
Surrounds me, from the cheerful ways of men
Cut off, and for the Book of knowledge fair
Presented with a Universal blanc
Of Natures works to mee expung'd and ras'd,
And wisdom at one entrance quite shut out.
So much the rather thou Celestial Light
Shine inward, and the mind through all her powers
Irradiate, there plant eyes, all mist from thence
Purge and disperse, that I may see and tell
Of things invisible to mortal sight.

Periodically, at moments of crisis in his epic, Milton is conscious of himself as the blind bard, and of the proud paradox of
his physical blindness yielding a greater spiritual vision. The verse
soars confidently up, yet the cadences are broken by pauses and
counter-movements suggestive, however faintly, of pathos and
regret. The ringing statement of his kinship with the great blind
bards of old is followed by a simile altogether different in tone and
feeling:

> as the wakeful Bird
> Sings darkling, and in shadiest Covert hid
> Tunes her nocturnal Note.

The bird singing in the dark has a romantic and even a self-
pitying suggestion, far removed from the prophetic grandeur of
the immediately preceding lines. The suggestion is adroitly
utilized by the conjunction *Thus* which links the bird passage with
the famous elegiac statement of the loss his physical blindness has
brought. The movement of the seasons, the different sights
appropriate to the different hours of the day and the different

times of the year, are denied him, and that this is a real loss is made abundantly clear by the whole tone of the passage. Yet the change of seasons was part of the curse which changed Eden's perpetual spring into the revolving agricultural year in which fallen man had to work for his living. And the human face, from which the divine light of prelapsarian innocence had for so long been absent— that, too, he mourned his inability to see. He calls it 'the human face divine' in spite of everything, emphasizing the paradox of the human and the divine together by dropping the word 'face' between the two mutually contradictory adjectives. The memory of the sons of Belial flown with insolence and wine was not able to destroy his respect and affection for men, even ordinary post-lapsarian men, for he speaks (surprisingly, if we take the professed theme of *Paradise Lost* too literally) of 'the cheerful ways of men' still. All this, as we shall see, is related to the underlying poetic theme of the poem, as distinct from its overt logical and theo-logical argument. On the theological surface, Milton justifies the ways of God to men by arguing that Adam and Eve abused the free-will with which they were endowed and so deserved a much worse punishment than they in fact received, while the Christian scheme of redemption showed God bringing good out of evil. At the deeper poetic level *Paradise Lost* suggests that the Fall was necessary, not because of the *felix culpa* which enabled God to bring good from evil, but because only in conditions of change and struggle could there emerge any kind of human virtue in which Milton could really believe.

After the invocation, Milton proceeds to describe God con-templating His works from His high heavenly throne, surrounded by the hierarchies of His angels. He looks down on 'our two first Parents' in Eden,

> yet the onely two
> Of mankind, in the happie Garden plac't,
> Reaping immortal fruits of joy and love,
> Uninterrupted joy, unrivald love
> In blissful solitude.

It was a fine stroke to have the first description of Eden simple and general, yet highly charged; 'the happie Garden' carries a world of meaning in its elemental suggestiveness. The discussion that follows is less successful. Milton is versifying parts of his *De Doctrina Christiana*, making God insist on man's free-will and responsibility in spite of God's omnipotence and foreknowledge. God foresees that Adam will fall (which makes subsequent deliberation in Heaven about ways of preventing his fall singularly otiose), and with an insistent literalness Milton must remind the reader that when God speaks to the Son of the possibility of Adam's fall, God already foreknows it :

> . . . Thus to his onely Son foreseeing spake.

A similar tactless literalism leads Milton to make God address His Son by his full Christian theological title : Christ is God's only begotten son, so God opens His speech to him thus :

> Onely begotten Son, seest thou what rage
> Transports our adversarie, . . .

Milton wants to achieve divine dignity and formality to set against the exhibitionist heroics of the fallen angels' speeches ; but the result is curiously stilted. The verse in these passages of divine argument is, however, supple and adroitly manipulated. It is not on technical points of versification that Milton falls down in Book III ; it is rather that here he is committing himself to logic in order to achieve his poetic intention, so that the reader, however much he wishes to read *Paradise Lost* 'as a poem', is forced to read it at this point as logical argument, and to answer back as he reads. It is no use for critics to tell us that this is an epic poem, to be read as such, and if we want to see Milton's logical arguments about free-will and other points we must go to the *De Doctrina*. Milton himself here forces the argument on us *as an argument*, and if we see weaknesses in it our whole participation in the poem momentarily lessens. With God continually giving the logical rather than the poetic answer to all the doubts we feel about the fairness of allowing an innocent couple to be so cunningly tempted and then drastically punishing both them and their descendants, we are forced to examine the arguments adduced, and as they are far from invulnerable, the poem suffers. It would be tedious to devote space here to pointing out the contradictions and inadequacies in Milton's formal case for God, though it might be mentioned that there is no *logical* answer to the question of evil existing in a world ruled by a power who is both omnipotent and benevolent. Man could have been created with a will both strong and free; in *Paradise Regained* Milton has God say

> He [Satan] now shall know I can produce a man
> Of femal Seed, far abler to resist
> All his solicitations,

which suggests that Adam was an early and inferior model. But perhaps the most disturbing aspect of the case which Milton makes God argue in Book III of *Paradise Lost* is his handling of the question of vicarious atonement. God predicts man's fall, and says that after his fall

> Hee with his whole posteritie must die,
> Die hee or Justice must; unless for him
> Som other able, and as willing, pay
> The rigid satisfaction, death for death.

Quite apart from the knotty point suggested here about the position of Justice (is Justice above God, a force which binds God against His inclination?), this picture of a judge telling the court after a murderer has been found guilty that in order that justice be done somebody, the guilty man or some member of the jury or the public, must be hanged—it doesn't matter who, so long as there is a hanging—is very far from the Christian doctrine of atonement. Clearly, Milton's heart was not fully in this sort of justification, whatever he might have consciously thought. His poetic instinct was better than his logical powers, and the true justification of the ways of God to men in *Paradise Lost* lies in the way in which it emerges as the poem develops that virtue can only be achieved by struggle, that the Fall was inevitable because a passive and ignorant virtue, without the challenge of an imperfect world, cannot release the true potentialities of human greatness. Of course, the cost of making such a release possible was enormous; but that was part of the nature of things and the paradox of the human condition.

Nevertheless, Book III has its fine poetic moments. The moving cadences of the Son's speech in reply to God's first announcement of the impending fall of man, and man's culpable responsibility for that fall, shows how effectively Milton can employ and vary the simple device of repetition:

> For should Man finally be lost, should Man
> Thy creature late so lov'd, thy youngest Son
> Fall circumvented thus by fraud, though joind
> With his own folly? that be from thee farr,
> That farr be from thee, Father, who are Judge
> Of all things made, and judgest only right.

A similar device is used in God's answer to the Son, but the effect is quite different. The repetition of 'me' in the following lines serves to emphasize God's knowledge of His own omnipotence and of man's total dependence on Him:

> Man shall not quite be lost, but sav'd who will,
> Yet not of will in him, but grace in mee
> Freely vouchsaf't; once more I will renew
> His lapsed powers, though forfeit and enthralld
> By sin to foul exorbitant desires;
> Upheld by me, yet once more he shall stand
> On even ground against his mortal foe,
> By me upheld, that he may know how frail
> His fall'n condition is, and to mee owe
> All his deliv'rance, and to none but me.

This almost suggests that if free-will existed in man before the Fall, it did not exist in him afterwards. In Book I of the *De Doctrina* Milton attempts to reconcile God's election of some few men by His grace with freedom of the will, but the argument, though ingenious, is unsatisfactory. As enunciated in Book III of *Paradise Lost*, the argument is no less confusing; the lines beginning

> Some I have chosen of peculiar grace
> Elect above the rest; so is my will:

which follow immediately on those quoted above show Milton

trying hard to reconcile several conflicting elements in Christian thought. But their main poetic interest lies in the sense of power and control which pervades God's idiom as contrasted with the warmer and more emotional tone of the Son. God may tell the Son that the latter has spoken 'as my thoughts are, all / As my Eternal purpose hath decreed', but the tone of their conversation emerges more as that of debate than as that of announcement of agreed truths. One of the troubles with Milton's God is that, unlike the God of the Bible, He is not content to announce, but He must go on to argue. Modern criticism has tended to pooh-pooh this traditional quarrel with Milton's portrait of the deity, but no candid reader can fail to see the force of it.

The other difficulty with the heavenly scenes in *Paradise Lost* is that Milton tended to be too detailed in his anthropomorphism. As we have observed, the nonsensical charge that he lacked a specific visual imagery (as though specific visual imagery was always essential to great poetry) is irrelevant, and particularly so here, where the trouble is that there is too much visual imagery. If Milton had been content, as he was in the magnificent description of Eden, to use large general terms highly charged with the appropriate emotion as a result of their cadence and tone and of the whole poetic movement of the context, he would have done better. Abstract images of light and joy would have rendered God more effectively than literal anthropormorphic description and earnest defensive arguments put into His mouth. Sometimes we almost feel that Milton had too little sense of the numinous.

The Son's offer to become man and suffer man's punishment for Him—'Be thou in *Adams* room' is how God sums it up—is followed by his exaltation and celebration. It is interesting that in Milton's view Christ is exalted to God's level as a reward for good behaviour, as it were:

> . . . because in thee
> Love hath abounded more than Glory abounds,
> Therefore thy Humiliation shall exalt
> With thee thy Manhood also to this Throne;
> Here shalt thou sit incarnate, here shalt Reign
> Both God and Man, Son both of God and Man,
> Anointed universal King; all Power
> I give thee, . . .

The hailing of the Son by the angelic host makes it clear that in a purely formal sense—but only in a purely formal sense—he is the hero of the poem. It is he who by voluntarily offering himself to 'be in Adam's room' enables God to bring good out of evil. Yet he plays far too small a part in *Paradise Lost* to be the real hero. One must distinguish, as so often in the poem, between the overt intention and the underlying poetic meaning. According to the overt intention, Christ is the hero and Adam merely the object of conflict between God and Satan—the Troy of this epic. But such an interpretation is contradicted at every point; ultimately, in terms of the fully realized poetic meaning, Adam is the hero; his and Eve's recovery and their going out in the end to face an uncertain and testing future constitute the final heroic act.

The verse in Book III gains in liveliness and complexity when Milton turns from the scene in Heaven to show Satan making his way towards Eden. Metaphor and simile leap into life, and all the known, tarnished world of fallen man is pressed into service to give richness and moral implication to Satan's behaviour. Satan lands on the sun, and from there contemplates the universe; there, too, he meets Uriel, whom he questions about the direction of Adam's abode, having first disguised himself as 'a stripling Cherube'. The priggish way in which he informs Uriel that he wants to find Adam's home in order to admire and to find a further reason for praising God is matched by the tone of Uriel's reply, which is rather like that of a headmaster speaking to a boy who has asked for extra homework:

> Faire Angel, thy desire which tends to know
> The works of God, thereby to glorifie
> The great Work-Maister, leads to no excess
> That reaches blame, but rather merits praise
> The more it seems excess, . . .

It is hard to believe that Milton was not conscious of the note almost of parody here. The situation is all the more ironical because the stripling cherub is really Satan, undetectable as such by Uriel:

> For neither Man nor Angel can discern
> Hypocrisie, the onely evil that walks
> Invisible, except to God alone, . . .

This excuses Uriel; but should it not also excuse Eve, who had no power to discern Satan's hypocrisy or to see through the serpent disguise to the true character behind? When, in *Paradise Regained*, Christ is tempted by Satan he knows all along that it is Satan whom he is dealing with; but Eve believes that she is talking to a genuine serpent whose powers of speech have been acquired as a result of eating of the forbidden tree. Man hardly seems to have had a fair deal.

Uriel, unsuspecting, points out Paradise to the disguised Satan, and it is significant that we should first see Paradise through Satan's eyes:

> That spot to which I point is *Paradise*,
> *Adams* abode, those loftie shades his Bowr.

The splendid emphatic quality of this simple demonstrative statement focuses both on the gesture of the pointer and on the vision of the beholder for whom he is pointing. It is the second reference to the Garden of Eden so far; the first mentioned simply 'the happie Garden', and this is equally forceful and appropriate in its elemental generality. In Book IV Milton brings us nearer and nearer to Eden, still looking through Satan's eyes, until finally we are close enough to look into the garden and see our first parents in all their primal dignity.

A new kind of excitement manifests itself in the poem with Satan's arrival at Eden in Book IV. As we see Paradise, in all its unfallen glory, through Satan's eyes we are aware of a complex moral symbolism at work. Satan, in his speech to the sun, has already revealed the frustrations and contradictions of his inner state; his tortured soliloquy is both morally and psychologically illuminating, and ends with a desperate and irrational cry of 'Evil be thou my Good'. At the same time (as Dr. Rajan has shown) it helps to modulate Satan down from the grand energetic figure of Books I and II to the more familiar tempter and perverter. So also his description in lines 183 to 192, in which he is compared to a prowling wolf attacking sheep and a thief breaking into a rich burgher's house, with the culminating line of monosyllables,

> So clomb this first grand Thief into Gods Fold,

helps to reduce Satan to the level of the cunning deceiver, the guileful tempter warned against by generations of Christian preachers. The new tone is set in lines 120–122 :

> ... Each perturbation smooth'd with outward calm,
> Artificer of fraud ; and was the first
> That practis'd falsehood under saintly shew, ...

The description of Eden is built up with deliberate suspense. All human longings for an ideal garden are suggested by Milton's employment of many different mythological elements together with contemporary notions of garden beauty (though Eden represented natural, not artificial, beauty, with no sign of 'nice Art / In Beds and curious Knots' but only profuse Nature), keeping on and on, sustaining and varying image and reference until the picture of ideal nature almost bursts with its own richness. The bursting is prevented by the careful punctuation of the description with grand elemental phrases, 'A happy rural seat of various view', 'Flowrs of all hue, and without Thorn the Rose'. Finally, the camera, which has already climbed up over Eden's steep sides and then roved round the luxuriance of the garden, picks out (but again the lens is Satan's eye) the great prelapsarian couple, the only man and woman ever to have walked in complete innocence and true human dignity :

> Two of far nobler shape erect and tall,
> Godlike erect, with native Honour clad
> In naked Majestie seemd Lords of all,
> And worthie seemd, for in thir looks Divine
> The image of thir glorious Maker shon,
> Truth, Wisdom, Sanctitude severe and pure,
> Severe, but in true filial freedom plac't ; ...

For all the large generalities in which this description is (very properly) couched, Milton is making specific points about man's place in creation, about woman's relation to man, and about the part played by sex in man's unfallen state. 'Hee for God only, shee for God in him', a line which has often been taken as evidence of Milton's anti-feminism, is of course the expression of a commonplace of contemporary and earlier thought. More interesting is

Milton's repeated emphasis on sex, on Eve's nakedness, on the beauty and propriety of unfallen sexuality. The pair come nearer and nearer to the camera, and then move off across the screen, as it were, Milton following them with a benedictory statement of their greatness and uniqueness:

> So passd they naked on, nor shunnd the sight
> Of God or Angel, for they thought no ill:
> So hand in hand they passd, the loveliest pair
> That ever since in loves imbraces met,
> *Adam* the goodliest man of men since born
> His Sons, the fairest of her Daughters *Eve*.

Nature, both animal and vegetable, is described with an almost baroque luxuriance, but a heraldic formality controls the profusion and prevents any suggestion of the florid:

> About them frisking playd
> All Beasts of th' Earth, since wild, and of all chase
> In Wood or Wilderness, Forrest or Den;
> Sporting the Lion rampd, and in his paw
> Dandl'd the Kid; Bears, Tigers, Ounces, Pards
> Gambold before them, th' unwieldy Elephant
> To make them mirth us'd all his might, and wreath'd
> His Lithe Proboscis; close the Serpent sly
> Insinuating, wove with Gordian twine
> His beaded train, and of his fatal guile
> Gave proof unheeded; others on the grass
> Coucht, and now filld with pasture gazing sat,
> Or Bedward ruminating: . . .

This half-humorous picture of the innocence of the animal world before the change wrought by the Fall emphasizes the fact that the only way we can now imagine such a scene is as both naïve and grotesque. Thus both vegetable profusion and animal life are described in Eden with an appropriate kind of symbolic simplicity, while such a phenomenon as sunset in Paradise is presented with a cosmic largeness which suggests that scenes in the postlapsarian world are pettier and less involved in a whole cosmic pattern:

for the Sun
Declin'd was hasting now with prone career
To th' Ocean Iles, and in th' ascending Scale
Of Heav'n the Starrs that usher Ev'ning rose : . . .

And later :

Mean while in utmost Longitude, where Heav'n
With Earth and Ocean meets, the setting Sun
Slowly descending, and with right aspect
Against the eastern Gate of Paradise
Leveld his ev'ning Rays : . . .

Satan's tortured speech on beholding the happy pair in their
innocent affection marks a further stage in his degeneration. At
first he pretends to pity them, and in a confused and indeed
almost meaningless outburst tries to maintain the note of political
necessity he had used with his own followers :

Ah gentle pair, ye little think how nigh
Your change approaches, when all these delights
Will vanish and deliver ye to woe,
More woe, the more your taste is now of joy ;
Happie, but for so happie ill secur'd
Long to continue, and this high seat your Heav'n
Ill fenc't for Heav'n to keep out such a foe
As now is enterd ; yet no purpos'd foe
To you whom I could pittie thus forlorne
Though I unpittied : League with you I seek,
And mutual amitie so strait, so close,
That I with you must dwell, or you with me
Henceforth ; . . .

But later, after hearing the gentle dignity of Adam and Eve's
mutual conversation, he looks at them 'with jealous leer maligne'
and savours with bitter joy the prospect of their destruction
through his cunning. He has learned of the fatal tree and its
prohibition from their own conversation, and there is a complex
irony in having Satan discover the one way in which he can
succeed in his plan from their obsessive interest in that 'one

easie prohibition' which, it seems, they cannot help talking about. Indeed nearly everybody in *Paradise Lost* seems to be obsessed with that one prohibition. God talks about it continually, and in the very first speech which Adam makes to Eve he comes to it almost at once :

> Sole partner and sole part of all these joys,
> Dearer thy self than all; needs must the Power
> That made us, and for us this ample World
> Be infinitly good, and of his good
> As liberal and free as infinite,
> That rais'd us from the dust and plac'd us here
> In all this happiness, who at his hand
> Have nothing merited, nor can performe
> Aught whereof he hath need, hee who requires
> From us no other service than to keep
> This one, this easie charge, of all the Trees
> In Paradise that beare delicious fruit
> So various, not to taste that onely Tree
> Of Knowledge, planted by the Tree of Life, . . .

The primal dignity and courtesy of Adam's speech is effectively rendered, and Eve's reply, though couched in similar terms, has a tone of its own, more liquid, more feminine. Her account of her experiences immediately after her creation—and in particular of her almost falling in love with her own reflection in a lake—has a winning innocence which is differentiated from Adam's more self-conscious dignity. It may be that Milton intended hers to symbolize woman's inherent vanity; but the effect is rather to emphasize Eve's lack of knowledge of the world, her naïve charm, her simple trust in experience, her vulnerability. Later, when she is on the point of being fooled by Satan in the guise of the serpent, Milton calls her '*Eve* our credulous Mother'.

The scenes between Adam and Eve in Book IV are some of the most charming and fragrant in the poem. They talk together against the background of a paradisial evening :

> Now came still Ev'ning on, and Twilight gray
> Had in her sober Liverie all things clad;
> Silence accompanied, for Beast and Bird,

> They to thir grassie Couch, these to thir Nests
> Were slunk, all but the wakeful Nightingale;
> Shee all night long her amorous descant sung;
> Silence was pleas'd: now glowd the Firmament
> With living Saphirs: *Hesperus* that led
> The starrie Host, rode brightest, till the Moon
> Rising in clouded Majestie, at length
> Apparent Queen unveild her peerless light,
> And ore the dark her Silver Mantle threw.

They talk about labour and repose, and in doing so illustrate Milton's dilemma in having to accept the scriptural view that labour was imposed on man as a curse after the Fall. 'Man hath his daily work of body or mind / Appointed,' Adam explains to Eve, speaking for Milton, for whom the daily round of labour and the thought of appointed work well done were always symbolic of all that was most satisfying in human experience. A life of pure contemplation was as difficult for Milton to praise as a fugitive and cloistered virtue: it might be said that the contemplative tradition of Christian thought was the one European tradition that Milton was unable to work into his great synthesis. Though he had spent so many years in quiet preparation for his own poetic achievement, he never regarded these years, either at the time or later, as a period devoted to contemplation merely. He would have been happier to see Adam and Eve really working in that garden, not merely trimming its luxuriant abundance for lack of anything better to do—for lack of imperfections to remedy and evils to struggle against. Though he succeeds in giving magnificent expression to the state of innocent dignity in which Adam and Eve lived before the Fall, he is unable to make their daily life convincing, because he cannot really believe in it. As Rose Macaulay once remarked, if Milton had been in Adam's place he would have eaten of the forbidden tree and then written a pamphlet to prove that his act was right and necessary.

The lilt and balance of Eve's speech have often been noted, and nowhere are these qualities better shown than in Eve's quietly eloquent expression of love for her husband, which stands out as a delicate love poem embedded in the text of the epic:

Sweet is the breath of morn, her rising sweet,
With charm of earliest Birds; pleasant the Sun
When first on this delightful Land he spreads
His orient Beams, on herb, tree, fruit, and flowr,
Glistring with dew; fragrant the fertil earth
After soft showers; and sweet the coming on
Of grateful Ev'ning mild, then silent Night
With this her solemn Bird and this fair Moon,
And these the Gemms of Heav'n, her starrie train:
But neither breath of Morn when she ascends
With charm of earliest Birds, nor rising Sun
On this delightful land, nor herb, fruit, flowr,
Glistring with dew, nor fragrance after showers,
Nor grateful Ev'ning mild, nor silent Night
With this her solemn Bird, nor walk by Moon,
Or glittering Starr-light without thee is sweet.

The theme is simple enough, and has long been a stock one in love poetry from the mediaeval lyric to the love songs of Hollywood—nature is beautiful, but without the loved one its beauty is meaningless. Any less simple and elemental a theme would have been inappropriate in this primal and innocent expression of love.

When Adam and Eve retire for the night, Milton hails wedded love, in which innocent sexuality gets free and proper play, and contrasts it with mere lust on the one hand and on the other with the artificial sighings and servitudes of the courtly love tradition. It is one of the strongest expressions of Milton's views of the place of sex, and makes clear once and for all that his views were far from those conventionally labelled Puritan:

Haile wedded Love, mysterious Law, true source
Of human offspring, sole proprietie,
In Paradise of all things common else.
By thee adulterous lust was driv'n from men
Among the bestial herds to range, by thee
Founded in Reason, Loyal, Just and Pure,
Relations dear, and all the Charities
Of Father, Son, and Brother first were known.
Farr be it, that I should write thee sin or blame,
Or think thee unbefitting holiest place,

Perpetual Fountain of Domestic sweets,
Whose bed is undefil'd and chaste pronounc't,
Present or past, as Saints and Patriarchs us'd.
Here Love his golden shafts imploys, here lights
His constant Lamp, and waves his purple wings,
Reigns here and revels; not in the bought smile
Of Harlots, loveless, joyless, unindear'd,
Casual fruition, nor in Court Amours
Mixt Dance or wanton Mask, or Midnight Bal,
Or Serenate which the starv'd Lover sings
To his proud fair, best quitted with disdain.

And then he turns to contemplate his sleeping lovers:

These lulled by Nightingales imbracing slept,
And on thir naked limbs the flowrie roof
Showrd Roses, which the Morn repaird. Sleep on,
Blest pair; and O yet happiest if ye seek
No happier state, and know to know no more.

The emotion rises and comes to a climax with 'Sleep on, Blest pair', where we can almost hear the catch in Milton's throat as he thinks of what the future has in store.

Satan's further adventures, though fraught with the promise of evil, seem stagey and hollow after this. His squatting like a toad by Eve's ear to give her corrupting dreams is merely nasty (though this weakening of Eve's will in sleep is surely something for which she cannot be held responsible?), and his haughty boast to Gabriel when discovered—

Know ye not then said *Satan*, filld with scorn
Know ye not mee? ye knew me once no mate
For you, there sitting where ye durst not soar;
Not to know mee argues your selves unknown,

—sounds forced and theatrical, as it is meant to. Gabriel punctures Satan's rhetoric with a sharp exposure of his self-contradictions, and their flyting concludes with a curious image, derived from both Homer and Isaiah, of God weighing Satan's lot in the celestial balances, so that

> The Fiend lookd up and knew
> His mounted scale aloft : nor more ; but fled
> Murmuring, and with him fled the shades of night.

An epic combat between Gabriel and Satan would have been
wholly inappropriate at this stage, and Milton contrives to end
the argument with a demonstration of God's superior power and
the temporary frustration of Satan. The book ends on a note of
sullen darkness, full of foreboding, which is fitting enough ; yet
having seen a demonstration of God's intervention we are inevitably reminded again of the whole question of why God should
stand idly by and allow Satan to corrupt and destroy His creatures, a question which Milton should not have allowed to emerge
at this point.

Book V opens with a description of dawn in Paradise and the
awakening of Adam and Eve. Eve tells Adam the nightmare she
has had (inspired, we are left to assume, by Satan, and fore-
shadowing the temptation and Fall), and the strange, trance-like
atmosphere of a bad dream is very finely captured :

>   methought
> Close at mine ear one calld me forth to walk
> With gentle voice, I thought it thine ; it said,
> Why sleepst thou *Eve* ? now is the pleasant time,
> The cool, the silent, save where silence yields
> To the night-warbling Bird, that now awake
> Tunes sweetest his love-labord song ; now reigns
> Full Orbd the Moon, and with more pleasing light
> Shaddowie sets off the face of things ; in vain,
> If none regard ; Heav'n wakes with all his eyes,
> Whom to behold but thee, Natures desire,
> In whose sight all things joy, with ravishment
> Attracted by thy beauty still to gaze.
> I rose as at thy call, but found thee not ;
> To find thee I directed then my walk ;
> And on, methought, alone I passd through ways
> That brought me on a sudden to the Tree
> Of interdicted Knowledge : fair it seemd,
> Much fairer to my Fancie than by day :
> And as I wondring lookd, beside it stood
> One shap'd and wingd like one of those from Heav'n

By us oft seen; his dewie locks distilld
Ambrosia; on that Tree he also gaz'd;
And O fair Plant, said he, with fruit surcharg'd,
Deigns none to ease thy load and taste thy sweet,
Nor God, nor Man; is Knowledge so despis'd?
Or envie or what reserve forbids to taste?
Forbid who will, none shall from me withhold
Longer thy offerd good, why else set here?
This said he paus'd not, but with ventrous Arme
He pluckd, he tasted; mee damp horror chilld
At such bold words voucht with a deed so bold:
But hee thus overjoyd, O Fruit Divine,
Sweet of thy self, but much more sweet thus cropt,
Forbidden here, it seems, as onely fit
For Gods, yet able to make Gods of Men:
And why not Gods of Men, since good, the more
Communicated, more abundant grows,
The Author not impaird, but honourd more?
Here, happie Creature, fair Angelic *Eve*,
Partake thou also; happie though thou art,
Happier thou mayst be, worthier canst not be:
Taste this, and be henceforth among the Gods
Thy self a Goddess, not to Earth confin'd,
But sometimes in the Air, as wee, somtimes
Ascend to Heav'n, by merit thine, and see
What life the Gods live there, and such live thou.
So saying, he drew nigh, and to me held,
Ev'n to my mouth of that same fruit held part
Which he had pluckt; the pleasant savourie smell
So quickend appetite, that I, methought,
Could not but taste. Forthwith up to the Clouds
With him I flew, and underneath beheld
The Earth outstretcht immense, a prospect wide
And various: wondring at my flight and change
To this high exaltation: suddenly
My Guide was gon, and I, me thought, sunk down,
And fell asleep; but O how glad I wak'd
To find this but a dream!

This is the authentic accent of nightmare, with its abrupt transitions and shifts of perspective and the final immense relief on awakening to find it all but a dream. Adam cheers her, and they then join, like good English Puritans, in 'unmeditated' prayer, a prayer in which Milton weaves together themes from the Psalms and notions from classical and mediaeval astronomy. The scene then moves to Heaven, to show God, moved by pity at the prospect before Adam and Eve, deciding to send Raphael down to give them a final warning. But as God has foreknowledge of the Fall and has already told His angelic host that it will take place, this action seems quite meaningless. All it can achieve is to make the pair more culpable in that they will fall after an extra warning, and surely it is an odd sign of pity to take steps to make the people whom you pity more culpable and so deserving of worse punishment than they would otherwise be. This kind of thought is forced on the reader by Milton's falling back on the argumentative style, bringing in discussion of free-will again that he had employed in the earlier scene in Heaven.

Raphael's descent gives Milton the opportunity of painting one of his finest prelapsarian portraits, that of unfallen man, in all the dignity of innocent nakedness, greeting an angelic guest:

> Mean while our Primitive great Sire, to meet
> His god-like Guest, walks forth, without more train
> Accompanied than with his own complete
> Perfections, in himself was all his state,
> More solemn than the tedious pomp that waits
> On Princes, when thir rich Retinue long
> Of Horses led and Grooms besmear'd with Gold
> Dazles the crowd, and sets them all agape.

Eve, too, is described again in her innocent and naked beauty:

> but *Eve*
> Undeckt, save with her self more lovely fair
> Than Wood-Nymph, or the fairest Goddess feignd
> Of three that in Mount *Ida* naked strove,
> Stood to entertain her guest from Heav'n; . . .

In both descriptions simile is used for the purpose of contrast. Unclothed Adam has more dignity than can be conferred by all the luxurious trappings and ceremonies with which fallen man loads himself, and naked Eve is more beautiful than the utmost which the pagan imagination can conceive. There is a moral as well as a descriptive purpose at work here.

The open-air feast to which Raphael is invited is culled from Nature and requires no cooking or other artificial treatment: 'No fear lest Dinner cool'. This phrase is not gauche, or awkward with the awkwardness of Wordsworth at his most banal, which it has been taken to be by some of those very critics who at the same time reproach Milton with being consistently grandiloquent and organ-voiced. The humour is intended, the domestic simplicity of the language employed for a deliberate effect. Milton is glancing with humorous irony at some of the unnecessary troubles of fallen man, the fretfulness of cooks and housewives while guests, absorbed in conversation, allow the meal to cool. The world of kitchen worries and dining-room tragedies is very far from Eden.

Milton is fascinated at his mental image of naked Eve ministering in complete innocence to her husband and their angelic guest, and comes back to it again and again:

> Mean while at Table *Eve*
> Ministerd naked, and thir flowing cups
> With pleasant liquors crownd: O innocence
> Deserving Paradise!

The conversation between Adam and Raphael, full of respectful attention on the one hand and of friendly advice and information on the other, shows how flexibly Milton could handle his blank verse in discussion and exposition (as opposed to argument, where he tends to be less happy, as we have seen). But Raphael's account of the war in Heaven, which occupies part of Book V and all of Book VI, is poetically the least original part of *Paradise Lost*. There is an inherent difficulty in a situation where one of the protagonists is Almighty God, all-knowing and all-powerful, who can bring anything to pass merely by willing it. Military conflicts seem purposeless, and God's deliberations on what to do ('Nearly it now concerns us to be sure / Of our omnipotence') appear absurd. In the same way the posting of angelic guards round Eden to prevent Satan's entry, when God has already told the angels that Satan will enter and successfully tempt Adam and Eve, is mere gesturing. Even the building up of Abdiel into a hero as the

only one of Satan's group to defy him to his face seems pointless :
what was Abdiel doing among Satan's host anyway ? The nearer
Milton approaches the defiances and conflicts of classical epic
the less convincing *Paradise Lost* is. Angelologists like Professor
Lewis can argue that the wounds suffered by the angels in the
conflict are perfectly consistent with Milton's conception of the
angelic nature, but that is beside the point. The whole physical
conflict, which falls between allegory and history, is misconceived.
There are memorable descriptive passages in this part of the poem,
but they do not possess the rich suggestive power of other parts.
Raphael's account of the Creation in Book VII is more poetically
effective, with Milton drawing ingeniously on imagery from
Genesis, the Psalms, Proverbs, Job and Plato, but here too the
poem is marking time, its true progress is halted. We return to the
true Miltonic poetic texture in Book VIII, where Adam tells
Raphael of his own experiences after his creation.

Book VII marks the beginning of the second half of *Paradise
Lost* ('Half yet remains unsung') and Milton gathers his forces
again before proceeding with an account of the Creation. As
always before turning to a new phase of the poem, he invokes
divine aid again and introduces the personal note :

> Descend from Heav'n *Urania*, by that name
> If rightly thou art calld, whose Voice divine
> Following, above th' *Olympian* Hill I soar,
> Above the flight of *Pegasean* wing.
> The meaning not the Name I call : for thou
> Nor of the Muses nine, nor on the top
> Of old *Olympus* dwellst, but Heav'nlie born.
> Before the Hills appear'd, or Fountain flowd,
> Thou with Eternal wisdom didst converse,
> Wisdom thy Sister, and with her didst play
> In presence of th' Almightie Father; pleas'd
> With thy Celestial Song.

Milton is associating his divine Muse with the Wisdom of Proverbs
(viii, 30) and of the *Wisdom of Solomon*, interpreting the passage in
Proverbs in which Wisdom speaks ('and I was daily his delight,
rejoicing always before him') in the light of the original Hebrew
meaning of the word translated in the Authorized Version as

'rejoicing' but also having connotations of a child's playing. There is no foundation whatever for Professor Saurat's elaborate Cabalistic interpretation of the lines.

Milton's sense of himself as poet, and of his own personal circumstances, rises up, with a familiar reference to the fate of Orpheus and a contrast between the divine and the secular Muse:

> Standing on Earth, not rapt above the Pole,
> More safe I Sing with mortal voice, unchang'd
> To hoarce or mute, though fall'n on evil days,
> On evil days though fall'n, and evil tongues;
> In darkness, and with dangers compast round,
> And solitude; yet not alone, while thou
> Visitst my slumbers Nightly, or when Morn
> Purples the East: still govern thou my Song,
> *Urania*, and fit audience find, though few.
> But drive farr off the barbarous dissonance
> Of *Bacchus* and his revellers, the Race
> Of that wilde Rout that tore the *Thracian* Bard
> In *Rhodope*, where Woods and Rocks had Eares
> To rapture, till the savage clamor drownd
> Both Harp and Voice; nor could the Muse defend
> Her Son. So fail not thou, who thee implores:
> For thou are Heav'nlie, shee an empty dream.

Parts of the account of the Creation are little more than a skilful padding out of the biblical narrative, but occasionally the blending of several biblical sources with Platonic and other notions produces an impressive description, and the imagery is often arresting in its combination of stylized movement with heraldic colour and form:

> The grassie Clods now Calv'd, now half appear'd
> The Tawnie Lion, pawing to get free
> His hinder parts, then springs as broke from Bonds,
> And Rampant shakes his Brinded mane; the Ounce,
> The Libbard and the Tiger, as the Moale
> Rising, the crumbl'd Earth above them threw
> In Hillocks; the swift Stag from under ground
> Bore up his branching head: . . .

In Book VIII, in the words of the prose 'argument' which Milton prefixed to each book, 'Adam inquires concerning celestial Motions, is doubtfully answer'd, and exhorted to search rather things more worthy of knowledg.' The Humanist and the Christian are not fully reconciled in the arguments brought forward here, though Milton's dilemma is far from original with him and he employs the long familiar distinction between vain knowledge and proper knowledge, which was self-knowledge. (The background of the whole question of forbidden knowledge in the seventeenth century has been carefully assembled by Professor Howard Schultz in his *Milton and Forbidden Knowledge*.)

Raphael's astronomical information hovers 'doubtfully' between the different systems known in the seventeenth century, with many hypothetical questions and suppositions. 'What if that light . . . be as a Starr . . . ?', '. . . other suns perhaps with thir attendant Moons . . . ;', 'whether thus these things or whether not' —hardly a satisfactory account from a superior being to an inferior. Milton, of course, was bound by the extent of his own knowledge of these subjects; but as he was professing to illustrate angelic wisdom he would have done better to suggest the whole matter in more abstract terms. However, a poet who had not hesitated to tell us exactly what God in His divine wisdom spoke in moments of profound deliberation could hardly be expected to boggle at angelic discourse. The conclusion is more Christian than Humanist:

> Solicit not thy thoughts with matters hid,
> Leave them to God above, him serve and fear; . . .
>   be lowlie wise:
> Think onely what concernes thee and thy being;
> Dream not of other Worlds, what Creatures there
> Live, in what state, condition or degree,
> Contented that thus farr hath been reveal'd
> Not of Earth onely but of Highest Heav'n.

And Adam declares himself satisfied, agreeing that

>   to know
> That which before us lies in daily life,
> Is the prime Wisdom.

The importance Milton attached to turning to the task at hand and avoiding worry about long-term possibilities is reflected in much of his early work, as we have seen; here it is given a new twist by being attached to the argument against vain speculation.

Adam's account of his first days on earth (given at Raphael's request, because the archangel had been absent on the day of man's creation, is full of lively and charming touches, of which one of the most attractive is the conversation between God and Adam on the question of a mate. God asks Adam how he is getting on, and Adam, with some trepidation, points out that it is no fun being alone:

> In solitude
> What happiness, who can enjoy alone,
> Or all enjoying, what contentment find?

God replies 'as with a smile' that Adam is not solitary at all:

> is not the Earth
> With various living creatures, and the Aire
> Replenisht, and all these at thy command
> To come and play before thee, . . . ?

To this Adam firmly though humbly points out that animals are not his equals, and

> Among unequals what societie
> Can sort, what harmonie or true delight?

God then proceeds to tease Adam:

> A nice and suttle happiness I see
> Thou to thyself proposest, in the choice
> Of thy Associates *Adam*, and wilt taste
> No pleasure, though in pleasure, solitarie.
> What thinkst thou then of mee, and this my State,
> Seem I to thee sufficiently possest
> Of happiness, or not? who am alone
> From all Eternitie, for none I know
> Second to me or like, equal much less.

Adam, who has not quite the courage to say, 'Don't be a tease, God,' patiently answers this argument too. God is all perfect in Himself, and needs no companion; man is different; he requires 'collateral love, and dearest amitie'. In the end God admits that He had been teasing all the time:

> Thus farr to try thee *Adam*, I was pleas'd,
> And finde thee knowing not of Beasts alone,
> Which thou hast rightly nam'd, but of thy self,
> Expressing well the spirit within thee free,
> My Image, not imparted to the Brute,
> Whose fellowship therefore unmeet for thee
> Good reason was thou freely shouldst dislike,
> And be so minded still; . . .

And He goes on to tell Adam that He had all along intended to give him a mate. The half-humorous anthropomorphism here is more attractive than the more ambitious anthropomorphism of the scenes in Heaven.

In talking of his first encounter with Eve, Adam whips himself up into an excited account of her beauty and its power over him. This is psychologically sound and poetically effective, and when the chiding voice of Raphael breaks in to remind Adam that man is the superior being, that whatever happens Adam must never allow his reason to be overcome, that

> In loving thou dost well, in passion not,

the scene becomes dramatic, not merely argumentative or didactic. The distinction between true love and irrational passion, as between sacred and profane love, was a common enough Renaissance theme, and Milton was here enunciating a moral commonplace. It is nevertheless central in his poem, and it is introduced here in such a way as to give it maximum life and force. True love, and sexual union (for Milton held that true love was not necessarily above sex), existed among the angels, Raphael tells Adam, as well as among men; indeed, the angels can unite more fully than man and woman can, because of their more rarefied bodies:

                                    if Spirits embrace,
         Total they mix, Union of Pure with Pure
         Desiring.

Yet immediately after this exaltation of sex to an angelic if not a
divine principle, Raphael repeats his warning about passion and
reason :

                    take heed lest Passion sway
         Thy Judgement to do aught, which else free Will
         Would not admit; thine and of all thy Sons
         The weal or woe in thee is plac't; beware.

   Book IX is one of the great books. After a brief introduction,
in which Milton, as he approaches the crisis of his poem, proclaims that his theme is not less but more heroic than the conventional themes of epics, we turn to Adam and Eve and find them
having a sweetly courteous difference of opinion about the
propriety of Eve's gardening alone in another part of Eden that
morning for a change. We are left to assume, though this is never
stated, that this suggestion was put into Eve's mind by Satan
when he lay by her ear in the form of a toad as she slept the
previous night. But neither she nor Adam is yet fallen, and the
quiet grace of their discourse illustrates at its best a quality which
Milton always tried to bring into his verse when describing the
behaviour and conversation of the pair before the Fall. When
Adam consents to let Eve go, knowing that 'thy stay, not free,
absents thee more', we feel that Eve, having, woman-fashion, won
her point, does not really want to act on it and she only goes
because she feels her previous insistence makes it necessary that
she should. They part reluctantly, and as Eve slowly slides her
hand out of her husband's Milton uses the richest resources of
classical mythology to dwell for the last time on her innocence
and beauty :

         Thus saying, from her Husbands hand her hand
         Soft she withdrew, and like a Wood-Nymph light
         Oread or *Dryad*, or of *Delia's* Train,
         Betook her to the Groves, but *Delia's* self
         In gait surpassd and Goddess-like deport,
         Though not as shee with Bow and Quiver armd,

> But with such Gardning Tools as Art yet rude
> Guiltless of fire had formd, or Angels brought.
> To *Pales*, or *Pomona*, thus adornd,
> Likest she seemd, *Pomona* when she fled
> *Vertumnus*, or to *Ceres* in her Prime,
> Yet Virgin of *Proserpina* from *Jove*.

Milton draws out and lingers over the comparisons as though,
like Adam, reluctant to see her go. Adam charges her again and
again to be back by noon, and again and again she promises that
she will:

> Oft he to her his charge of quick returne
> Repeated, shee to him as oft engag'd
> To be returnd by Noon amid the Bowr,
> And all things in best order to invite
> Noontide repast, or Afternoons repose.

She will be back to make lunch, in fact. But that lunch was never
made or eaten. At noon Eve was standing beneath the forbidden
tree, the arguments of the cunning serpent reinforced by her own
appetite; and the noontide repast that both she and her husband
eventually ate was the fatal apple. Milton's lingering on this final
moment when prelapsarian man and woman stood hand in hand
for the last time produces its own plangent emotion. We are made
to realize fully that Eve, for all her promises, will never return—
not *this* Eve, not the unfallen bride with her innocent display of
her naked beauty; the woman who tripped back to Adam with a
glib and tipsy speech on her lips and a branch of the forbidden
tree in her hand was a very different person.

> O much deceiv'd, much failing, hapless *Eve*,
> Of thy presum'd return! event perverse!
> Thou never from that houre in Paradise
> Foundst either sweet repast or sound repose;
> Such ambush hid among sweet Flowrs and Shades
> Waited with hellish rancour imminent
> To intercept thy way, or send thee back
> Despoild of Innocence, of Faith, of Bliss.

The temptation scene itself shows the skilled orator taking

advantage of simplicity. Eve is 'our credulous mother', and she is
fooled by the cunning serpent. (Incidentally, Milton, who cannot
do violence to the biblical text, is somewhat embarrassed by the
fact that the story in Genesis has the serpent as the tempter, and
says nothing of Satan. Though later tradition made the serpent
merely the disguise of Satan, the clear statement in Genesis of the
serpent's own guilt and punishment leads to some odd prevari-
cation on Milton's part.) Satan's (or the serpent's) final effort is
significantly compared by Milton to the speech of 'som Orator
renownd / In *Athens* or free *Rome*'. If she had known more Eve
would have been more suspicious of this plausible eloquence; but
she could not know more without eating of the forbidden Tree of
Knowledge; and so the paradox is emphasized. Her sin was
disobedience, it is true; but what caused her to commit that sin
was credulity. She was taken in by cunning lies, never having met
with lies or cunning before. Is credulity sinful and suspicion a
virtue? It is the problem of Othello's trusting Iago. There is no
solution; only a moral paradox at the heart of the matter.

Eve falls through credulity; Adam falls because he does not
realize that the duty of an unfallen man who wants to help a
fallen beloved is not to share her sin, and so render them both
helpless, but to intercede for her while he is yet sinless. In a
cunning parody of the courtly love tradition, Milton has Adam
eat the apple as (in Eve's delighted words) a 'glorious trial of
exceeding Love'. And so they both become irresponsible and
fatuous. Eve had changed as soon as she had eaten the apple,
bowing to the tree in drunken worship, and spilling out her story
to Adam in the most brilliant of all 'Sorry I'm late, but——'
speeches in English poetry.

> Hast thou not wonderd, *Adam*, at my stay?
> Thee I have misst, and thought it long, depriv'd
> Thy presence, agonie of love till now
> Not felt, nor shall be twice, for never more
> Mean I to trie, what rash untri'd I sought,
> The paine of absence from thy sight. But strange
> Hath bin the cause, and wonderful to hear:
> This Tree is not as we are told, a Tree
> Of danger tasted, nor to evil unknown
> Op'ning the way, but of Divine effect

> To open Eyes, and make them Gods who taste;
> And hath bin tasted such: the Serpent wise,
> Or not restraind as wee, or not obeying,
> Hath eaten of the fruit, and is become,
> Not dead, as we are threatend, but thenceforth
> Endu'd with human voice and human sense,
> Reasoning to admiration, and with mee
> Persuasively hath so prevaild, that I
> Have also tasted, and have also found
> Th' effects to correspond, op'ner mine Eyes,
> Dimm erst, dilated Spirits, ampler Heart,
> And growing up to Godhead; which for thee
> Chiefly I sought, without thee can despise.
> For bliss, as thou hast part, to me is bliss,
> Tedious, unshar'd with thee, and odious soon.
> Thou therefore also taste, that equal Lot
> May joine us, equal Joy, as equal Love;
> Lest thou not tasting, different degree
> Disjoine us, and I then too late renounce
> Deitie for thee, when Fate will not permit.

The tumbling rush of words, the breathlessness and the drunken lilt, distinguish this speech sharply from the gentle, liquid tones of Eve before her Fall. Milton emphasizes the flushed excitement:

> Thus *Eve* with Countnance blithe her storie told,
> But in her Cheek distemper flushing flowd.

The picture of Adam, smitten by horror and letting fall from his slack hand the garland of roses he had woven for Eve while awaiting her return, is full of dramatic power:

> On th' other side, *Adam*, soon as he heard
> The fatal Trespass don by *Eve*, amaz'd,
> Astonied stood and Blank, while horror chill
> Ran through his veins, and all his joints relaxd;
> From his slack hand the Garland wreath'd for *Eve*
> Down dropd, and all the faded Roses shed:

It is a situation which has been exploited again and again by subsequent writers, and which is now a commonplace in Hollywood: the lover preparing some special treat for his beloved, to be forced to forget it or leave it unused by some unexpected betrayal or disaster. So many of the situations in *Paradise Lost* have their debased romantic counterparts in later literature. This, of course, is not a criticism of Milton's poem, but an indication of how many elemental situations it contains. Perhaps the most used of all has been the ending, with the couple walking hand in hand into the sunset.

The shift in *tempo* from Eve's rapid speech to the description of Adam's reaction, slow and horror-struck, is emphasized by the lingering cadence of 'and all the faded Roses shed'. The control and dignity of Adam's reply to Eve show him as yet unfallen, but gradually allowing his compassion and affection to lead him to the wrong course of action. He does not reproach her (reproaches only come after both have fallen), and his opening words are still of admiration and compliment:

> O fairest of Creation, last and best
> Of all Gods works, Creature in whom excelld
> Whatever can to sight or thought be formd,
> Holy, divine, good, amiable, or sweet!
> How art thou lost, how on a sudden lost,
> Defac't, deflowrd, and now to Death devote?
> Rather how hast thou yielded to transgress
> The strict forbiddance, how to violate
> The sacred Fruit forbidden! som cursed fraud
> Of Enemie hath beguil'd thee, yet unknown,
> And mee with thee hath ruind, for with thee
> Certain my resolution is to Die;
> How can I live without thee, how forgoe
> Thy sweet Converse and Love so dearly joind,
> To live again in these wilde Woods forlorn?
> Should God create another *Eve*, and I
> Another Rib afford, yet loss of thee
> Would never from my heart; no no, I feel
> The Link of Nature draw me: Flesh of Flesh,
> Bone of my Bone thou art, and from thy State
> Mine never shall be parted, bliss or woe.

This is brilliantly done. Though Adam has reached the wrong conclusion, it is difficult to put one's finger on the exact point where he went wrong. Milton was only too well aware of the way in which man may be led astray even by his own virtues. There Is, too, in this and subsequent speeches an awareness on Milton's part of the curious relationship between love and selfishness. if one loves someone so much that injury to the beloved becomes a pain to oneself, is it the ultimate in selflessness or the ultimate in selfishness to sacrifice everything in order to keep the beloved from pain? Of course in Adam's case it is not a question of his sacrificing himself in order to redeem Eve; he wishes to share her fate so that they will not be separated; but the moral paradox is clearly there.

In a later speech Adam argues himself into a belief that God would not dare to destroy His own handiwork—that would simply be playing into the hands of His enemies. It is an elaborate piece of self-deception, in which Milton shows us that logic as well as rhetoric can lead astray. So Adam too eats of the fatal tree, and immediately a change is wrought in him as it had been wrought in Eve. He addresses Eve in a nasty parody of the teasing tone in which God had spoken to him about a mate:

> *Eve*, now I see thou art exact of taste
> And elegant, of Sapience no small part,
> Since to each meaning savour we apply,
> And Palate call judicious; I the praise
> Yield thee, so well this day thou hast purveyd.

He goes on, with blasphemous levity, to wish that

> For this one Tree had bin forbidden ten,

since there seemed to be such pleasure in things forbidden.

Sex becomes guilty now; images suggesting drunkenness and irresponsibility are rife in Milton's account of the first post-lapsarian sexual act, and they awake from the restless sleep that follows with the new knowledge of shame. A new kind of self-consciousness is present, and it destroys all their satisfaction in their mutual relationship. The pair bicker with sullen regret and mutual reproachfulness (how different the tone of their speech now from that of their prelapsarian discourse!) and Book IX ends in disillusion and bitterness.

Book X charts the change that begins to take place on earth

and in Hell as a result of the Fall, but its most interesting passages
are those showing the gradual process of recovery on the part of
Adam and Eve. Adam's bitter repudiation of Eve, in the speech
beginning 'Out of my sight, thou Serpent', is followed by Eve's
beautifully modulated penitential speech:

> Forsake me not thus, *Adam*, witness Heav'n
> What love sincere and reverence in my heart
> I bear thee, and unweeting have offended,
> Unhappilie deceiv'd; thy suppliant
> I beg, and clasp thy knees; bereave me not,
> Whereon I live, thy gentle looks, thy aid,
> Thy counsel in this uttermost distress,
> My onely strength and stay: forlorn of thee,
> Whither shall I betake me, where subsist?
> While yet we live, scarce one short hour perhaps,
> Between us two let there be peace, both joining,
> As joind in injuries, one enmitie
> Against a Foe by doom express assign'd us,
> That cruel Serpent: On mee exercise not
> Thy hatred for this miserie befall'n,
> On me already lost, mee than thy self
> More miserable; both have sinnd, but thou
> Against God onely, I against God and thee,
> And to the place of judgement will return,
> There with my cries importune Heaven, that all
> The sentence from thy head remov'd may light
> On me, sole cause to thee of all this woe,
> Mee mee onely just object of his ire.

This is not quite the tone of prelapsarian Eve, but its quietly
elegiac cadence, with its balances and repetitions ('forsake me
not ... bereave me not ... on mee exercise not'), does have echoes
of the early Eve, together with its own liturgical overtones. If Eve
began the Fall, she also began the process of recovery. Adam
responds to her repentant speech with words of compassion and
comfort, and from this point on the pair's recovery develops—
not in a straight line, for Milton was too knowing a psychologist
to think that that was how such things happened, but in a halting
and winding manner, to end in their joint prayer to God of submission and penitence.

The immediate punishment of the guilty pair—the curse of work and of pain in childbirth—is somewhat perfunctorily described early in Book X. Here Milton mechanically follows the narrative in Genesis (to the point of having God punish the serpent as well), and he seems glad to get away from it to his own account of the recovery of Adam and Eve. Adam's later reference to his part of the curse is curiously light-hearted:

> On mee the Curse aslope
> Glanc'd on the ground, with labour I must earn
> My bread; what harm? Idleness had bin worse; . . .

It is true that Adam is still deluded, with some rude shocks to come. But here he seems to be speaking for Milton, who is asserting once again his belief in the dignity of work. Adam goes on to reconcile himself rather too readily to the changing seasons which will now replace Eden's perpetual spring, and here again he seems to be reflecting Milton's own satisfaction in contemplating the revolving seasons, each with its own duties and its own pleasures.

The final part of *Paradise Lost* shows Michael first displaying and then narrating the future history of the world to Adam. It is a miserable story, from Cain's committing the first murder to the final picture of the world going on

> To good malignant, to bad men benign,
> Under her own weight groaning, till the day
> Appear of respiration to the just,
> And vengeance to the wicked, . . .

The story of Christ's passion and triumph, which breaks the dismal chronicle with a momentary gleam of light and elicits in Adam his great hail to the 'fortunate Fall'—

> O goodness infinite, goodness immense!
> That all this good of evil shall produce,
> And evil turn to good;

—is not, as Michael reveals the story, the culmination, but only an incident in the long history, and in some respects a less cheering incident than the quiet beauty of the picture of the earth returning to normal after the flood, never again to be so overwhelmed :

> but when he brings
> Over the Earth a Cloud, will therein set
> His triple-colourd Bow, whereon to look
> And call to mind his Cov'nant : Day and Night,
> Seed time and Harvest, Heat and hoary Frost
> Shall hold thir course, till fire purge all things new,
> Both Heav'n and Earth, wherein the just shall dwell.

This, with its sense of satisfaction in the procession of the seasons and man doing his daily agricultural labour, everything in its due time, gets us close to the real comfort in the poem.

In the end Milton and Adam turn from grandiose public hopes to the 'paradise within', content with the prospect of

> with good
> Still overcoming evil, and by small
> Accomplishing great things, . . .

Michael specifically tells Adam that since man will allow unworthy powers to rule his own reason, then 'God in Judgement just / Subjects him from without to violent Lords', and

> Tyrannie must be,
> Though to the Tyrant thereby no excuse,

which seems to mark Milton's complete repudiation of any political hopes and his way of accommodating himself to living under Charles II. Yet the note of patience and purpose rises above everything. Adam and Eve leave their former Paradise with quiet confidence, to face a world of work and endeavour and mutual help. Milton could not praise a fugitive and cloistered virtue, could not conceive of a life of pure meditation, could not imagine life in Eden lasting. At the same time he had lost his earlier confidence that Heaven on Earth could be restored by a regenerate, fully reformed England. Public virtue became for him almost a contradiction in terms, and only private virtue was real. The arts of public virtue, notably rhetoric, were suspect. In

Paradise Regained he was to make this point even clearer, for Satan tempts Christ there to the public life, which he rejects, with all its accompanying splendours. This was not a wholly new view of Milton's, for, together with the great public ambitions of his earlier years, he had felt also the necessity of submitting himself quietly and patiently to God's purpose for him—as Christ does in *Paradise Regained*. The sonnets on his twenty-third birthday and on his blindness should not be forgotten when we come to consider how far the turn to the 'paradise within' represented a radical change in Milton as a result of the failure of his political hopes for England. On the other hand, the change, though it should not be exaggerated, cannot be denied.

All great works of literature contain more than their ostensible subject. Starting from a particular set of beliefs, a story such as the biblical story of the Fall or a journey through the underworld, the true poet, in presenting his material, keeps reaching out at every point to touch aspects of the human situation which are real and recognizable whatever our beliefs may be. By turns of phrase, handling of imagery, simultaneous exploitation of the musical and semantic aspects of words and of all the evocations and suggestions that can be obtained from allusions to the great mythological imaginings of mankind, the poet turns his story and his creed into a unique means of shedding light on man. The combined knowledge of man's nobility and his weakness, the sense of man's looking back or forward to a Golden Age coupled with the knowledge that, partly because of the very characteristics of man as man, such a Golden Age can only be envisioned but never realized, the sense that man's life is governed by change and linked always with the movements of day to night and back to day, with the passing of the seasons, and affected by resolutions that fluctuate and moods that alter, but a sense, too, that only a determination to do what can be done at the moment of decision can ever achieve anything—all this and a thousand more such archetypal ideas are carried alive and passionately into the mind of the reader by *Paradise Lost*. The poem has its barren patches, and the arguments in Heaven about free-will may leave us unconvinced. But as a poem the subject of *Paradise Lost* is less the logical or theological justification of the ways of God to men than the essential and tragic ambiguity of the human animal. Expanding his meaning by every poetic device to include almost all that Western man had thought and felt and imagined, pivoting the action on a scene which, as Milton describes it, illuminates immediately the paradox of man's ambition (at once good because noble and bad because arrogant) and human love (both bad because selfish and because passion clouds the judgment and good because unselfish and self-sacrificing), linking the grandiose action at every point to suggestions of man in his daily elemental activities in fields, cities, and on the ocean, developing all the implications of man's perennial desire for a better world with the continuous awareness of man's tendency to trip himself up and turn his very virtues into snares—achieving all this in spite of the plot, or at least by expanding the plot into something infinitely more than its summarizable meaning, by placing an image where it will speak most suggestively and by linking up units to each other so that the chorus of implication grows ever richer, reverberates ever more widely, Milton, operating as a poet rather than as a theologian, probes more deeply into man's fate than his formal scheme would seem to allow. Work was a punishment for the Fall, but images of daily work well done are used throughout the poem to establish a note of satisfaction and recovery. Perpetual spring gave way after the Fall to the procession of the seasons, yet it is the procession of the seasons itself that gives meaning and dignity to human life as Milton reveals it by the pattern of image and suggestion in his poem. And in the end, Paradise, the ideal world of innocent idleness, has become uninhabitable. As they look back on it for the last time, the angels guarding it seem dreadful figures from another world. It is a great and memorable ending:

> for now too nigh
> Th' Archangel stood, and from the other Hill
> To thir fixt Station, all in bright array
> The Cherubim descended; on the ground
> Gliding meteorous, as Ev'ning Mist
> Ris'n from a River ore the marish glides,
> And gathers ground fast at the Labourers heel
> Homeward returning. High in Front advanc't,
> The brandisht Sword of God before them blaz'd
> Fierce as a Comet; which with torrid heat,

And vapour as the *Libyan* Air adust,
Began to parch that temperat Clime; whereat
In either hand the hastning Angel caught
Our lingring Parents, and to th' Eastern Gate
Led them direct, and down the Cliff as fast
To the subjected Plain; then disappear'd.
They looking back, all th' Eastern side beheld
Of Paradise, so late thir happie seat,
Wav'd over by that flaming Brand, the Gate
With dreadful Faces throngd and fierie Arms:
Som natural tears they dropd, but wip'd them soon;
The World was all before them, where to choose
Thir place of rest, and Providence thir guide:
They hand in hand with wandring steps and slow,
Through *Eden* took thir solitarie way.

The image of the labourer returning homeward in the evening sets the emotional tone of this concluding passage: as we have already sufficiently emphasized, for Milton daily agricultural labour duly accomplished was a highly charged symbol of satisfaction in human achievement. Eden becomes hot and frightening. Below, the 'subjected plain' awaits them—subjected in the literal Latin sense of lying below them and in the other sense of awaiting their conquest of it. The simple phrase 'so late thir happie seat' renews the elegiac tone with memories of lost felicity. But natural tears give way to the pioneering spirit of hope. 'The World was all before them'. And so they go forth, hand in hand yet in a sense solitary: they know now that, while mutual love and help sweeten all human toil, complete communion between individuals is impossible, for love and companionship are bound up with self-interest. All is here said that can be said about man's capacity to hope in spite of despair, about loneliness and companionship, about the healing effects of time and the possibility of combining bewilderment with a sense of purpose, about man as both elegist and pioneer. The style, with its quiet gravity, is more characteristically Miltonic than the Milton-Satan style which most people think is the invariable style of *Paradise Lost*. The manipulation of the pauses alone shows the highest art.

Much modern criticism of *Paradise Lost* has considered either only the language or only the theology, attacking Milton for his

diction or defending him for his Christian orthodoxy. The real
critical question, however, is how the language and the ideas
work in the poem. The degree of Milton's Christian orthodoxy is
of less literary interest than the kinds of craftsmanship he employs
in order to make his ideas proper material for poetry and achieve
adequate poetic expression of his theme. *Paradise Lost* is not a
piece of Christian theology put into a grand epic style in order to
sound persuasive any more than it is the expression of a piece of
exploded mythology in magnificent verse or a wilful piece of
barren virtuosity. It is a poem about the nature of man which
uses the Christian story of the Fall and its consequences as a
framework. Occasionally Milton confuses the framework with
the fabric of the poem, and these are the less interesting and less
important parts. The most interesting and the most important
parts—and the most impressive and enjoyable—are those where
Milton's use of language expands the core of literal meaning to
produce a complex and moving statement of the great paradox of
the human condition.

V

PARADISE REGAINED AND *SAMSON AGONISTES*

THOMAS ELLWOOD, a young Quaker who had studied with Milton in 1662, visited him in 1665 at Chalfont St. Giles whither Milton had retired to escape the plague, and in his memoirs gives an account of his borrowing the manuscript of *Paradise Lost* and returning it later with the remark, 'Thou hast said much here of Paradise Lost, but what has thou to say of Paradise Found?' To which, Ellwood goes on, Milton made no reply, 'but sat some time in a muse; then brake off that discourse, and fell on another subject'. Some time after Milton's return to London Ellwood was given the manuscript of *Paradise Regained*, Milton remarking (again according to Ellwood): 'This is owing to you; for you put it in my head by the question you put to me at Chalfont, which before I had not thought of.' Ellwood's story, though no one has questioned its accuracy, has generally been dismissed as the report of a simpleton who did not understand that Milton was gently making fun of him. Had not Milton dealt with Paradise regained in his first epic, which embraced the whole history of man, and was it not dense of Ellwood not to see this? Yet the fact remains that *Paradise Lost* is primarily about the Fall and the moral paradoxes it involved, with only a brief and formal mention of Christ's re-enacting of Adam's role, with a different ending, to secure salvation for men. In a sense it can be said that, for Milton in *Paradise Lost*, Paradise could be regained only by a willed confrontation of the fallen world. From the more purely theological standpoint, Paradise was regained by Christ's incarnation and passion. At yet another level—and one which particularly interested Milton—it could be said that the regaining of Paradise was made possible when another Adam faced Adam's temptation and resisted it instead of succumbing to it. Adam and Eve abused their free-will by making a wrong moral choice. If Christ, acting as man and not as God (and Milton always preferred to think of Christ as man), was faced with a similar moral

216

choice and used his free-will properly by choosing right, would that not be a symbolic reversal of the Fall? Perhaps Ellwood's remark set Milton thinking along those lines. For what he produced in *Paradise Regained* was a poem not about Christ's passion but about his re-enactment of Adam's part in order to prove that Satan could be and had been resisted.

Paradise Regained was published together with *Samson Agonistes* in 1671, and it was apparently written in its entirety after the completion of *Paradise Lost* and perhaps after its publication in 1667. There is no clear evidence as to when *Samson* was written, but theme and versification together with the date of publication suggest that it was one of Milton's latest works if not his final achievement, though some scholars have suggested an earlier date. Its theme, however, had been in Milton's mind for a longer period than the theme of *Paradise Regained*. The idea of treating Christ's temptation in the wilderness as a ritual re-enactment of the Fall seems to have come to him late in life, though it was a well-established tradition to see the temptation as some kind of undoing of the Fall. Taking the order of the temptations from the account in Luke (not in Matthew, where the order is different), Milton shows Christ facing the wiles of Satan *quasi homo*, and his triumph is, therefore, redemptive for mankind. As God tells His angels:

> He now shall know I can produce a man
> Of femal Seed, far abler to resist
> All his solicitations, and at length
> All his vast force, and drive him back to Hell,
> Winning by Conquest what the first man lost
> By fallacy surpriz'd. But first I mean
> To exercise him in the Wilderness,
> There he shall first lay down the rudiments
> Of his great warfare, ere I send him forth
> To conquer Sin and Death, the two grand foes,
> By Humiliation and strong Sufferance:
> His weakness shall orecome Satanic strength
> And all the world, and mass of sinful flesh;
> That all the Angels and Ethereal Powers,
> They now, and men hereafter may discern,
> From what consummat vertue I have chose
> This perfet Man, by merit calld my Son,
> To earn Salvation for the Sons of men.

The statement of theme at the opening of the poem is equally explicit: man's disobedience lost Paradise, and Christ's firm obedience will regain it:

> I who erewhile the happy Garden sung,
> By one mans disobedience lost, now sing
> Recoverd Paradise to all mankind,
> By one mans firm obedience fully tri'd
> Through all temptation, and the Tempter foild
> In all his wiles, defeated and repulst,
> And *Eden* rais'd in the waste Wilderness.

Adam's action produced a wilderness in the midst of Eden, and Christ's raised Eden in the wilderness. 'Be thou in *Adams* room', God told Christ in Book III of *Paradise Lost*, and *Paradise Regained* shows him doing so.

Satan's motive in tempting Christ—and again, as Elizabeth Pope has shown, Milton is following a well-established tradition here—is both to find out if he is really the prophesied Messiah and to tempt him to destroy his perfection and messianic claims by committing specific sins. Satan is here a rather seedy character compared with the rebellious angel of *Paradise Lost*; his address to his fellows in Book I, announcing his determination to find out who this man is, is a sullen and shabby affair, the rhetoric sounding hollow, as though Satan did not believe himself in the possibility of his success. (This, of course, is an effect deliberately aimed at on Milton's part, and shows his mastery of tone.) After a brief interlude in Heaven, where we see God with a confident smile telling Gabriel that He is about to expose Christ to Satan's 'utmost suttlety', the interest shifts to the mind of Christ himself. We see him communing with himself after his forty days in the wilderness without food, wondering what God has in store for him, and determined to await patiently the revelation of His purpose. It showed considerable daring on Milton's part to enter into the unspoken meditations of Christ, even of Christ *quasi homo*, and it is interesting that we find Christ meditating on matters which had much exercised Milton during his life:

> When I was yet a child, no childish play
> To me was pleasing, all my mind was set

> Serious to learn and know, and thence to do
> What might be public good; my self I thought
> Born to that end, born to promote all truth,
> All righteous things : therefore above my years,
> The Law of God I read, and found it sweet, . . .
> . . . yet this not all
> To which my Spirit aspir'd, victorious deeds
> Flam'd in my heart, heroic acts, one while
> To rescue *Israel* from the *Roman* yoke,
> Thence to subdue and quell ore all the earth
> Brute violence and proud Tyrannic power,
> Till truth were freed, and equity restor'd : . . .

The dedicated man with political ambitions to free his country from tyranny and bring about the reign of truth and justice is a familiar picture to those who have studied the young Milton.

Satan's first appearance to Christ, in the likeness of 'an aged man in rural weeds', produces a quiet dialogue in which the cunning persuasiveness of the supposed innocent old pauper, as he suggests that by turning stones into bread Christ would both save himself from starvation 'and us relieve with food', is met by a quietly firm, slightly contemptuous reply, which is characteristic of Christ's speech to Satan throughout the poem. His first remark is simply :

> Who brought me hither
> Will bring me hence, no other Guide I seek.

When Satan's suggestion becomes more specific, Christ calmly points out that God supported Moses on the mount and Elijah in the wilderness: 'Why dost thou then suggest to me distrust?' Christ also states that he knows Satan's identity—which, we cannot help feeling, gives him a quite unfair advantage over Eve, who had not known that the serpent was really Satan. Christ's calm refusal to do anything which might suggest distrust of God produces a change in Satan's style, which becomes steadily more persuasive and more rhetorical. That rhetoric, the art of persuasion, is here on the side of evil is abundantly clear. Christ's language is quiet, precise, even homely, the language of private, not public, discussion. Satan, having been recognized, proceeds to build himself up as at once heroic and pitiful, a character worthy

of respect and at the same time deserving compassion, an
flattery is added to this cunning mixture of boasting and self-pity
It is a remarkable speech, ending with deliberate art on an elegia
note:

> but long since with woe
> Nearer acquainted, now I feel by proof,
> That fellowship in pain divides not smart,
> Nor lightens aught each mans peculiar load.
> Small consolation then, were Man adjoind:
> This wounds me most (what can it less) that Man,
> Man fall'n shall be restor'd, I never more.

Christ is not fooled:

> To whom our Saviour sternly thus repli'd.
> Deservedly thou griev'st, compos'd of lies
> From the beginning, and in lies wilt end; . . .

He goes on to taunt Satan with having been the deceiver of mar
through the oracles of the pagan world; but 'God hath now sen
his living Oracle / Into the World'. Satan counters this hopelessly
with the argument that he loves virtue though he does not follow
it, adding that God allows sinners to approach His altar, and
therefore, Christ should give access to him. Christ replies tersely

> Thy coming hither, though I know thy scope,
> I bid not or forbid; doe as thou find'st
> Permission from above; thou canst not more.

So the first temptation ends, Satan temporarily disappears, and
Jesus is left alone in the wilderness:

> for now began
> Night with her sullen wing to double-shade
> The Desert, Fowls in thir clay nests were coucht;
> And now wild Beasts came forth the woods to roam.

The quiet desolation of the scene is significant. (The last line is
made up entirely of simple monosyllabic words.) The hero is alone
in the waste land. Satan tempts him to take easy ways out, later

rying to persuade him to exchange his lonely private life for the
glories and satisfactions of a successful public career. But all
emptations to public life are refused, and Jesus, trusting in God's
plan for him, remains a private man at the end of the poem.

Book II gives us a glimpse of the disciples wondering what has
happened to their master, then moves to Satan reporting to his
devils his lack of success and repudiating contemptuously
Belial's fatuous advice to 'set women in his eye' to propose
instead further temptation 'of worth, or honour, glory and
popular praise'. The devils have completely lost their grip, and
Belial's suggestion has the ring of routine advice trotted out
because his imagination is now incapable of rising to anything
further. Satan's rejection of the temptation through female beauty
reveals at least some degree of clear understanding of the last
infirmity of noble minds. But his words—

> for Beauty stands
> In th'admiration only of weak minds
> Led captive

—which are so often taken to be the direct voice of Milton repudiating part of his humanist legacy are after all the words of Satan;
they represent a truth distorted. If Milton and not Satan were
speaking he would discriminate between different kinds of beauty
and different kinds of admiration, distinguishing rational admiration of God's work in creating woman from irrational self-
abasement before feminine beauty. *Paradise Regained* is a
dialogue, with the dramatic elements of a dialogue, and to take
Satan's plausible distortions and self-deceptions as at any point
reflecting Milton's views is oddly naïve.

We then turn to Jesus, communing with himself again,
wondering what is to happen to him. He feels hunger, but his
bodily strength is not impaired, so that while he has a desire for
food he has not an absolute need of it :

> But now I feel I hunger, which declares
> Nature hath need of what she asks ; yet God
> Can satisfie that need som other way,
> Though hunger still remain : so it remain
> Without this bodys wasting, I content me, . . .

As Elizabeth Pope has pointed out, this whole passage reflects the Protestant interpretation of the temptation : Jesus is hungry, but not wasting, and therefore he can afford to disregard his hunger. His position is thus in some respects similar to that of Eve at that fatal noon—longing for food, but not actually requiring it. The analogy between Christ in the Wilderness and Adam and Eve in the Garden was a familiar one in both Protestant and Catholic thought. But to Protestants, with their distrust of the Catholic ascetic tradition, the temptation to turn stones into bread was a temptation to distrust, not to gluttony (for would it be gluttony to eat bread after forty days' fasting ?), and Milton's introduction in Book II of *Paradise Regained* of temptation by a luxurious banquet showed that he wished his hero to be tempted by gluttony and sensuality while accepting the Protestant view that the temptation of the stones could not be so interpreted. Eve's eating the apple indicated distrust and disobedience of God, but, because of the splendour and the sensual appeal of the fatal fruit, it also showed her succumbing to luxury and sensuality.

Before Satan reappears to attack Jesus with the temptation of the banquet, we see Jesus sleeping after his silent walking and meditation, dreaming of food 'as appetite is wont to dream'. He dreams of nothing luxurious, but of 'Natures refreshment', of the ravens bringing food to Elijah and Daniel's diet of pulse. And in the morning he rises, still fasting, to look in vain for some comforting sign of human habitation or activity :

> Up to a hill anon his steps he rear'd,
> From whose high top to ken the prospect round,
> If Cottage were in view, Sheep-cote or Herd ;
> But Cottage, Herd or Sheep-cote none he saw, . . .

The simplicity of the diction here carries on the suggestion of temperance in the account of his dream. The human symbols which he looks for are the most elemental and primitive. The repetition of 'Cottage, Herd or Sheep-cote' adds to the effect of sober simplicity.

Satan arrives for the second temptation clad this time in courtly garments, and he brings on a magnificent banquet :

A Table richly spred, in regal mode,
With dishes pil'd, and meats of noblest sort
And savour, Beasts of chase or Fowl of game,
In pastry built or from the spit or boild,
Gris-amber-steam'd; all Fish from Sea or Shore,
Freshet or purling Brook, of shell or fin,
And exquisitest name, for which was draind
Pontus and *Lucrine* Bay and *Afric* Coast.
Alas how simple, to these Cates compar'd,
Was that crude Apple that diverted *Eve*!
And at a stately side-board by the wine
That fragrant smell diffus'd, in order stood
Tall stripling youths rich clad, of fairer hue
Than *Ganymed* or *Hylas*; distant more
Under the Trees now tripd, now solemn stood
Nymphs of *Diana's* train, and *Naiades*
With fruits and flowrs from *Amalthea's* horn,
And Ladies of th' *Hesperides*, that seemd
Fairer than feignd of old, or fabl'd since
Of Fairy Damsels met in Forest wide
By Knights of *Logres*, or of *Lyoness*,
Lancelot or *Pelleas* or *Pellenore*;
And all the while Harmonious Airs were heard
Of chiming strings or charming pipes, and winds
Of gentlest gale *Arabian* odours fannd
From thir soft wings, and *Flora's* earliest smells.
Such was the Splendor, and the Tempter now
His invitation earnestly renewd.

This is in the style of the richer passages of *Paradise Lost*, but instead of classical mythology being employed to build up a powerful and moving suggestion of ideal beauty (as it is in the first account of Eden and of Eve), it is used almost ironically to suggest excess and exhibitionism. This effect is achieved partly by describing domestic objects and activities in a high epic language, as in

> Beasts of chase or Fowl of game,
> In pastry built or from the spit or boild,
> Gris-amber-steam'd;

and partly by a note almost of parody in the exaggeration of such passages as those describing the two youths who stood by the sideboard or the nymphs under the trees. These are waiters and waitresses, and to describe the latter as

> Ladies of th' *Hesperides*, that seemd
> Fairer than feignd of old, or fabl'd since
> Of Fairy Damsels met in Forest wide
> By Knights of *Logres*, or of *Lyoness*,
> *Lancelot* or *Pelleas* or *Pellenore*

is a deliberate violation of decorum in order to achieve irony. Yet there is beauty and splendour in the description, too, for it *is* a temptation.

Jesus replies 'temperately' to Satan's urging that he should sit and eat, his short speech concluding with contemptuous acerbity :

> And with my hunger what hast thou to do?
> Thy pompous Delicacies I contemn,
> And count thy specious gifts no gifts, but guiles.

Satan then turns to a more forceful argument—Christ's lack of followers and authority. How can he save the world without these ? 'Money brings Honour, Friends, Conquest and Realms'—

> They whom I favour thrive in wealth amain,
> While Virtue, Valour, Wisdom sit in want.
>   To whom thus Jesus patiently repli'd.
> Yet Wealth without these three is impotent.

Significantly, Jesus goes on, in the quietly assured style which Milton has by now established as the anti-Satanic style, to cite examples from both biblical and classical history of heroes who, their work over, returned to private life. As for power, 'he who reigns within himself, and rules / Passions, Desires and Fears, is more a King'—a Stoic as well as a Christian ideal. He goes on :

> But to guide Nations in the way of truth
> By saving Doctrin, and from error lead
> To know, and knowing worship God aright,
> Is yet more Kingly; . . .

Satan is defeated in both logic and ethics.

In Book III Satan, with increasing cunning and all kinds of verbal trickery, makes more explicit the contrast between private and public life:

> These God-like Vertues wherefore dost thou hide,
> Affecting privat life, or more obscure
> In savage Wilderness? Wherefore deprive
> All Earth her wonder at thy acts, thy self
> The fame and glory? glory the reward
> That sole excites to high attempts the flame
> Of most erected Spirits, . . .

This is coming more shrewdly home: Milton in 'Lycidas' had recognized that 'Fame is the spur . . .' But Jesus replies with cold contempt that the praise of the rabble is not worth having. (An un-Christlike argument, surely, but one that reflects Milton's disillusion with majority public opinion in England.) Conventional glory is won by meaningless and destructive wars. Patience and temperance are the true virtues, and Job and Socrates are cited. This leads Satan to press the moral aspect of the conquest of evil by good: would not the deliverance of Israel from the Roman yoke be a good thing? (Even as Milton had thought the deliverance of England from episcopacy and Charles I would be a good thing.) The argument is here pressed closely, with Satan making adroit use of biblical and other phrases long hallowed in Christian exhortation. A righteous war against the heathen is urged. But again Jesus replies coldly: 'All things are best fulfilld in thir due time.' ('They also serve who only stand and wait', in fact.) *If* he is the promised Messiah (he will not come out into the open and say explicitly that he is, for one of Satan's purposes is to confirm that he really is the Saviour and the Son of God), God will see that whatever is decreed will come to pass in the proper season. Meanwhile, he will continue 'suffering, abstaining, quietly expecting / Without distrust or doubt'. Satan now presses his point with a magnificent picture, both historical and geographical, of the power-pattern in the Middle East and Mediterranean, employing place names with the ringing sonority that is found in *Paradise Lost*, and he offers his help and advice to Jesus in regaining David's throne. But again Jesus answers coldly, repudiating with quiet contempt 'much ostentation vain of fleshly arm'. As for the people of Israel, they serve for their sins, and will be called back to God in His own time.

The fourth and last book of *Paradise Regained* opens with an account of Satan's perplexity and confusion. He had succeeded easily with Eve, 'but *Eve* was *Eve*, / This far his over-match'. He makes one final effort and puts forth all 'the persuasive Rhetoric that sleekd his tongue' to build up a glorious picture of the civilization of Greece and Rome. It is in the grandest style of *Paradise Lost*. A brilliant evocation of the whole of Roman civilization, with a sense of the colour and movement and variety of the whole Roman world, is followed by an equally brilliant evocation of the wisdom of Greece:

> Look once more ere we leave this specular Mount
> Westward, much nearer by Southwest, behold
> Where on the *Ægean* shore a City stands
> Built nobly, pure the air, and light the soil,
> *Athens* the eye of *Greece*, Mother of Arts
> And Eloquence, native to famous wits
> Or hospitable, in her sweet recess,
> City or Suburban, studious walks and shades.
> See there the Olive Grove of *Academe*,
> *Plato's* retirement, where the *Attic* Bird
> Trills her thick-warbl'd notes the summer long;
> There flowrie hill *Hymettus* with the sound
> Of Bees industrious murmur oft invites
> To studious musing; there *Ilissus* rouls
> His whispering stream. Within the walls then view
> The schools of ancient Sages; his who bred
> Great *Alexander* to subdue the world,
> *Lyceum* there, and painted *Stoa* next:
> There thou shalt hear and learn the secret power
> Of harmony in tones and numbers hit
> By voice or hand, and various-measurd verse,
> *Æolian* charms and *Dorian Lyric* Odes,
> And his who gave them breath, but higher sung,
> Blind *Melesigenes* thence *Homer* calld,
> Whose Poem *Phœbus* challeng'd for his own.
> Thence what the lofty grave Tragœdians taught

In *Chorus* or *Iambic*, teachers best
Of moral prudence, with delight receiv'd
In brief sententious precepts, while they treat
Of fate and chance and change in human life;
High actions and high passions best describing.
Thence to the famous Orators repair,
Those ancient, whose resistless eloquence
Wielded at will that fierce Democratie,
Shook th'Arsenal and fulmind over *Greece*
To *Macedon*, and *Artaxerxes* Throne.
To sage Philosophy next lend thine ear,
From Heav'n descended to the low-rooft house
Of *Socrates*, see there his Tenement,
Whom well inspir'd the Oracle pronounc'd
Wisest of men; from whose mouth issu'd forth
Mellifluous streams that waterd all the schools
Of Academics old and new, with those
Sirnam'd *Peripatetics*, and the Sect
Epicurean, and the *Stoic* severe;
These here revolve, or, as thou lik'st, at home,
Till time mature thee to a Kingdoms weight;
These rules will render thee a King complete
Within thy self, much more with Empire joind.

This is the Greece of the humanist imagination, and nowhere in English poetry is it so eloquently described. The panoramic view from the air (Milton was particularly good at aerial views; his imagination preferred to look down on a scene from above) is bathed in clear Aegean light, and in a verse-movement both swift and loving we are taken round the great scenes of Greek philosophy and poetry, to end with a reminder that Greek philosophy can teach that very self-mastery which Jesus earlier had so praised. It is difficult this time not to believe that one side of Milton was speaking here. There is no hint of irony through exaggeration or deliberate lack of decorum, there is no exhibitionism, no heroics, but a vivid and clearly apprehended picture of a great civilization at work.

To the civilization of imperial Rome, control of which is offered by Satan in exchange for Jesus' homage, Jesus replies (becoming ever more contemptuous of the now desperate Satan), 'I never lik'd thy talk, thy offers less.' As for the Roman Empire, control of which would bring control of all the kingdoms of the world, Jesus, like Milton, preferred the Republic, and regarded the Roman people, 'victor once, now vile and base', as deservedly made vassal to tyrants, because they abandoned their former justice and temperance for lust and rapine. To the offer of mastery of Greek wisdom and literature Jesus replies with more careful arguments. The wisdom of the Greeks is not dismissed with contempt. There is a note of genuine compassion when he says of the Greek philosophers:

> Alas what can they teach, and not mislead?
> Ignorant of themselves, of God much more, . . .

But though Greek philosophy has its virtues (and Jesus has already praised Socrates), they are pale beside those of the Hebrew prophets. 'Sions songs' are better than Greek literature, and 'our Prophets' the greatest orators.

> In them is plainest taught, and easiest learnt,
> What makes a Nation happy, and keeps it so,
> What ruins Kingdoms, and lays Cities flat;
> These only with our Law best form a King.

Though Jesus is drawing here on a long Christian tradition of attacks on vain secular learning, the balanced tone of the argument shows Milton the Christian arguing with Milton the Humanist in a highly personal manner. Does this passage really show the collapse of Milton's Christian humanism, the repudiation of the high ideals of secular learning combined with Christian wisdom and piety which we find in his pamphlet on education and elsewhere? We must remember that *Paradise Regained* is a poem much more restricted in scope than *Paradise Lost*, dealing only with one moment in history, a critical and symbolic debate between the perfect man and his tempter. In this deliberately narrowed context the issue is inevitably both sharpened and simplified. In the last analysis, only the Bible has total truth; all other literature, whatever specific useful functions it may serve, is defective and potentially misleading. Milton perhaps would not have denied this in his earlier years, but he would have viewed the whole matter in a different perspective. There *is* some degree of hardening and narrowing in Milton's later thought, and it would be disingenuous to pretend that there is not; but it is less than it is sometimes taken to be by those who read passages from *Paradise Regained* outside their context.

Paradise Regained now moves rapidly towards its close. Satan, frustrated and furious and fast losing all self-control, carries Jesus back to the wilderness and tries, ridiculously, to frighten him with a night of storm and 'hellish furies'. The next morning Jesus replies quietly to Satan's attempt to frighten him, 'Mee worse than wet thou find'st not.' Enraged and desperate, Satan brings Jesus to a pinnacle of the Temple, on which he sets him, hoping that he will call on angels to support him and thus both reveal his identity and at the same time lose it by invoking divine aid for his personal safety, or else fall and be destroyed. But neither of these things happens: Jesus stands unaided, and Satan is confounded. An angelic choir hails Jesus' triumph over temptation, and Jesus himself

Home to his Mothers house privat returnd.

The identification of the private life with virtue and the public with evil could not be more emphatic. This is how Milton's own experience had led him to interpret the story of the temptation in the wilderness.

The Book of Job as well as Spenser's *Faerie Queene* (Book II, Canto VIII) and Giles Fletcher's *Christ's Victory and Triumph* gave suggestions to Milton for *Paradise Regained*, and of course he drew on a variety of Christian traditions. But the 'brief epic' is nevertheless remarkably original in treatment, in its presentation of the conflict between public ambition and quiet trust. If the character of Jesus suffers somewhat as a consequence—he seems an oddly cold and stoical character, with none of the warmer virtues—it must be remembered that in this poem he is opposing the false claims of rhetoric and resisting the temptation to exchange the 'Paradise within' for grandiose public action. *Paradise Regained* is a more perfect poem than *Paradise Lost* from the point of view of consistency of tone and subordination of all the parts to the whole. But it is far more limited not only in subject but also in the poetic devices employed for expanding the area of suggestion. *Paradise Regained* is about Christ resisting Satan in a symbolic and model *débat*; *Paradise Lost* is about *la condition humaine*.

In *Samson Agonistes* Milton finally produced the biblical tragedy which he had long ago prescribed as the kind of literature to be encouraged in a Christian society. The form is that of Greek tragedy, with Sophocles' *Oedipus at Colonus* and Aeschylus' *Prometheus Bound* serving as models. Milton explains in an introduction that 'Tragedy, as it was antiently compos'd, hath been ever held the gravest, moralest, and most profitable of all other Poems: therefore said by *Aristotle* to be of power by raising pity and fear, or terror, to purge the mind of those and such like passions, that is to temper and reduce them to just measure with a kind of delight, stirr'd up by reading or seeing those passions well imitated'. He goes on to cite other evidence of the gravity and high seriousness of tragedy, testified to by Cicero, Plutarch, Seneca and others, among them a Father of the Church. His models, he continues, are both the Greeks and the Italians, and 'the measure of verse us'd in the Chorus is of all sorts'. The introduction concludes:

> Of the style and uniformitie, and that commonly call'd the Plot, whether intricate or explicit, which is nothing indeed but such œconomy or disposition of the fable as may stand best with verisimilitude and decorum; they only will best judge who are not unacquainted with *Æschulus*, *Sophocles*, and *Euripides*, the three Tragic Poets unequall'd yet by any, and the best rule to all who endeavour to write Tragedy. The circumscription of time wherein the whole Drama begins and ends, is according to antient rule, and best example, within the space of 24 hours.

A Greek tragedy on a biblical theme may be considered Milton's final way of reconciling his Christianity with his human-ism, and perhaps taken as evidence (assuming that *Samson* really was his last work, which cannot be proved) that Christ's repudia-tion of Greek literature in *Paradise Regained* does not mean Milton's own repudiation of his classical interests. At any rate, he takes up again the theme of temptation and the trials to which a good man could be subjected, but choosing as his hero this time not a perfect man, of whom there was only one example in history and who, as the Son of God, was in a very special position and so not entirely satisfactory as a symbol of man in the world, but a man guilty of human weaknesses. Samson had long been established in Christian tradition as a hero and a saint (though the primitive violence of the story in Judges made it a tricky business for patristic and other commentators to establish him as such), largely as a result of the reference to him in the eleventh chapter of the Epistle to the Hebrews as an example of those who triumphed through faith. And, as Professor Michael Krouse has shown in his *Milton's Samson and the Christian Tradition*, the story of Samson developed at the end of generations of mediaeval ecclesiastical and other writers as a tragedy in the mediaeval sense, an 'account of a great man, a saint, counterpart of Hercules, a type of Christ, who falls from happiness to misery'. And in non-ecclesiastical texts he appears as a great man who fell through weakness, his foolish love and trust of a bad woman. Renaissance poets developed the mediaeval view of Samson as a great man brought low by his trust of a faithless woman. His weakness, his *hamartia*, was lust or passion or imprudence or all three. The emphasis was on the latter part of Samson's career, and the stories in Judges of his earlier exploits were for the most part glossed over—as well they might be, for they are a very odd collection of acts of violence and brutality on all sides, which, though allegorized into edifying meanings by Church writers, were not easily amenable to serious literary treatment.

Milton's choice of Samson as a hero is not as arbitrary and as personal as has often been thought. Christian traditions about Samson available to Milton were strong and numerous. In Professor Krouse's words: 'During Milton's own lifetime Samson was remembered by many as a tragic lover; as a man of prodigious strength; as the ruler and liberator of Israel; as a great historical personage whose downfall was caused by the treachery of a woman, and therefore as an example of the perils of passion; as a sinner who repented and was restored to grace; as the original of Hercules; as a consecrated Nazarite; as a saint resplendent in unfailing faith; as an agent of God sustained by the Holy Spirit; and as a figure of Christ.' Milton, of course, brought to his treatment of the theme his own experience and his own interest in the temptations of the dedicated man and in the conflicting claims of public and private life. The result is an interesting blend of traditional and personal interpretations of the meaning of the last phase of Samson's life. Technically, too, Milton was inspired by the complex nature of Greek dramatic verse and by hints from the dramatic verse of such Italian poets as Tasso and Guarini to go beyond the relatively restricted scope of his epic blank verse, to develop in the choruses new kinds of poetic rhythms and to use variety of line-lengths and intermittent rhyme and suggestions of rhyme with a virtuosity unparalleled elsewhere in English poetry.

The tragedy is in the form of a series of dialogues between Samson and the various people who visit him, one at a time, with intervening monologues by Samson, comments by the Chorus, and the final reported account of Samson's death in pulling down the heathen temple on the Philistines. In the course of the action Samson gradually (and not always in a continuous forward movement) recovers a proper state of mind, which combines penitence, recognition of the nature of his earlier fault and of the justice of his present fate, and a confident submission to whatever destiny God has in store for him. The temptations which face him, a blind prisoner of the heathen Philistines, are despair on the one hand and a belief in his own ability to decide his destiny (instead of waiting on God's revelation of His purpose) on the other. In the end, God's purpose is revealed, and Samson goes to participate in the Philistine festival knowing that that is what God wishes him to do. His death in destroying his enemies was the destiny prepared for him.

The theme of the play is the process of Samson's recovery, and each of the characters who visit him—his father Manoah, his wife Dalila, the Philistine giant Harapha (an invention of Milton's), and the Philistine officer who comes to bid him to the festival—represent different temptations, in resisting which he proceeds further towards recovery and establishes his status as a hero. Only on some such reading of *Samson Agonistes* can full sense be made out of it, can all its features be reconciled and understood, and can Johnson's charge that it has a beginning and an end but no middle be refuted. We see Samson first lamenting his present state, in a blank verse distinctly Sophoclean in movement

but breathing a note of self-pity which Samson has to learn to
lose :

> A little onward lend thy guiding hand
> To these dark steps, a little furder on;
> For yonder bank hath choice of Sun or shade;
> There I am wont to sit, when any chance
> Relieves me from my task of servile toil,
> Daily in the common Prison else enjoind me,
> Where I a Pris'ner chaind, scarce freely draw
> The air imprisond also, close and damp,
> Unwholsom draught : but here I feel amends,
> The breath of Heav'n fresh-blowing, pure and sweet,
> With day-spring born; here leave me to respire. . . .
> Why was my breeding orderd and prescrib'd
> As of a person separate to God,
> Design'd for great exploits, if I must die
> Betrayd, Captiv'd, and both my Eyes put out,
> Made of my Enemies the scorn and gaze,
> To grind in Brazen Fetters under task
> With this Heav'n-gifted strength? O glorious strength
> Put to the labour of a Beast, debas't
> Lower than bondslave! Promise was that I
> Should *Israel* from *Philistian* yoke deliver;
> Ask for this great Deliverer now, and find him
> Eyeless in *Gaza* at the Mill with slaves,
> Himself in bonds under *Philistian* yoke:

There is a weight and a controlled passion in these lines that is
very different from the rhetorical splendour of Satan's early
speeches in *Paradise Lost*. The question—why was he dedicated
from birth to great exploits for his people if he is to end blind
and helpless?—has, of course, overtones from Milton's personal
situation, but it is a real question in terms of the unfolding plot
of the tragedy.

Having questioned the ways of God to man he immediately
recollects himself:

> Yet stay, let me not rashly call in doubt
> Divine Prediction; what if all foretold
> Had been fulfilld but through mine own default,
> Whom have I to complain of but my self?

Samson is already resigned to God's justice at the opening of the play. But intellectual assent is not the same thing as emotional conviction, and though Samson recognizes the justice of his being punished for his own sin in parting with the secret of his strength 'weakly to a woman . . . orecome with importunity and tears`, the thought of his former strength leads him to reflect bitterly on the fact that it lay only in his hair, so easily sheared:

> God, when he gave me strength, to shew withall
> How slight the gift was, hung it in my Hair.

Self-pity rises again, to be checked once more:

> But peace, I must not quarrel with the will
> Of highest dispensation, which herein
> Haply had ends above my reach to know.

Then the thought of his blindness overcomes him, and as he reflects on it the passion rises, the bounds of blank verse are broken, and he bursts forth into a great lyric cry:

> O dark, dark, dark, amid the blaze of noon,
> Irrecoverably dark, total Eclipse
> Without all hope of day!
> O first created Beam, and thou great Word,
> Let ther be light, and light was over all;
> Why am I thus bereav'd thy prime decree?
> The Sun to me is dark
> And silent as the Moon,
> When she deserts the night
> Hid in her vacant interlunar cave.
> Since light so necessary is to life,
> And almost life itself, if it be true
> That light is in the Soul,
> Shee all in every part; why was the sight
> To such a tender ball as th' eye confin'd,
> So obvious and so easie to be quencht,
> And not as feeling through all parts diffus'd,
> That she might look at will through every pore?
> Then had I not bin thus exil'd from light;
> As in the land of darkness yet in light,

> To live a life half dead, a living death,
> And buried; but O yet more miserable!
> My self, my Sepulcher, a moving Grave,
> Buried, yet not exempt
> By priviledge of death and burial
> From worst of other evils, pains and wrongs,
> But made hereby obnoxious more
> To all the miseries of life,
> Life in captivity
> Among inhuman foes.

With this passage the verse moves, as Mr. Prince has pointed out, from speech to chant, just as it moves from chant back to speech again in the conclusion:

> But who are these? for with joint pace I hear
> The tread of many feet steering this way; . . .

The repetitions of individual words, the very occasional rhyme, startling and emphatic because of its rarity, the many hints of rhymes and deliberate echoes of sounds, the short lines thrust out with moving force between the longer lines, the dwindling down to hopelessness at the end—

> . . . To all the miseries of life,
> Life in captivity
> Among inhuman foes.

—all contribute to the bodifying forth of the speaker's emotion as it rocks to and fro between self-reproach and self-pity, between resignation and despair. There is little point in analysing the rhythms of this kind of verse in formal metrical terms: the unit is the rhythmic phrase. The rising anguish in the line

> My self, my Sepulcher, a moving Grave,

is achieved by the sequence of three rhythmic phrases each longer than the preceding one, and a formal scansion in traditional feet would quite obscure this.

The Chorus now enter, and in a similar varied measure

comment on Samson's state and contrast it with his former heroic exploits for his people. They speak first in tones of exaggerated quiet, appropriate to someone entering a sick chamber :

> This, this is he; softly a while,
> Let us not break in upon him : . . .

They show almost a certain embarrassment in approaching their former champion in his present pitiful state. But as they look on him and the contrast between his present state and his former glory is borne in upon them, the tone of their chant becomes stronger, passionate with shock and incredulity :

> Or do my eyes misrepresent? Can this be hee?
> That Heroic, that Renowned,
> Irresistible *Samson*?

The emphatic 'hee', the short demonstrative line 'That Heroic, that Renowned', rising to the climactic 'Irresistible *Samson*', expresses brilliantly the nature of their emotion. Now they no longer say 'hush!' to each other, but rush on to an account of Samson's former exploits, wondering at the contrast between what Samson was and what he now is. They then turn to his present state, and see Samson as the hero of a mediaeval tragedy, cast low from his former position at the top of fortune's wheel :

> By how much from the top of wondrous glory,
> Strongest of mortal men,
> To lowest pitch of abject fortune thou art fall'n.

The long third line here trundles along the ground, as it were.

This is no comfort to Samson, to hear how shaken the Chorus are by his reversal of fortune, to listen to them recalling the glories of his former career. But then, as is made clear as the tragedy proceeds, only Samson can comfort Samson. All his visitors are tempters in one way or another. To hear his friends saying how incredible it is that he should be in this awful state can only encourage despair. But he receives them with friendliness and dignity :

> Your coming, Friends, revives me, for I learn
> Now of my own experience, not by talk,
> How counterfeit a coin they are who friends
> Bear in thir Superscription (of the most
> I would be understood) : in prosperous days
> They swarm, but in adverse withdraw their head
> Not to be found, though sought.

But once again as he goes on to talk of his present state his bitterness rises, and resignation gives way to protest:

>   tell me Friends,
> Am I not sung and proverbd for a Fool
> In every street, do they not say, how well
> Are come upon him his deserts? yet why?
> Immeasurable strength they might behold
> In me, of wisdom nothing more than mean ;
> This with the other should, at least, have paird,
> These two proportiond ill drove me transverse.

This is almost saying that it is God's fault for having endowed him with more strength than wisdom, and the Chorus now play the part of the reproving superior, admonishing him:

> Tax not divine disposal ; . . .

They go on to needle him (but with the best of motives) by asking why on earth he should have married a Philistine woman rather than someone of his own tribe or at least his own nation. Samson, talking to himself rather than to the Chorus, goes over the history of his relations with Dalila, concluding with a proud humility that

> She was not the prime cause, but I my self,
> Who vanquisht with a peal of words (O weakness!)
> Gave up my fort of silence to a Woman.

When the Chorus reproach him with the fact that, in spite of his heroic deeds against the Philistines, 'Yet *Israël* still serves with all his Sons', Samson sharply replies that he is not responsible for *this* disaster. The fact that Israel is still under the Philistine yoke must be blamed squarely 'On *Israels* Governors, and Heads of

Tribes', who refused to take proper advantage of his exploits. He goes on to recall his own unacknowledged and unappreciated activity and tells his story with rising confidence. He has no cause for self-reproach here. If the leaders of his people had followed up his individual campaigns—'had *Judah* that day joind, or one whole Tribe'—the Philistines would by now have been conquered. This is an interesting passage, for it not only shows some obvious autobiographical elements (Milton will not reproach himself for the ultimate failure of his political pamphleteering) but also reflects Milton's view that proper self-esteem is consistent with true humility, and that a good man gone astray through weakness is not showing a proper moral recovery by abjectly blaming himself for *everything* he has done; his task is to discriminate between what he accepts and what he rejects in his own conduct. Abjectness is akin to despair rather than to true humility.

The Chorus then break into their well-known vindication of God's justice, which is really less a vindication than an expression of the nature of the problem:

> Just are the ways of God,
> And justifiable to Men; . . .

Here the Chorus speak no longer as visitors to Samson, whose visit plays a specific part in the development of the play, but rather as the impersonal mouthpiece of some of the general moral ideas in the play. (This double function of the Chorus is common enough in Greek drama.) Once more, the occasional rhyme, the varying line-lengths, the to-and-fro movement of the whole, are devices which effectively project a sense of inner mental and emotional struggle.

Manoah, Samson's first visitor (apart from the Chorus, who remain throughout the play), comes to rub salt into his son's wound, though of course not intentionally, by saying 'I told you so' about his marriage to a Philistine woman. Like the Chorus, he begins by noting with shocked surprise, and then lamenting, the great change in Samson's position:

> O miserable change! is this the man,
> That invincible *Samson*, . . .

His picture of Samson's present state is vivid and bitter, but its basis is less sympathy for Samson than disappointment and frustration in his own hopes for his son:

> I prayd for Childern, and thought barrenness
> In wedlock a reproach; I gaind a Son,
> And such a Son as all Men haild me happy;
> Who now would be a Father in my stead?

With no thought now of comforting Samson he goes on with masochistic fury to describe his present degradation:

> . . . then in an hour
> Ensnar'd, assaulted, overcome, led bound,
> Thy Foes derision, Captive, Poor, and Blind
> Into a Dungeon thrust, to work with Slaves.

It is not fair of God, he goes on, to have chosen Samson 'to worthiest deeds' and then so overwhelm him merely because he erred 'through frailty'. This results in the ironical picture of Samson telling his father not to rail against Heaven:

> Appoint not heav'nly disposition, Father,
> Nothing of all these evils hath befall'n me
> But justly; I my self have brought them on,
> Sole Author I, sole cause; . . .

This, we may feel, is complete moral recovery at last, the note of true humility and repentance. But once again as Samson goes on to recall to his father how it all came about the note of acceptance of God's will disappears or at least diminishes and his bitterness rises—this time at his own monstrous folly, rather than at what God has done to him:

> O indignity, O blot
> To Honour and Religion! servil mind
> Rewarded well with servil punishment!
> The base degree to which I now am fall'n,
> These rags, this grinding, is not yet so base
> As was my former servitude, ignoble,
> Unmanly, ignominious, infamous,
> True slavery, and that blindness worse than this,
> That saw not how degenerately I serv'd.

There is a self-torturing savagery here, which represents yet another of the temptations that lie in wait for the lapsed hero on
the road to moral recovery. Manoah replies by almost smugly
reminding Samson of his original error:

> I cannot praise thy Marriage choices, Son, . . .

But worse than all that has happened to you yet, he goes on to
tell Samson,

> This day the *Philistines* a popular Feast
> Here celebrate in *Gaza*; and proclaim
> Great Pomp and Sacrifice and Praises loud
> To *Dagon*, as their God who hath deliverd
> Thee *Samson* bound and blind into thir hands,
> Them out of thine, who slewst them many a slain.
> So *Dagon* shall be magnifi'd, and God,
> Besides whom is no God, compar'd with Idols,
> Disglorifi'd, blasphem'd, and had in scorn
> By th' Idolatrous rout amidst thir wine; . . .

This, he concludes, is the heaviest of all Samson's sufferings and
reproaches. It is a speech full of conscious cruelty, but its very
excess helps to calm Samson, who replies with a quiet humility
which has its own dignity:

> Father, I do acknowledge and confess
> That I this honour, I this pomp have brought
> To *Dagon*, . . .

Having rubbed his salt in his son's wounds, Manoah proceeds to the real business he has in hand, proposals for Samson's
recovery. With a bustling optimism (which is perfectly consistent
with the other traits in his character so far revealed) he explains
that he will be able to arrange ransom with the Philistian lords
and that if Samson is penitent God will surely restore his sight
and bring about a happy ending. Manoah here reminds us somewhat of Oceanus in *Prometheus Bound*, who also exhibits an optimistic vanity in imagining that he can arrange everything between
Prometheus and Zeus if only Prometheus will behave himself.

His facile optimism succeeds only in depressing Samson, who becomes more and more hopeless, verging on the sin of despair. Manoah departs to try to arrange Samson's ransom, leaving Samson to give passionate expression to his hopelessness and the Chorus to ponder the baffling ways of God, who raises a man up from earliest youth to a high destiny, only to dash him down again in middle life.

The entry of Dalila, Samson's faithless Philistine wife who by betraying the secret of his strength to his enemies was responsible for his present condition, is announced by the Chorus in terms which make clear that she is decked out in all her finery:

> But who is this, what thing of Sea or Land?
> Female of sex it seems,
> That so bedeckt, ornate and gay,
> Comes this way sailing
> Like a stately Ship
> Of *Tarsus*, bound for th' Iles
> Of *Javan* or *Gadier*
> With all her bravery on, and tackle trim,
> Sails filld, and streamers waving, . . .

In its deliberate exaggeration, and in the ironic pretence not to know 'what thing of Sea or Land' this dressed-up creature can be, there is a world of criticism of female vanity. But the new temptation which Dalila brings is not the simple one of luxury or sensuality. She explains that she betrayed Samson for love of him, not expecting the Philistines to blind and imprison him, but hoping that they would simply cut his hair to remove his great strength and leave him to her luxurious protective care. She is not lying: she is proffering Samson a dangerous kind of love, and wants him back as

> Mine and Loves pris'ner, not the *Philistines*.

This is not Milton's concept of marriage, and when Dalila actually suggests that a blind Samson is better off than a seeing one, as being more completely under her loving protection, we see clearly that Milton is attacking here a variant of the courtly love tradition (with the man as 'Loves pris'ner') which he attacked in other ways in *Paradise Lost*. Her speech, with its rapid movement and tone of special pleading (a little reminiscent of Eve's speech to Adam on returning from the fatal tree), is brilliantly done; there is real emotion behind it. She begins hesitantly, 'still dreading thy displeasure, *Samson*', only to meet with the fierce rebuff:

> Out, out *Hyaena*; these are thy wonted arts, . . .

Her reply to this is an impressive piece of pleading:

> Yet hear me *Samson*; not that I endevor
> To lessen or extenuate my offence,
> But that on th' other side if it be weighd
> By it self, with aggravations not surcharg'd,
> Or else with just allowance counterpois'd,
> I may, if possible, thy pardon find
> The easier towards me, or thy hatred less.
> First granting, as I do, it was a weakness
> In me, but incident to all our sex,
> Curiosity, inquisitive, importune
> Of secrets, then with like infirmity
> To publish them, both common femal faults:
> Was it not weakness also to make known
> For importunity, that is for naught,
> Wherein consisted all thy strength and safety?
> To what I did thou shewdst me first the way.
> But I to enemies reveal'd, and should not:
> Nor shouldst thou have trusted that to womans frailty;
> Ere I to thee, thou to thy self wast cruel.
> Let weakness then with weakness come to parl,
> So near related, or the same of kind,
> Thine forgive mine; that men may censure thine
> The gentler, if severely thou exact not
> More strength from me, than in thy self was found.
> And what if Love, which thou interpretst hate,
> The jealousie of Love, powerful of sway
> In human hearts, nor less in mine towards thee,
> Caus'd what I did? I saw thee mutable
> Of fancy, fear'd lest one day thou wouldst leave me
> As her at *Timna*, sought by all means therefore
> How to endear, and hold thee to me firmest:
> No better way I saw than by importuning

> To learn thy secrets, get into my power
> Thy key of strength and safety: thou wilt say,
> Why then reveal'd? I was assur'd by those
> Who tempted me, that nothing was design'd
> Against thee but safe custody and hold:
> That made for me, I knew that liberty
> Would draw thee forth to perilous enterprises,
> While I at home sate full of cares and fears
> Wailing thy absence in my widowd bed;
> Here I should still enjoy thee day and night
> Mine and Loves pris'ner, not the *Philistines*,
> Whole to my self, unhazarded abroad,
> Fearless at home of partners in my love.
> These reasons in Loves law have past for good,
> Though fond and reasonless to some perhaps:
> And Love hath oft, well meaning, wrought much woe,
> Yet always pitty or pardon hath obtain'd.

It must be quoted at length if its movement and texture are to be illustrated.

This is a real temptation, because sex and a plausible if distorted view of love are involved; the savagery with which Samson forbids Dalila to approach him indicates his fear of succumbing if once he allows physical contact between them. His repudiation of her stings her into a spiteful declaration of her determination to seek appreciation from the Philistines, and she goes, leaving the Chorus to ponder over the strange power of physical love. In a sense, both Samson and the Chorus—who see her as a hypocrite throughout—misjudge her. Milton is subtler than they, and can see that she may well be sincere and yet represent something evil. There has developed such a strong tradition of Milton's anti-feminism that critics have too readily assumed that Milton's portrait of Dalila is simply a nasty attack on women through a portrait of a hypocritical traitress. But Dalila is surely telling the truth when she explains that

> conjugal affection
> Prevailing over fear and timorous doubt
> Hath led me on desirous to behold
> Once more thy face, and know of thy estate.

And she is also telling the truth when she gives her version of how and why she gave in to the Philistine lords. She wanted Samson at home and in her power. That was her way of loving him. It was a wrong way, but she is not lying in her account of it. This is an important point, because Milton's whole reputation as a dramatic poet is at stake. If we see the scene between Dalila and Samson as a subtle portrait of sincere but perverse love appealing to righteous disillusion, and recognize the various tensions and overtones that result from the remarkable conflict between the two, we can appreciate Milton's achievement in making this complex situation the centre of his play. Samson is right in believing that 'weakness' (of a kind) was the cause of the whole trouble; but it was not Dalila's 'weakness to resist / *Philistian* gold'. It is only by seeing it in these terms and by affirming that

> if weakness may excuse,
> What Murtherer, what Traitor, Parricide,
> Incestuous, Sacrilegious, but may plead it?
> All wickedness is weakness

that Samson can maintain his moral position. It is an axiom of art that the creator has more insight than the characters he creates (or how could he create them?) and it is odd that so many critics have denied this insight to Milton.

Samson's next visitor is Harapha, the Philistine champion, who comes to taunt him, but Samson answers Harapha's bravado with calm and confident words. There is an insolent swagger about Harapha's speech:

> I come not *Samson*, to condole thy chance,
> As these perhaps, yet wish it had not been,
> Though for no friendly intent. I am of *Gath*,
> Men call me *Harapha*; of stock renownd
> As *Og* or *Anak* and the *Emims* old
> That *Kiriathaim* held, thou knowest me now
> If thou at all art known.

This is Satan's idiom reduced to petty proportions. It stimulates an opposite tone in Samson (whose reactions throughout the play tend to be the contrary of what is acting on him):

> Boast not of what thou wouldst have don, but do
> What then thou wouldst; thou seest it in thy hand. . . .

And again:

> All these indignities, for such they are
> From thine, these evils I deserve and more,
> Acknowledge them from God inflicted on me
> Justly, yet despair not of his final pardon
> Whose ear is ever open; . . .

This is a proper combination of humility and self-respect; the calmness and dignity of the tone show that Samson is well on the way to complete recovery. He vindicates his earlier career with equal dignity, and in the end chases Harapha from the scene by merely making a pretended motion towards him. The Chorus hail Samson's reviving spirits, and note that patience is the true exercise of the saints.

The Philistine officer now enters and summons Samson to give an exhibition before the Philistine lords at their festival in honour of Dagon. Samson returns a contemptuous negative, but then, contemplating his growing hair and returning strength, suddenly begins to feel 'som rouzing motions in me', indicating a divine impulse to go with the messenger after all. Samson has at last reached the state which Milton describes at the end of the sonnet on his blindness, at the end of 'Lycidas' (by implication) and early in *Paradise Regained*, in the self-communings of Jesus: he is waiting for God to reveal what He has in store for him. It is not enough to repent, to absolve God of blame, to avoid despair, to resist the various temptations to sensuality and violence and other wrong states of mind; one must also resign oneself patiently to the will of God, whose purpose for the recovered hero (that God has a purpose for such characters Milton of course could not doubt) will be revealed in due time. So Samson leaves in high dignity, telling the Chorus:

> Happen what may, of me expect to hear
> Nothing dishonourable, impure, unworthy
> Our God, our Law, my Nation, or my self,
> The last of me or no I cannot warrant.

Manoah then returns, confident that he can secure his son's release, looking forward to a completely restored Samson, with eyesight as well as strength given back. This moment of apparent light before the final tragedy can be paralleled in many of Shakespeare's plays. But the irony of the situation is very Sophoclean. Manoah's optimistic speculations are interrupted by a shout from the temple of Dagon, and he exchanges apprehensive speculations with the Chorus. The announcement by a messenger, in a set speech in the true Greek dramatic tradition, of Samson's end brings comment by the Chorus (who are careful to point out that Samson died 'self-killd not willingly'—he was not guilty of the sin of suicide) and a final realization by Manoah that the end is heroic and fitting:

> Come, come, no time for lamentation now,
> Nor much more cause; *Samson* hath quit himself
> Like *Samson*, and heroicly hath finisht
> A life Heroic; . . .
> Nothing is here for tears, nothing to wail
> Or knock the brest, no weakness, no contempt,
> Dispraise or blame, nothing but well and fair,
> And what may quiet us in a death so noble.

The play concludes with the Chorus echoing this thought in well-known lines:

> All is best, though we oft doubt,
> What th' unsearchable dispose
> Of highest wisdom brings about,
> And ever best found in the close.
> Oft he seems to hide his face,
> But unexpectedly returns
> And to his faithful Champion hath in place
> Bore witness gloriously; whence *Gaza* mourns
> And all that band them to resist
> His uncontroulable intent.
> His servants he with new acquist
> Of true experience from this great event
> With peace and consolation hath dismist,
> And calm of mind all passion spent.

Samson Agonistes is a moral and psychological tragedy (perhaps the qualifications are superfluous, for all tragedy should be moral and psychological, but it is worth insisting on both terms in describing a play that has been so much misunderstood), largely Greek in form and in spirit largely Hebraic and Christian. In the questionings of the ways of God to men that Milton puts into the mouth of the Chorus—

> God of our Fathers, what is man!
> That thou towards him with hand so various,
> Or might I say contrarious,
> Temperst thy providence through his short course,
> Not evenly, . . .

—we are often reminded of the Book of Job. There is also a distillation of much Christian tradition here, exegetical, homiletic and ethical, and, as perhaps has been over-emphasized by critics, much of Milton's personal views and circumstances. Milton employs Aristotle's theory of *katharsis* in a simple and impressive way, his final words, 'And calm of mind all passion spent', having an obvious reference to this theory. Yet in a sense *Samson Agonistes* is not a tragedy; its hero recovers and does God's work. That he dies in the process cannot be tragic to a Christian who believes that death, and certainly such a death, is but the prelude to greater and eternal glory. The moral law remains above all the characters, firm and clear. There is no disproportion between sin and punishment, no temporary dislocation of the universal order, no sense of waste, nor—for all the passionate precision with which Samson's blind state is described—any real sense of 'the pity of it' or of the sad paradoxes of human nature which can make a man's very virtues the instrument of evil. From one point of view, a Christian tragedy is a contradiction in terms : nothing to a Christian can be tragic if seen in its proper perspective. Tragedy involves a certain element of injustice, of disproportion, of slight defect, *hamartia*, turning everything to corruption until a whole cycle of human woe has been completed. But where God, all-just, all-powerful and merciful, is in control, no injustice and disproportion can exist. Justice in real tragedy works with difficulty under distorting conditions and through intractable material.

All this is not to deny that *Samson Agonistes* is a remarkable play. But it is not, in the full sense of the word, a great *tragedy*. We lack a name for the kind of play which it is. There is no other play like it in English, and no other really like it, despite superficial resemblances of form or theme, in any other European literature. Technically it is a remarkable achievement. Milton went back to the experiments in the balancing and cadencing of verse which he had made in 'At a Solemn Musick' and 'Lycidas' and now went very much further, producing effects—in the rapid shifting of tone, the distribution of emphases, the marking of the rise and fall of passion—peculiarly suited to dramatic verse. And *Samson Agonistes* is dramatic. It is not, however, any more than *Paradise Regained*, as complex and profound an interpretation of the human situation as *Paradise Lost*, which remains the greatest if not the most perfect of his works.

When Milton died in November 1674 his reputation as a great English poet was assured. But he had long been out of touch with the spirit of the age, and though he was admired it was rarely for what we would consider the right reasons. His reputation and influence in the eighteenth century are well-known facts of English literary history, but the influence was generally unfortunate and the reputation grounded on the critically irrelevant facts that he was both a religious poet and an epic poet. Modern criticism, which in so many respects is better placed for a fuller and more discriminating appreciation of Milton than that of any previous age, has all too often chosen either to attack him because he does not write like Donne or to offer by way of defence a consideration of his poems as documents in his biography or as proofs of his theological heterodoxy or orthodoxy. The present account of his work, limited as it inevitably is and scrappy and ill-balanced as it may be considered to be, is offered primarily as a critical appreciation, made on strictly literary grounds, in the hope of increasing the reader's understanding of the nature and value of his achievement.

SELECT BIBLIOGRAPHY

1. SOME MODERN EDITIONS OF MILTON

The Poetical Works of John Milton, edited by Helen Darbishire. Vol. I, *Paradise Lost*, 1952; Vol. II, *Paradise Regained, Samson Agonistes* and the *Minor Poems*, 1955.

The Student's Milton (the complete poems and much of the prose), edited by F. A. Patterson, New York, 1936.

Milton: Complete Poetry and Selected Prose, edited by E. H. Visiak (Nonesuch edition), n.d.

John Milton, Complete Poems and Major Prose, edited by M. Y. Hughes, New York, 1937.

Poems, edited by B. A. Wright (Everyman edition), 1956.

2. SOME MODERN CRITICAL AND HISTORICAL WORKS

A Milton Handbook, by J. H. Hanford, 1926 (4th ed., 1946).

Milton, by E. M. W. Tillyard, 1936.

Milton and the Puritan Dilemma, by Arthur Barker, 1942.

Milton's Lycidas: The Tradition and the Poem, edited by C. A. Patrides, New York, 1961.

A Preface to 'Paradise Lost', by C. S. Lewis, 1942.

'Paradise Lost' and the Seventeenth Century Reader, by B. Rajan, 1947.

Some Graver Subject: an essay on Paradise Lost, by J. B. Broadbent, London, 1960.

'Paradise Regain'd': The Tradition and the Poem, by Elizabeth M. Pope, 1947.

Milton's Samson and the Christian Tradition, by F. M. Krouse, 1949.

The Italian Element in Milton's Verse, by F. T. Prince, 1954.

Liberty and Reformation in the Puritan Revolution, by William Haller, 1955.

3. BIOGRAPHY

Early Lives of Milton, ed. Helen Darbishire, 1932.

John Milton, Englishman, by J. H. Hanford, 1949.

INDEX

251

In the Norton Library

CRITICISM AND THE HISTORY OF IDEAS